FINANCIAL INSTITUTIONS AND SERVICES

MODERNIZING FINANCIAL REGULATION

Financial Institutions and Services

Additional books in this series can be found on Nova's website at:

https://www.novapublishers.com/catalog/index.php?cPath=23_29&seriesp=Financial+Institutions+and+Services

Additional E-books in this series can be found on Nova's website at:

https://www.novapublishers.com/catalog/index.php?cPath=23_29&seriespe=Financial+Institutions+and+Services

FINANCIAL INSTITUTIONS AND SERVICES

MODERNIZING FINANCIAL REGULATION

LAWRENCE P. COWELL
EDITOR

Nova
Nova Science Publishers, Inc.
New York

For permission to use material from this book please contact us:
Telephone 631-231-7269; Fax 631-231-8175
Web Site: http://www.novapublishers.com

LIBRARY OF CONGRESS CATALOGING-IN-PUBLICATION DATA
Modernizing financial regulation / editor, Lawrence P. Cowell.
p. cm.
Includes index.
ISBN 978-1-60741-442-1 (hardcover)
1. Financial services industry--United States. 2. Financial
institutions--Law and legislation--United States. 3. Banking law. I.
Cowell, Lawrence P.
HG181.M5717 2010
346.73'08--dc22
2010012875

Published by Nova Science Publishers, Inc. + New York

CONTENTS

PREFACE

The current U.S. financial regulatory system has relied on a fragmented and complex arrangement of federal and state regulators, put into place over the past 150 years, that has not kept pace with major developments in financial markets and products in recent decades. As the nation finds itself in the midst of one of the worst financial crises ever, the regulatory system increasingly appears to be ill-suited to meet the nation's needs in the 21st century. This book explores a framework for modernizing the outdated U.S. financial regulatory system to help policymakers weigh various regulatory reform proposals and consider ways in which the current regulatory system could be made more effective and efficient.

Chapter 1 - Today, financial services, banking, insurance and securities trading are no longer specific to an institution, but are delivered by almost every financial services institution in most cases with little or no differentiation. Since the 1980s, financial services companies increasingly commingle products and services. The passage of P.L. 106-102, the Gramm-Leach-Bliley Act (GLBA), incorporated the commingling of financial services within institutions into U.S. financial services law. In this new GLBA framework, the responsibilities of regulating financial institutions are more difficult to achieve because their business activities have become more interrelated.

Technological advances have helped to erase the traditional lines of demarcation in financial services products upon which the regulatory structure was built. Bank regulators, for example, continue to lower barriers to bank entry into commodity futures and the options business, and insurance has become a popular bank product. As bankers get more involved in the securities business, the business has been changing rapidly. As financial instruments or products become more complicated, the riskiness (probability of default) of the products is more difficult to determine for regulatory purposes. Maintaining a regulatory structure and control based on past market demarcations that are now slowly disappearing raises questions about the effectiveness of the regulatory structure that has responsibility for the safety and soundness of the financial institutions under its jurisdiction.

This chapter is a brief overview of the U.S. federal financial services regulatory structure. The first section is a brief historical analysis of the functional and competitive regulatory structure of the three major financial services — banking, insurance, and securities, including commodities futures and options. The second section deals with the difficulties in regulating institutions when they begin to provide services outside their demarcated lines of business. The third section discusses some of the recent proposals to consolidate regulatory agencies in the United States. The fourth section briefly assesses the consolidated financial services regulatory structures in the United Kingdom, Japan, and Germany, and the report concludes with some implications.

Chapter 2 - As the financial services industry has become increasingly concentrated in a number of large, internationally active firms offering an array of products and services, the adequacy of the U.S. financial regulatory system has been questioned. GAO has identified the need to modernize the financial regulatory system as a challenge to be addressed in the 21st century. This chapter, mandated by the Financial Services Regulatory Relief Act of 2006, discusses (1) measurements of regulatory costs and benefits and efforts to avoid excessive regulatory burden, (2) the challenges posed to financial regulators by trends in the industry, and (3) options to enhance the efficiency and effectiveness of the federal financial regulatory structure. GAO convened a Comptroller General's Forum (Forum) with supervisors and leading industry experts, reviewed regulatory agency policies, and summarized prior reports to meet these objectives

Chapter 3 - The United States and other countries are in the midst of the worst financial crisis in more than 75 years. While much of the attention of policymakers understandably has been focused on taking short-term steps to address the immediate nature of the crisis, these events have served to strikingly demonstrate that the current U.S. financial regulatory system is in need of significant reform.

To help policymakers better understand existing problems with the financial regulatory system and craft and evaluate reform proposals, this chapter (1) describes the origins of the current financial regulatory system, (2) describes various market developments and changes that have created challenges for the current system, and (3) presents an evaluation framework that can be used by Congress and others to shape potential regulatory reform efforts. To do this work, GAO synthesized existing GAO work and other studies and met with dozens of representatives of financial regulatory agencies, industry associations, consumer advocacy organizations, and others. Twenty-nine regulators, industry associations, and consumer groups also reviewed a draft of this chapter and provided valuable input that was incorporated as appropriate. In general, reviewers commented that the report represented an important and thorough review of the issues related to regulatory reform.

Chapter 4 - This chapter is based upon a statement of Gene L. Dodaro, Acting Comptroller General of the United States, before the Congressional Oversight Panel on Financial Regulation who discussed a January 8, 2009, report that provides a framework for modernizing the outdated U.S. financial regulatory system. We prepared this work under the authority of the Comptroller General to help policymakers weigh various regulatory reform proposals and consider ways in which the current regulatory system could be made more effective and efficient. My statement today is based on our report, which (1) describes how regulation has evolved in banking, securities, thrifts, credit unions, futures, insurance, secondary mortgage markets and other important areas; (2) describes several key changes in financial markets and products in recent decades that have highlighted significant limitations and gaps in the existing regulatory system; and (3) presents an evaluation framework that can be used by Congress and others to shape potential regulatory reform efforts. To do this work, we synthesized existing GAO work and other studies and met with representatives of financial regulatory agencies, industry associations, consumer advocacy organizations, and others. The work upon which the report is based was conducted in accordance with generally accepted government auditing standards. Those standards require that we plan and perform the audit to obtain sufficient, appropriate evidence to provide a reasonable basis for our findings and conclusions based on our audit objectives. We believe that the evidence obtained provides a reasonable basis for our findings and conclusions based on our audit objectives. This work was conducted between April 2008 and December 2008.

Chapter 5 - This chapter is based upon a speech made by Timothy F. Geithner, President and CEO, Federal Reserve Bank of New York, at the Economic Club of New York, June 9, 2008, who spoke about reducing systemic risk in a dynamic financial system.

In: Modernizing Financial Regulation
Editor: Lawrence P. Cowell

ISBN: 978-1-60741-442-1

Chapter 1

FEDERAL FINANCIAL SERVICES REGULATORY CONSOLIDATION: AN OVERVIEW

Walter W. Eubanks

SUMMARY

Among the arguments offered for consolidating the federal regulatory structure of the financial services industry is that the industry has changed in ways that blur the clear- cut boundaries between the functional areas of banking, insurance, securities, and commodities markets. It has also been argued that while the financial services firms are primarily responsible for effectively managing their risks, the new nature of those risks has created a need for the government to take a more comprehensive approach to financial regulation. Moreover, a consolidated financial services regulator at the national level is more suited to accommodate international regulatory negotiations on financial services regulations such as capital, accounting, and privacy standards. The most recent proposal to consolidate the federal regulatory structure is the *Department of the Treasury Blueprint for a Modernized Regulatory Structure* (page 13), which would merge several federal regulatory agencies' functions into five distinct functional supervisory agencies. The proposal consolidates regulatory functions, not agencies.

Even though a number of proposals to consolidate the federal regulatory structure of the financial services industry have been put forth, the United States has yet to make any significant move to do so. A key reason is that the functional, competitive regulatory structure of the United States was, and continues to be, viewed by most policymakers and knowledgeable observers as being sound over time, despite a number of crises. For example, significant federal regulation of banks first occurred during the Civil War when states' management of their currencies failed dramatically. In another example, financial regulators addressed the savings and loan associations failures of the 1980s with risk-based capital requirements for all insured-depository institutions for the first time. The Sarbanes-Oxley Act established accounting standards for publicly traded companies in response to the accounting frauds leading to the bankruptcy of several large publicly traded firms. The structure has often been able to successfully address such problems quickly before they disrupt the economy.

To improve their ability to regulate the modern financial services sectors, many countries including the United Kingdom, Japan, and Germany have recently consolidated their financial services regulatory agencies. Financial Services Authority of the United Kingdom (FSA-UK), the Financial Services Agency of Japan (FSA- Japan), and the Federal Financial Supervisory Authority (BaFin) in Germany provide a point of comparison for the U.S. regulatory structure. These foreign regulatory structures are said to offer more effective methods of regulating modern financial services firms.

This chapter is a brief overview of the U.S. federal financial services regulatory structure. It briefly provides an historical analysis of the current U.S. functional and competitive regulatory structure. It discusses some of the recent proposals to consolidate the U.S. regulatory agencies, and it assesses three consolidated financial services regulatory structures abroad.

INTRODUCTION

Today, financial services, banking, insurance and securities trading are no longer specific to an institution, but are delivered by almost every financial services institution in most cases with little or no differentiation. Since the 1980s, financial services companies increasingly commingle products and services. The passage of P.L. 106-102, the Gramm-Leach-Bliley Act (GLBA), incorporated the commingling of financial services within institutions into U.S. financial services law. In this new GLBA framework, the responsibilities of regulating financial institutions are more difficult to achieve because their business activities have become more interrelated.

Technological advances have helped to erase the traditional lines of demarcation in financial services products upon which the regulatory structure was built. Bank regulators, for example, continue to lower barriers to bank entry into commodity futures and the options business, and insurance has become a popular bank product. As bankers get more involved in the securities business, the business has been changing rapidly. As financial instruments or products become more complicated, the riskiness (probability of default) of the products is more difficult to determine for regulatory purposes. Maintaining a regulatory structure and control based on past market demarcations that are now slowly disappearing raises questions about the effectiveness of the regulatory structure that has responsibility for the safety and soundness of the financial institutions under its jurisdiction.

This chapter is a brief overview of the U.S. federal financial services regulatory structure. The first section is a brief historical analysis of the functional and competitive regulatory structure of the three major financial services — banking, insurance, and securities, including commodities futures and options. The second section deals with the difficulties in regulating institutions when they begin to provide services outside their demarcated lines of business. The third section discusses some of the recent proposals to consolidate regulatory agencies in the United States. The fourth section briefly assesses the consolidated financial services regulatory structures in the United Kingdom, Japan, and Germany, and the report concludes with some implications.

THE MAJOR FINANCIAL SERVICES REGULATORS

There are currently seven major federal regulators for the financial services industry. The following is a summary of the supervisory duties of the Office of the Comptroller of the Currency (OCC), the Federal Reserve System (the Fed), the Federal Deposit Insurance Corporation (FDIC), the Office of Thrift Supervision (OTS), the National Credit Union Administration (NCUA), the Securities and Exchange Commission (SEC), and the Commodity Futures Trading Commission (CFTC). All these agencies regulate for safety and soundness. The SEC and the CFTC emphasize consumer protection more than the others.

- **The Office of the Comptroller of the Currency (OCC)** The OCC is the regulator for just under 2,000 nationally chartered banks, and the U.S. branches and offices of foreign banks. The OCC conducts on-site examinations of each national bank at least three times within every two-year period.

- **The Federal Reserve System (Fed)** The Fed supervises about 950 state-chartered commercial banks that are members of the system and more than 5,000 bank holding companies and financial holding companies. Along with the OCC, it also supervises some international activities of national banks. The Fed uses both on-site examination and off-site surveillance and monitoring in its supervision process. Each institution is examined on-site every 12 to 18 months. The Fed's in-house examiners are to examine larger institutions continuously. The Board of Governors of the Fed coordinates the examination and compliance activities of the 12 regional banks.

- **The Federal Deposit Insurance Corporation (FDIC)** The FDIC regulates about 4,800 state-chartered commercial banks and 500 state-chartered savings associations that are not members of the Fed. They also insure deposits of the remaining 4,000 depository institutions without regulating them. The FDIC examines its supervised institutions about once every 18 months.

- **The Office of Thrift Supervision (OTS)** The OTS supervises about 950 federally chartered savings associations, savings banks, and their holding companies. Like the OCC, the OTS is located within, but is independent of, the Treasury. The OTS is to conduct on-site examinations of each institution at least three times every two years.

- **The National Credit Union Administration (NCUA)** The NCUA currently regulates 9,369 federally chartered credit unions and another 3,593 federally insured, state-chartered credit unions. Most credit unions are small and considered to have limited risk exposure. Consequently, credit unions and NCUA are not covered further in this chapter.
- **The Securities and Exchange Commission (SEC)** The SEC regulates to protect investors against fraud and deceptive practices in securities markets. It also has authority to examine institutions it supervises for regulatory compliance. This covers securities markets and exchanges, securities issuers, investment advisers, investment companies, and industry professionals such as broker-dealers. The SEC supervises

more than 8,000 registered broker-dealers with approximately 92,000 branch offices and 67,500 registered representatives.

- **The Commodity Futures Trading Commission (CFTC)** The CFTC protects market users and the public from fraud and abusive practices in markets for commodity and financial futures and options. The CFTC delegates regulatory examinations to its designated self-regulatory organizations (DSROs), of which the most prominent are the National Futures Association (NFA), the Chicago Board of Trade, and the New York Mercantile Exchange. NFA membership covers more than 4,000 firms and 50,000 individuals. The regulatory process generally starts at registration, when the DSRO screens firms and individuals seeking to conduct futures business. The DSROs monitor business practices and, when appropriate, take formal disciplinary actions that could prohibit firms from conducting any further business.

SAFETY AND SOUNDNESS REGULATIONS

Safety and soundness regulations for banks consist of basically five components: **federal deposit insurance** to reduce the likelihood of bank runs and panics; **deposit interest ceilings** to reduce the costs of bank deposits and weaken banks' incentives to invest in risky assets; **regulatory monitoring** to ensure that banks do not invest in excessively risky assets, have sufficient capital given their risk, have no fraudulent activities, and have competent management; **capital requirements** to provide incentives for banks not to take excessive risk; and **portfolio restrictions** to prohibit investment in risky assets.

Under regulatory monitoring, U.S. banking regulators adopted a uniform rating system known as CAMEL to monitor banks' safety and soundness. "C" stands for capital adequacy; "A" stands for asset quality; "M" stands for management ability, "E" stands for earnings, and "L" stands for liquidity. The bank's capital is evaluated on the basis of the bank's size as well as the composition of its assets and liabilities, on and off the balance sheet. The quality of the bank's assets is determined by assessing the bank's credit risk of loans in its portfolio, which are classified as good, substandard, doubtful, or loss. Management ability is determined by evaluating the bank's management as well as its board of directors. The examiners assess competence, management acumen, integrity, and willingness to comply with banking regulations. Earnings are evaluated in terms of trends relative to the bank's peers. In determining the bank's liquidity, the examiners assess credit conditions, deposit volatility, loan commitments, and other contingent claims against the bank's capital, current stock of liquid assets, and the bank's perceived ability to raise funds on short notice. From the list of regulators above, one can see that bank examiners have overlapping jurisdictions. For example, national banks are also FDIC-Insured. Often federal and state examiners accept each others' examinations, and sometimes they examine jointly. It is important to note that it is illegal to disclose a bank examination (for example, CAMEL ratings) outside the bank.[1]

BACKGROUND

A number of proposals to consolidate the federal regulatory structure of the financial services industry have been put forth. The United States, however, has yet to make any significant move in this direction. One reason is that most policymakers and knowledgeable observers believe that the functional, competitive regulatory structure of the United States has proven sound over time.[2] For example, the number of bank (a key financial services provider) failures would be among the indicators of the health of a financial services structure. **Figure 1** indicates that the number of bank failures have declined, since it peaked during the S&L crisis in 1989 when 206 depository institutions failed.

Figure 2 shows the ratio of the deposits of the failed institutions to the total deposits of FDIC-insured depository institutions (failed institutions' deposits divided by total deposits). At its peak in 1991, 124 institutions failed but only a little more than 2% of the total banking deposits were held by these failed institutions. In contrast, at the end of 2006 no depository institution failed for the first time two in consecutive years since 1934. But the subprime turmoil that started in August of 2007 and the credit crunch that followed contributed to the failure of three small banks in 2007 and four in the first quarter of 2008.

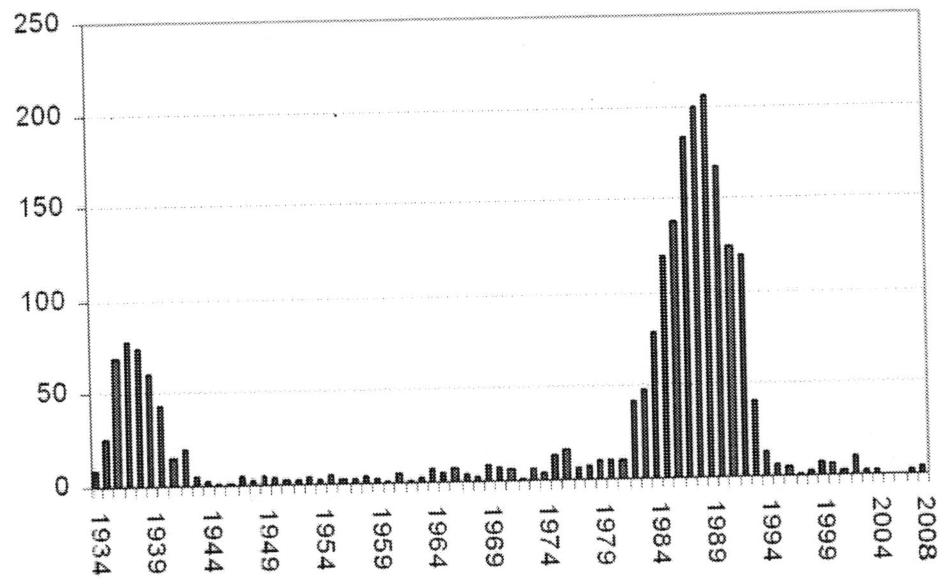

Source: FDIC 2007Annual Report. Appendix A, p.107, and FDIC 2008 Failed Bank List, [http://www.fdic.gov/about/strategic/report/2004highlight/arhighlight.pdf], and [http://www.fdic.gov/bank/individual/failed/banklist.html].

Figure 1. The Number of FDIC-Insured Bank Failures, 1934-2008

The regulatory structure of the United States is said to be functional because regulators supervise by line of business such as banking, insurance, or securities trading. The structure is said to be competitive because there are usually multiple regulators responsible for a single function, for example, banking services.[3] Regulatory responsibilities are widely dispersed among several regulators on the federal as well as the state level of government.

The U.S. regulatory structure reflects historical evolution rather than deliberate design. The structure has evolved by addressing regulatory deficiencies on whatever level they are found. For example, federal regulation of banks occurred for the first time after the Civil War when states' management of their currencies failed dramatically. For the first time in the 1980s, the financial regulators addressed the savings and loan associations'(S&Ls) failures by abolishing the Federal Saving and Loan Insurance Corporation (FSLIC), creating the OTS as the S&Ls' new regulator and requiring all insured-depository institutions to increase their capital by calculating their regulatory capital based on the riskiness of their assets. The purpose was to increase the protection of taxpayers from future bailouts of these institutions. More recently, the Sarbanes-Oxley Act created a new independent body, the Public Company Accounting Oversight Board to oversee auditors and established accounting standards for publicly traded companies in response to accounting fraud leading to the bankruptcy of several large publicly traded firms. In most cases, the U.S. regulatory structure has been able to handle most financial crises successfully before they significantly disrupt economy activity. The issue is the regulatory structure's capacity to continue to handle most financial crises given the increased interrelationships and functional commingling within the financial services industry.

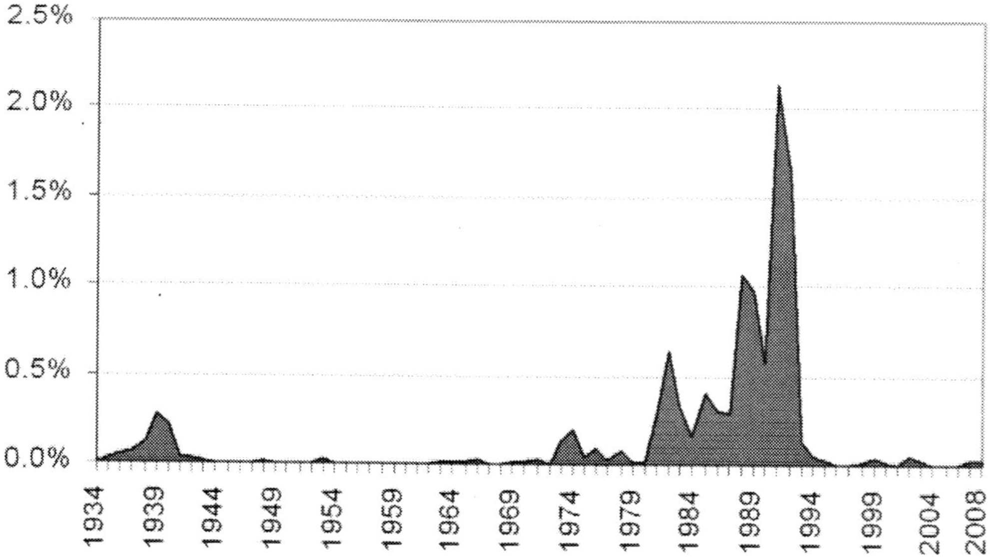

Source: FDIC 2007Annual Report. Appendix A, p.107, and FDIC 2008 Failed Bank List, [http://www.fdic.gov/about/strategic/report/2007highlight/arhighlight.pdf], and [http://www.fdic.gov/bank/individual/failed/banklist.html].

Figure 2. FDIC-Insured Bank Deposits: Ratio of Failed Bank Deposit to Total Bank Deposits, 1934-2008

The United Kingdom, Japan, and Germany recently consolidated and redesigned their financial services regulatory agencies to meet recent developments in the financial services markets. These recent developments included the blurring of boundaries among functions, need for a comprehensive approach to risk management, better allocation of regulatory resources, and the need to accommodate international regulatory negotiations on trade in financial services.

The Financial Services Authority in the United Kingdom (FSA-UK), the Financial Service Agency in Japan (FSA-Japan), and the Federal Financial Supervisory Authority (BaFin) in Germany provide a point of comparison for the U.S. structure. These foreign regulatory structures are said to offer more effective methods of regulating modern financial services firms.

U.S. FUNCTIONAL AND COMPETITIVE REGULATORY STRUCTURE

U.S. regulation of financial services is dispersed among a number of regulators. For example, the FDIC and the OCC have regulatory responsibilities for national banks that are FDIC-insured. The OCC holds these banks' charters, and therefore determines the activities in which they may engage. The FDIC insures each of the institutions' deposit accounts for up to $100,000 on which it must make good if the institutions fail. Proponents of the framework contend that competing regulatory bodies regulate less but do it more efficiently. The redundancy of regulators is more likely to detect and correct risky market behaviors before they develop into financial crises.[4]

The structure allows regulations to be tailored to the specific deficiencies at the appropriate level of the abusing firm(s). Also, the structure promotes innovations and competition among financial services providers. Opponents argue that the overlapping regulations are costly and allow astute financial services firms to exploit weaknesses along the regulatory seams. The structure also allows financial services providers to shop for the regulator that best suits their business plan. This was confirmed in a recent FDIC survey that shows that the top reasons given by the 34 banks that changed their charter to the FDIC were that "the FDIC was less expensive and more banker friendly, and that other regulators were stricter, and that institutions could more readily pursue market share increases."[5] On the other hand, the ability to shop for regulators could lead to more institutions being regulated by the weakest regulators, which would increase systemic risk.

Regulatory Competition in Banking

In the beginning of the nation, the federal government exercised an indirect role in the regulation of banking through the First and Second Banks of the United States. When President Andrew Jackson refused to renew the Second Bank's charter, states' regulatory banking commissions filled the regulatory vacuum that was created.[6] The Civil War and the disarray of the national currencies led to the reintroduction of the federal government into regulating banks by establishing the national bank charter system, which was governed by the Comptroller of the Currency (OCC) established in 1863.[7] Its creation immediately began the dual banking system which exists today and placed the federal government in competition with states for the number and size of banks under their respective jurisdictions. Until recently, most bankers preferred state charters because states' regulations were considered less burdensome.

More layers to the regulatory structure, and therefore competition between regulators, were added with the creation of the Federal Reserve Board after the Panic of 1907 and the creation of the Federal Deposit Insurance Corporation (FDIC) after the banking failures of the Great Depression in the 1930s. Further layers of regulatory competition were added when saving banks and credit unions were provided with separate federal regulators which evolved into the Office of Thrift Supervision (OTS) and the National Credit Union Administration (NCUA).[8] The Great Depression also led Congress to pass the Glass-Steagall Act of 1933 (Ch.89, 48 Stat. 162) to further seal off banking from other financial services enterprises by prohibiting banks from engaging in investment banking activities until it was repealed by the Gramm-Leach-Bliley Act of 1999 (GLBA) (P.L. 106-102). It repealed the Glass-Steagall Act and allows financial companies owning or operating institutions to commingle financial services.

Regulatory Competition in Insurance

Like banking, the insurance industry owes its competitive regulatory structure to correcting deficiencies. States began regulating insurance in 1837, starting with Massachusetts and New York, to ensure that insurance companies maintained adequate reserves to meet claims.[9] In the early 1920s, states significantly increased legislative restrictions on insurance companies, starting in New York and copied by other states. A New York legislature's investigation uncovered massive insurance companies' abuses that left them without adequate reserves to pay claims. That led to the New York state's legislature passing laws barring companies from underwriting insurance while underwriting other securities.

Copying New York state's regulations, states separated insurance companies from the banking industry.[10] These regulatory provisions also protected the insurance industry from the excesses of the securities industry in the late 1920s that led to the stock market crash. Consequently, when the stock market crashed in 1929, the insurance companies were in relative good shape.[11] Having escaped the massive failures of the other parts of the financial services sector, the insurance companies were not included in New Deal regulatory legislation, even though in 1934 the Securities and Exchange Commission (SEC) proposed a federal agency to regulate insurance companies. The proposal was soundly rejected upon objections from the industry and state regulators.[12]

Another possible expansion of federal regulation of insurance came in 1944 out of a Supreme Court ruling which held that the insurance industry was subject to the federal antitrust laws.[13] The insurance industry feared that this ruling would preempt their state regulation. As a result, the industry lobbied Congress heavily to pass the McCarran-Ferguson Act, which granted insurance companies immunity from the antitrust laws to the extent that they were regulated by state insurance laws.[14] The McCarran-Ferguson Act protected the insurance industry until the early 1950s when insurance companies began selling variable annuities, which the SEC challenged. The SEC argued that variable annuities were securities subject to its regulation because the returns on these investments were based on investment of the annuitants' premium payments in securities. The Supreme Court found for the SEC. Insurance companies selling variable annuity contracts are now regulated by states and the SEC.[15]

The insurance industry was able to stave off other federal intrusions, despite suffering significant losses from contracts sold in the 1980s.[16] The industry, however, could not avoid competition from the banking and securities industries.[17] One reason was that variable annuities became a growing line of financial services products sold by stockbrokers. In addition, federal bank regulators began allowing banks to sell insurance products in the 1990s.[18] This competition resulted in many insurance companies demutualizing[19] and expanding their own financial service offerings, such as more securities-like products with banking services options.[20] In sum, even though regulatory competition was maintained with the states, state insurance regulators could not protect insurance companies from competition from other financial services providers. There have been several legislative proposals in recent years to impose federal regulation on some companies who offer securities- like products with banking services options.[21]

Regulatory Competition in Securities

When the Securities and Exchange Commission was created by Congress in 1934 — in the wake of the stock market crash of 1929 — it was to establish a strong federal regulatory presence in the market for corporate securities.[22] The SEC's main focus was full disclosure in the securities markets. The Securities and Exchange Act of 1934 did not preempt state securities regulations. Consequently, the SEC has competed with state securities regulators for most of its existence.[23] With the exception of mortgage-backed securities in 1984, it was not until the National Securities Markets Improvement Act of 1996 that some of the states' securities regulations were preempted or states were required to conform their standards to those of the SEC.[24] Federal securities law and SEC regulations apply to the markets where securities are traded and to all businesses that sell stocks or bonds to public investors. Other regulated entities include mutual funds, bidders in corporate mergers and acquisitions, certain investment advisers, public accountants, and power utilities (the SEC has some control over the market structure under the Public Utility Holding Company Act of 1935).[25]

In this securities regulatory structure, regulatory competition remains in the form of self-regulatory organizations (SROs). These are non-governmental organizations that were given regulatory authority and shelter from the antitrust laws by the Securities and Exchange Act of 1934.[26] SROs like the securities exchanges and the National Association of Securities Dealers, Inc. (NASD) are required to regulate the conduct of their members. The SEC's role is to oversee the exchanges, as well as act directly when the SROs' oversight fails.[27]

In addition to the SROs, the structure of securities regulation also includes accountants that certify the financial statements of public companies and broker- dealers as well as the Nationally Recognized Statistical Ratings Organizations (NRSROs). The NRSROs include rating agencies such as Moody and Standard & Poor's. The SEC's ability to enforce its rules over accountants and broker-dealers has been strengthened by the Sarbanes-Oxley Act of 2002, which created a Public Company Accounting Oversight Board to oversee the auditing principles of auditors. Sarbanes-Oxley also requires the SEC to conduct a study of NRSROs and to report to Congress on any deficiencies. Concerns about conflict of interest and certification have resulted in the Senate Committee on Banking, Housing, and Urban Affairs holding hearings on the regulation of NRSROs.[28]

Regulatory Competition in Commodity Futures and Options

Like the other financial services, commodities futures were separated from the rest of the industry as part of historical regulatory development in the United States. The agricultural recession of 1921 following World War I, and speculative manipulation of commodity prices prompted Congress to pass the Grain Futures Act of 1922 under its commerce powers.[29] The Grain Futures Act required commodity futures trading to be conducted on organized exchanges, such as the Chicago Board of Trade, which would register with the government as contract markets. With commodity speculation and market manipulation unchecked in the Great Depression, President Roosevelt added regulation of the commodity markets to his request for regulation of the securities market. Congress responded with the Commodity Exchange Act of 1936 (CEA), which continued many of the requirements of the Grain Futures Act, but required futures commission merchants (the equivalent to broker-dealers in the securities business) to register with the government.[30]

For decades, even though options trading of regulated commodities, and manipulation of commodity prices, were prohibited, the government was unable to stop speculation and manipulation in commodity prices, particularly in options on unregulated commodities which added to the rapid rise in commodity prices in the early 1970s. The Commodity Futures Trading Commission Act of 1974 was enacted in response to developments in the commodities markets which carried forward the Commodity Exchange Act and created the CFTC.[31]

The CFTC was given exclusive jurisdiction over the trading of commodity futures and commodity options on all commodities and it was given more enforcement powers than its predecessor. Its regulatory reach included commodity trading advisors, commodity pool operators, and associated persons of futures commission merchants.[32] Despite the increased federal regulation of the commodity trade, the regulatory control of commodity trade remained less stringent than SEC's control of trade in securities. Competition between the SEC and the CFTC developed when the financial services industry began developing new financial instruments and trading strategies that converged on products regulated by both regulators — stock index futures, and other equity-based derivatives. The difference in the level of regulation in the securities and the commodity futures and options markets became important to investors. Over-the-counter (OTC) instruments such as swaps, caps, collars, and floors were increasingly popular alternatives to exchange- traded commodity futures and options. Some of these instruments were abused by both SEC- and CFTC-regulated firms and traders. In 1978, Congress mandated that the two agencies consult with each other and with banking regulators in curtailing these abuses.[33]

The over-the-counter market for derivatives was the source of regulatory competition between the CFTC and the banking regulators — the Fed and the OCC. The banking regulators argued for no regulation of OTC financial derivatives, even though Congress had given the CFTC exclusive jurisdiction over all contracts and mandated that all such contracts be traded on CFTC-regulated exchanges. However, the CFTC did not move to assert its regulatory jurisdiction over these derivative contracts. The lack of regulation provided a legal risk to swaps contracts. That is, if a court had ruled that swaps were illegal, trillions of dollars in OTC derivative contracts might have been rendered void and unenforceable.[34]

The Commodity Futures Modernization Act of 2000 (CFMA; P.L. 106-554) was enacted to clarify the situation. It specifies that the CEA does not apply to contracts between "eligible contract participants" (which include financial institutions, regulated financial professionals, units of government, nonfinancial businesses or individual persons with assets more than $10 million, and others whom the CFTC may approve) based on "excluded commodities." Excluded commodities are defined as financial products and indicators, and are thought to be less susceptible to manipulation than physical commodities with finite supplies. Derivatives based on agricultural commodities, however, may be traded only on CFTC-regulated exchanges, because of concerns about price manipulation — "corners" and "squeezes" — in those markets.[35]

THE PROBLEM OF REGULATING IN THE CURRENT ENVIRONMENT

Today, financial services, such as banking, insurance and securities trading are no longer specific to an institution. Insurance, for instance, does not have to be bought from an insurance company; instead it can be purchased from a bank with little or no differentiation in the policy being delivered to the customer. Since the 1980s, financial services companies increasingly commingle financial services. The passage of P.L. 106-102, the Gramm-Leach-Bliley Act of 1999, incorporated the commingling of financial services within institutions into U.S. financial services law.

In this new GLBA framework, the responsibilities of regulating financial institutions are more difficult to achieve because the regulators no longer have the separation of the lines of businesses that they had in the past. Technological advances have helped to erase the traditional lines of demarcation in financial services products upon which the regulatory structure was built. Bank regulators, for example, continue to lower barriers to bank entry into commodity futures and options businesses, and insurance has become a popular bank product. As bankers get more involved in the securities business, the business has been changing rapidly. Maintaining a regulatory structure and control based on past established market behavior that is now slowly disappearing raises questions about the effectiveness of the structure to manage the changing risks. Most regulatory changes have occurred after the risks have risen sufficiently to show the deficiencies.

PROPOSED CONSOLIDATION SOLUTIONS

The most recent proposal to consolidate the federal regulatory structure of financial services industry is the *Department of the Treasury Blueprint for a Modernized Regulatory Structure* (the Blueprint). It was motivated by the Bush Administration's recognition that the existing functional regulatory framework no longer provides efficient and effective safeguards against poor prudential behavior of financial services firms.[36] The Administration believed that the existing framework is based on a structure that has been largely knitted together more than 75 years to address specific economic disruptions and is not optimal because financial institutions have become more opaque and more difficult to understand as the institutions develop new products and complex risk-hedging strategies that are difficult to evaluate.

For these reasons, on March 31, 2008, Treasury Secretary Henry Paulson offered the Blueprint as a more optimal federal financial regulatory structure. This proposed framework would consolidate similar functions more than it would consolidate agencies by renaming existing regulatory agencies and make significant changes in their responsibilities, and functions. There will be five major regulatory agencies which is the same number as there are federal banking regulators: a market stability regulator, which is essential the monetary and lender of last resort functions of the Federal Reserve; a prudential regulator, which would enforce the safety and soundness prudential regulations that are shared by all existing regulators; a business conduct regulator, which is a consumer and business protection regulator whose functions are now shared by all regulators and particularly the SEC/CFTC; a federal insurance regulator, which is essentially the Federal Deposit Insurance Corporation with additional insurance responsibilities preempted from states, and a corporate financial regulator, which is essentially the SEC/CFTC and related self regulated organizations, such as the securities exchanges.

The financial services industry's reaction to the Blueprint has been mixed with the criticisms outweighing the support of the proposal. Banking groups supported the prospects of regulatory modernization, but were critical of the Blueprint's plan to eliminate the thrift and credit unition charters along with their supervisory agencies — the Office of Thrift Supervision (OTS), and the National Credit Union Administration (NCUA). On the other hand, the mortgage bankers supported the Blueprint arguing that it would lead to resolving regulatory inconsistences in mortgage lending supervision at the state level. For insurance, most smaller insurance companies opposed the Blueprint's optional federal charter, which would give insurance companies the option of federal regulation rather than the existing state regulation of insurance companies. By contrast, large insurance companies operating in several states supported the optional federal charter proposal, while state insurance commissions were quick to oppose the Blueprint's insurance proposal. The commissioners argue that they support needed modernization but that does not mean federalization. On the securities and futures markets, the Blueprint proposes to merge the SEC with the CFTC, which has been proposed before as shown below, but has not happened.

Congress and regulators in the first term of the George W. Bush Administration raised the long-standing issue of consolidating federal financial services regulators.[37] The former U.S. Treasury Undersecretary for Domestic Finance, Peter R. Fisher, made an argument that the supervisory process of the financial services industry should remain diverse, and aimed at the risk-bearing parts of financial firms. However, he strongly advocated creating one regulator to write rules and regulations. This single regulatory agency — a super-regulator — should be responsible for only this activity.[38] Such an agency would absorb the regulation-making functions of all the major federal financial regulators. The George W. Bush Administration's restructuring efforts for financial services regulators was later shifted to oversight of particular institutions such as the government-sponsored housing enterprises Fannie Mae and Freddie Mac.

An even earlier suggested reform of the federal financial regulatory agencies was put forth in 2002 by Donald E. Powell, Chairman of the Federal Deposit Insurance Corporation. Chairman Powell proposed to design a new regulatory system that would reflect the modern financial services marketplace. Three federal financial services regulators would carry out federal supervision. One would be responsible for regulating the banking industry, another for the securities industry, and a third for insurance companies that choose a federal charter.[39] Under this proposal, regulators like the OCC would be restructured out of existence.

Along this line of thinking there have been other regulatory restructuring plans for the financial services industry by sectors:

Banking

During the Clinton Administration, Secretary of the Treasury Lloyd Bentsen proposed that certain functions of the Federal Reserve, the FDIC, the OCC, and the OTS be combined into an independent agency called the Federal Banking Commission. This commission would have been responsible for bank regulation and supervision. The FDIC would have remained responsible for administering federal deposit insurance, and the Federal Reserve would have retained its central banking responsibilities for monetary policy, liquidity lending, and the payments system. However, both the FDIC and the Fed would lose most of their bank supervisory rule- making authority to the Banking Commission.[40]

In 1994, former Federal Reserve Governor, John P. LaWare recommended combining the OCC with the OTS. The combined agencies would form an independent Federal Banking Commission. The Federal Reserve would supervise all independent state banks and all depository institutions in any holding company whose lead institution was state chartered. The commission would have supervised all independent national banks and thrifts. The FDIC would not have independent examination powers but would be authorized to join in the examination of problem banking institutions. In 1996, the GAO recommended that primary supervisory responsibilities of the OTS, OCC, and the FDIC be consolidated into a new, independent Federal Banking Commission. The Commission and the Federal Reserve would be responsible for supervision of banking organizations.[41]

Insurance

Since there is no federal insurance regulatory agency, the issue becomes, should one be created. Bills have been introduced in Congress to create some federal regulation of the insurance industry. These bills have been supported by several insurance trade associations. In the 107th Congress, the Insurance Industry Modernization and Consumer Protection Act (H.R. 3766)[42] proposed optional federal charters for insurance companies that would have created a dual system, on the federal and state levels of government. H.R. 3766 would have required the creation of a federal regulatory agency for insurance. In the 108th Congress, the Insurance Consumer Protection Act (S. 1373) would have created a federal commission within the Department of Commerce to regulate the interstate business of property-casualty and life insurance and require federal regulation of all interstate insurers. Unlike the bills in the 107th Congress which made federal regulation optional for insurance companies, the bill in the 108th Congress would have pre-empted most current state regulation of insurance.[43]

A draft bill which began circulating in August 2004 entitled the State Modernization and Regulatory Transparency Act, is quite different from previous proposals. It would establish uniform standards for almost every area of the insurance business including market conduct, product and producer licensing, life insurance, property and casualty insurance, and reinsurance. It would preempt state laws if these laws were not made to conform to its uniform standards[44]

Securities

The regulatory competition between the SEC and the CFTC has brought about several proposals to combine the two agencies. As mentioned previously, the changes in the financial services industry have led to the development of financial instruments that appear to fall into the jurisdiction of both the SEC and the CFTC.[45] To solve the problem, in the 1990s, the Treasury proposed three alternative solutions: combining the SEC and the CFTC, giving the SEC regulatory authority over all financial futures, or transferring regulation of stock index futures from the CFTC to the SEC. In a hearing concerning the Markets and Trading Reorganization and Reform Act of 1995, (H.R. 718) that would have merged the CFTC and the SEC, the GAO pointed out to those considering the merger the difficulty of quantifying both the potential benefits and risks. The GAO also noted that a merger might yield only small budgetary cost savings.[46] As an alternative to consolidation, the Commodity Futures Modernization Act of 2000 specified the respective jurisdictions of the two agencies and mandate that the two agencies negotiate their jurisdictional disputes as they may occur in the future. The Blueprint also proposed combining the SEC and the CFTC.

Consolidation in Other Countries

Most of the arguments used in other countries to justify a consolidation of financial services regulatory structure are applicable to the United States. These arguments were successful in convincing several of the United States' major trading partners to consolidate their financial services regulators into a single regulatory agency or authority. The key arguments were:[47]

- The financial services industry has changed in ways that blur the clear-cut boundaries between the functional areas of banking, insurance, securities, and commodities markets.
- While the financial services firms are primarily responsible for effectively managing their risks, the nature of the risks has created a need for the government to take a more comprehensive approach to regulating those firms' risk management procedures.
- The functional regulatory structure is not conducive to comprehensively understanding the appropriate risk-taking activities of large, complex, international firms. Furthermore, the functional regulatory structure does not have the ability to allocate resources across agencies to carry out strategically focused priorities.
- A consolidated financial services regulator at the national level is more suited to accommodate international regulatory negotiations on financial services regulations and supervision, such as capital, accounting, and privacy standards.

Among the countries that have adopted a single national regulator are the United Kingdom, Japan, and Germany. In all three countries, the new agencies are generally recognized as the sole financial services supervisors. However, to a varying extent, the traditionally dominant regulators such as the central bank, and/ or the ministry of finance still have important roles to play in the new consolidated framework. In addition, in contrast to the American competitive regulatory model, these countries' financial services sectors have been closer to a monolithic regulatory structure than the United States. In Europe, for example, through universal banking, banks have a long tradition of providing banking services as well as trade in securities and insurance, and the central banks and/or ministry of finance were the dominant regulators.[48]

Financial Services Authority of the United Kingdom

In 1997, the Financial Services Authority of the United Kingdom (FSA-UK) consolidated financial services regulation in the UK by combining nine regulatory bodies. FSAUK was given the responsibility to regulate virtually every aspect of financial services. To compare with the United States, FSA-UK has the roles played by the federal and state banking agencies, the SEC, the CFTC, insurance and securities commissions, as well as the SROs.[49] It was also given expanded independent enforcement powers enabling it to bring action against violators and impose sanctions. FSA-UK has a single ombudsman to handle complaints by consumers in all financial services. This is in contrast to the numerous hotlines to the various federal and state agencies in the United States. Another remarkable provision of the FSA-UK is that it assigns one office to develop policies on capital requirements for all financial sectors (similar to the Fisher proposal mentioned previously). By comparison, in the United States, the assessment of risks and capital requirements are developed separately for insurance, banks, broker-dealers, and futures commission merchants.

The FSA-UK is organized as a private corporation with a chairman and a chief executive officer and 16-person board of directors. Eleven members of the board are independent. The FSA-UK is answerable to the Treasury and the British Parliament. A practitioner panel and a consumer panel oversee FSA-UK for their respective constituencies. There is also a requirement for consultation on rules and an appeals process for enforcement. FSA-UK organization strategy is to focus on the most damaging potential risks to the financial system. Consequently, it generally targets larger financial firms. It is required to furnish cost-benefit analyses for its proposals and report annually on its costs relative to the cost of regulations in other nations.[50]

Most financial firms under the FSA-UK and the International Monetary Fund (IMF) have reported that the FSA-UK has been successful in regulating the financial services industry in the United Kingdom.[51] However, a major financial crisis came to light in 2001 that caused FSA-UK to reexamine its regulatory activities in the insurance sector. Equitable Life is a mutual insurer that sold policies in the high interest environment of the 1980s without setting aside the necessary reserves for these policies. While Equitable Life assured pensioners that its assets would exceed its liabilities for years, in 2001 the stated value of its customers' policies was £4.4 billion more than Equitable's assets were worth. Consequently, the company slashed its pension holders' policy value by 16%.[52] A major study of the crisis blamed the "light touch, reactive regulatory environment" that preceded the FSA-UK. In response to the crisis, FSA-UK has become more aggressive in regulating the insurance sector, and has begun a program of enforcement actions, imposing fines and banning wrongdoers from the industry.[53] In the 2002 the International Monetary Fund found that "the insurance industry is under considerable stress, reflecting depressed investment returns, declining profitability in base life insurance products, and, more recently, increasing regulatory compliance cost as the FSA introduces more stringent prudential supervision."[54]

The Financial Services Agency of Japan

In 2000, the Financial Services Agency (FSA-Japan) was established by renaming the Financial Supervisory Agency (created in 1998) and transferring the Securities Exchange Surveillance Commission (SESC) of the ministry of finance along with other functions and staff from the ministry of finance to FSA-Japan. The SESC was created in 1992 to police the securities markets. Besides SESC, there are three bureaus: the planning and coordination bureau, the inspection bureau, and the supervision bureau. The planning and coordination bureau is responsible for the administration of relevant laws including the deposit insurance law. The inspection bureau is responsible for examining and supervising the accounting profession and auditing standard for financial institutions as a whole. The supervision bureau is responsible for the supervision of insurance companies, securities firms, and all financial institutions under FSA's jurisdiction. FSA-Japan is responsible to the minister for financial services, a member of the Cabinet answerable to the Diet (Japan's legislature) for legislative matters. He has effective management control over FSA. All significant reports on individual institutions are referred to him. However, FSA's management is the responsibility of the Commissioner and his staff. There is no board of directors.[55]

The legislation creating FSA-Japan allowed the establishment of previously banned holding companies which increased the size and diversification of banks.[56] In addition, consumer protection was enhanced through the law concerning the sale of financial products. After World War II General Douglas MacArthur required Japan to adopt U.S. laws regulating finance, including securities, and the Glass- Steagall Act.[57] Although insurance is under FSA-Japan, the agency has not made a strong effort to bring about the promised reform of the insurance industry. It was not until several insurance companies failed that FSA-Japan increased regulatory control over the industry by requiring mark-to-market accounting and increased solvency margins.[58]

FSA-Japan' s performance to date has been criticized heavily. The IMF raised questions about the independence and enforcement powers of the agency.[59] The ministry of finance, combined with the Bank of Japan, was essentially the monolithic financial services regulator. They were the managers of the economy, business promoters, and it has been argued that they continue to exert significant influence over FSA-Japan limiting FSA-Japan's effectiveness. An example of this criticism is that SESC, a sub-agency of FSA-Japan, lacks a strong enforcement mechanism. It has only the power to investigate and not the authority to impose sanctions, but must refer matters of sanction to the commission.[60]

FSA-Japan' s poor regulatory performance was reflected in bank regulation. It has shored up some troubled large banks while allowing them to keep their bad debt instead of urging them to write off these bad debts.[61] The government nationalized Credit Bank of Japan and Nippon Credit Bank after they could be no longer kept afloat and public funds were also injected into all but one major bank.[62] Most recently, FSA-Japan has pushed for market solutions and encouraged banks to merge, and offering endorsed government guarantees.[63]

On the positive side, the financial condition of the banking system continues to improve. The ratio of nonperforming loans to total assets has declined from 8% in 2001 to 3% in 2004. In the same time period, the capital adequacy ratio has risen from less than 8% to 11.6%. FSA-Japan has improved recognition and provisioning or bad loans.[64] FSA-Japan increased public disclosures of financially troubled financial services firms. It raised overall bank capital in Japan, even though some bank capital remains below the Basel minimum international standard. In addition, FSA-Japan allowed banks to sell life and other insurance. It also allows banks to affiliate with brokers. FSA-Japan has also lowered barriers to entry by foreign financial services firms.[65]

The Federal Financial Supervisory Authority (BaFin)

In 2002, Germany consolidated its banking, securities, and insurance regulators into BaFin, which was the federal banking regulator. The new structure kept the old divisions of financial services — banking, securities, and insurance. While the banking and insurance divisions are in Bonn, the securities division is in Frankfurt, home of Germany's stock market. As a federal agency, BaFin is under the oversight of the ministry of finance. It has a board of directors composed of the ministers of finance, economics, and justice, members of Parliament, officials of the Bundesbank, and representatives of the banking, insurance, and securities sectors. Like the other consolidated regulators, BaFin has an advisory council made up of industry, unions, and consumer representatives.[66]

A significant part of the impetus for creating BaFin was the European Union's Financial Services Action Plan for a unified Europe-wide single financial services regulator.[67] BaFin facilitates interaction with Germany's regulators and the other EU regulators. At the same time, BaFin regulates institutions more equitably within Germany and throughout Europe than its predecessor framework. Conglomerate regulations are more comprehensive and the costs of regulations were expected to fall under this arrangement. BaFin helped Germany to interface with creation of the European Central Bank.[68] BaFin seems to have met most of its pre-establishment goals.

Germany has a state system of banking institutions, but their supervision takes place on the federal level similar to FDIC-insured state banks in the United States. This system consists of private as well as state-owned banks. Banks are also owned by cities as well as other governmental entities. Some insurance as well as securities activities are supervised on the state level. Even though BaFin is required to supervise financial services firms, the Bundesbank maintains its responsibilities to continuously monitor the financial services sector.[69] To date, most analysts consider BaFin to be successful in regulating financial services firms in its all-in-one framework.[70]

U.S. Regulators Are Trying to Speak with One Voice

A consolidated financial services regulator at the national level in the United States would better accommodate negotiations and implementation of international regulatory agreements such as Basel II. In the Basel II negotiations, while all the major banking regulators participated, they disagreed on specific aspects of the negotiations (Basel II sets a more comprehensive framework for judging and containing bank portfolio risks and capital adequacy than Basel I, the current system being used in most industrial countries. Basel II should be more easily fine-tuned to react to changes in risks that affect bank capital). Overall recently, all indications are that the banking regulators are now in agreement on Basel II, even though they do not always speak with one voice.[71] On April 1, 2008, 11 large banks were to begin submitting Basel II implementation plans to their primary regulator, despite the fact the FDIC remained concern about the internal models the banks are expected to use to determine the level of risk-based capital they are required to hold.[72]

Some Implications

The United States' functional and competitive regulatory structure has been effective primarily because of its ability to address deficiencies in financial institutions' management of risk wherever they may appear. While doing this, the structure promotes economic growth by encouraging innovation, competition, and risk taking in the financial services markets. In addition, this structure is able to maintain its flexibility, and resiliency. On the other hand, the federal regulatory structure is replete with costly redundancies that proponents call checks and balances, but opponents call needless duplication. All regulators in this structure write rules, conduct off-site monitoring, and examine financial services firms for compliance with their rules and regulations. Proponents also argue that the costs of these duplicated activities are affordable due to the benefits the stable financial services industry contributes to overall economic growth.

While Congress has heard the arguments promoting consolidation of U.S. financial services regulators at the federal level, Congress has not enacted legislation to bring this about. The industry and its regulators have argued against creating a monolithic regulator, because it could lead to unchecked extension of regulation beyond the established jurisdictional boundaries. A consolidated regulator would alter the existing regulatory checks and balances. If such a consolidated regulator extended its regulatory powers, it could stifle innovation in financial services and prevent firms from shopping for regulators that provide the greatest advantage to their business plans. On the other hand, shopping for regulators could undermine safety and soundness by allowing the least effective regulator to supervise an increasing number of financial services institutions.

Evidence from the experience in the other industrialized nations that have consolidated their financial services regulatory structures suggests that a single regulatory structure could watch for systemic risk more effectively, but that evidence is inconclusive. These nations have not had these new regulatory structures in place for a long time, making it difficult to draw conclusions from their experience with any certainty. Moreover, these nations continue to experience failures at rates not significantly different from before their consolidation took place

End Notes

[1] See Stuart I. Greenbaum and Anjan V. Thakor, *Contemporary Financial Intermediation* (Orlando, FL: Dryden Press, 1995), pp. 5 14-521, or most finance textbooks.

[2] Melanie L. Feir, "Functional Regulation: A Concept for Glass-Steagall Reform," *Stanford Journal of Law, Business & Finance*, Spring 1995, pp. 89-90, and Jerry W. Markham, *Banking Regulation: Its History and Future* (Chapel Hill, NC: North Carolina Banking Institute, 2000), pp. 277, 285.

[3] Bert Ely, "Functional Regulation Flunks: It Disregards Category Blurring," *American Banker*, February 27, 1997, p. 4.

[4] See the Board of Governors of the Federal Reserve System comments on the Government Accountability Report in U.S. Government Accountability Office, *Financial Regulation: Industry Changes Prompt Need to Reconsider U.S. Regulatory Structure*, GAO Report GAO-05-61, October 2004, p. 137, also see U.S. Task Group on Regulation of Financial Services, *Blueprint for Reform: The Report of the Task Group on Regulation of Financial Services* (Washington: GPO, 1984), pp. 29-33.

[5] BNA Banking Report, "Bank Supervision 'Burdensome' Regulations Complaint In FDIC Ombudsman Surveys, Agency Says," *BNA's Banking Report*, March 28, 2005, p. 1. See the original report at [http://www.fdic.gov /regulations

[6] Jerry W. Markham, *Banking Regulation: Its History and Future* (Chapel Hill, NC: North Carolina Banking Institute, 2000), pp. 226-227.

[7] National Bank Act of 1863, ch. 106, 13 stat. 99.

[8] Broome and Markham, Regulation of Bank Financial Service Activities (New York: West Publishing, 2001), pp. 78-81, 87.

[9] Broome and Markham, "Banking and Insurance: Before and After the Gramm-LeachBliley Act," *Journal of Corporation Law*, summer 2000, p. 727.

[10] Ibid., p. 731.

[11] Temporary National Economic Committee (TNEC), *Investigation of the Concentration of Economic Power*, Monograph No. 28A: Statement on Life Insurance, 76th Congress, 2nd sess., 1941, pp. 2, 107.

[12] Broome and Markham, "Banking and Insurance: Before and After the Gramm-LeachBliley Act," p. 732.

[13] United States v. South-Eastern Underwriters Association, 322 U.S. 533 (1944).

[14] Jerry W. Markham, "A Comparative Analysis of Consolidated and Functional Regulation: Super Regulator: A Comparative Analysis of Securities and Derivatives Regulation in the United States, the United Kingdom, and Japan," *Brooklyn Journal of International Law*, 2003, p. 4.

[15] Broome & Markham, "Banking and Insurance: Before and After the Gramm-Leach-Bliley Act," p. 737.

[16] Ibid., p. 739.

[17] Cedric V. Fricke, *The Variable Annuity: Its Impact on the Savings-Investment Market*, Bureau of Business Research, School of Business Administration, University of Michigan, 1959, 90 p.

[18] For example, states were unable to restrict banks from selling insurance following banks' victories in the courts. See *U.S. National Bank of Oregon v. Independent Agents of Agents of America*, 508 U.S. 439 (1993), and *Barnett Bank of Marion County N.A.B. Nelson*, 517 U.S. 25 (1996).

[19] Many insurance companies changed from being owned by their customers to publicly owned companies. See Broome & Markham, *Banking and Insurance: Before and After the Gramm-Leach-Bliley Act*, pp. 19, 745-746.

[20] See CRS Report RL32138, *Revising Insurance Regulation: Policy Considerations*, by Baird Webel and Carolyn Cobb.

[21] See U.S. Congress, Senate Committee on Commerce, Science, and Transportation, *Federal Involvement in the Regulation of the Insurance Industry*, hearing, 108th Cong., 1st sess., October 22, 2003, available at [http://www commerce].

[22] Joel Seligman, *The Transformation of Wall Street: A History of the Securities and Exchange Commission and Modern Corporate Finance* (New York: Aspen Publishing, 1995), p. 45.

[23] Jerry W. Markham, "A Comparative Analysis of Consolidated and Functional Regulation: Super Regulator: A Comparative Analysis of Securities and Derivatives Regulation in the United States, the United Kingdom, and Japan," p. 4.

[24] Ibid., p. 34.

[25] See the Securities and Exchange Commission section by Mark Jickling in CRS Report RL32309, *Appropriations for FY2005: Commerce, Justice, State, the Judiciary, and Related Agencies*, coordinated by Ian F. Fergusson and Susan E. Epstein.

[26] Self-regulation by the National Association of Securities Dealers was added in 1938 by the Maloney Act, 52 Stat. 1070 (Codified as amended at 15 U.S.C.§ 780-3 (2000)).

[27] Jerry W. Markham, "A Comparative Analysis of Consolidated and Functional Regulation: Super Regulator: A Comparative Analysis of Securities and Derivatives Regulation in the United States, the United Kingdom, and Japan," p. 5.

[28] Alec Klein, "Debt-Rating Firms Resist Prospect of More Supervision" *The Washington Post*, February 9, 2005, p. E-2. For testimonies presented at the Senate hearing, see [http://banking 136].

[29] The Futures Trading Act of 1921, Ch.86, 42 Stat. 187 (1921) was found unconstitutional by the Supreme Court as an impermissible use of the congressional taxing powers. See Jerry W. Markham, "A Comparative Analysis of Consolidated and Functional Regulation: Super Regulator: A Comparative Analysis of Securities and Derivatives Regulation in the United States, the United Kingdom, and Japan," p. 7.

[30] Ibid., pp.7-8.

[31] Jerry W. Markham, "Manipulation of Commodity Futures Prices — The Unprosecuteable Crime," *Yale Journal on Regulation*, vol. 8, 1991, p. 281.

[32] Jerry W. Markham, *History of Commodity Futures Trading and Its Regulation* (New York: Praeger, 1987), pp. 66-72.

[33] Ibid., pp. 99-100.

[34] CRS Report RS20560, *The Commodity Futures Modernization Act (P.L. 106-554)*, by Mark Jickling.

[35] Ibid., p. 3.

[36] The Department of the Treasury, *The Department of the Treasury Blueprint for a Modernized Financial Regulatory Structure*, March, 2008. 218pp.

[37] See Donald E. Powell, Federal Deposit Insurance Corporation Chairman, *Why Regulatory Restructuring? Why Now?*, Delivered at the Exchequer Club, Washington DC, November 16, 2002. The FDIC also sponsored a symposium entitled, "The Future of Financial Regulation: Structural Reform or the Status Quo?," March 13, 2003. The American Enterprise Institute conducted a similar conference on February 21, 2003 entitled, *Is Consolidated Financial Regulation Appropriate for the United States?* [http://www.aei.org].

[38] Kim Betz, "Super Regulator Could Aid Consistency in Financial Services Rule Writing Process," *BNA Banking Report*, September 23, 2002, p. 1.

[39] Don Powell, Remarks before the Conference on Bank Structure and Competition, Federal Reserve Bank of Chicago, Chicago, IL, May 2002, p. 2, [http://www.fdic.gov /news/news/speeches /archives/w00w/sp 1may02.html].

[40] U.S. Senate Committee on Banking, Housing, and Urban Affairs, *Banking Industry Regulatory Consolidation*, hearings, 103th Congress, 2nd sess., March 1, 1994, pp. 44-66.

[41] U.S. Government Accountability Office, *Financial Regulation: Industry Changes Prompt Need to Reconsider U.S. Regulatory Structure*, GAO Report GAO-05-61, October 2004, p. 77.

[42] See CRS Report RS21 153,*Optimal Federal Chartering for Insurers: Legislation and Viewpoints*, by S. Roy Woodall Jr.

[43] U.S. Government Accountability Office, *Financial Regulation: Industry Changes Prompt Need to Reconsider U.S. Regulatory Structure*, GAO Report GAO-05-61, October 2004, p. 81.

[44] CRS Report RL32789, *Insurance Regulation: Issues, Background, and Current Legislation*, by Baird Webel.

[45] Jerry W. Markham, "A Comparative Analysis of Consolidated and Functional Regulation: Super Regulator: A Comparative Analysis of Securities and Derivatives Regulation in the United States, the United Kingdom, and Japan," *Brooklyn Journal of International Law*, 2003, p. 17.

[46] U.S. Government Accountability Office, *Financial Regulation: Industry Changes Prompt Need to Reconsider U.S. Regulatory Structure*, GAO Report GAO-05-61, October 2004, p. 78.

[47] Ibid., p. 68; and see the Bafin's 2002 Annual Report, p. 9, at [http://www.bafin.de/j ahresbericht/ jb02_e_TeilA.pdf].

[48] Anthony Saunders and Ingo Walter, *Universal Banking in the United States* (New York: Oxford University Press, 1994), p. 276.

[49] Jerry W. Markham, "A Comparative Analysis of Consolidated and Functional Regulation: Super Regulator: A Comparative Analysis of Securities and Derivatives Regulation in the United States the United Kingdom, and Japan," *Brooklyn Journal of International Law*, 2003, p. 19.

[50] U.S. Government Accountability Office, *Financial Regulation: Industry Changes Prompt Need to Reconsider U.S. Regulatory Structure*, GAO Report GAO-05-61, October 6, 2004, p. 66.

[51] International Monetary Fund, *United Kingdom: 2002 Article IV Consultation — Staff Report; Staff Statement; Public Information Notice on the Executive Board Discussion; and Statement by the Executive Director for the United Kingdom*, Country Report no. 03/48, February 2003, pp. 3 1-32.

[52] Andrew Verity, "Where Equitable Life Went Wrong," *BBC News*, March 9, 2004, p. 1, [http://news.bbc.co.uk/1/hi/business/3547441.stm].

[53] U.S. Government Accountability Office, *Financial Regulation: Industry Changes Prompt Need to Reconsider U.S. Regulatory Structure*, GAO Report GAO-05-61, October 6, 2004, p. 66. Jerry W. Markham, "A Comparative Analysis of Consolidated and Functional Regulation: Super Regulator: A Comparative Analysis

of Securities and Derivatives Regulation in the United States, the United Kingdom, and Japan," p. 20, and James Mackintosh, and James Archer, "Banned from City Trading for Shares Deception," *Financial Times*, July 28, 2001, p. 3.

54 International Monetary Fund, *United Kingdom: 2002 Article IV Consultation — Staff Report; Staff Statement; Public Information Notice on the Executive Board Discussion; and Statement by the Executive Director for the United Kingdom*, Country Report no. 03/48, February 2003, p. 31.

55 International Monetary Fund, *Japan: Financial System Stability Assessment and Supplementary Information*, Country Report no. 03/287, Washington, September 2003, p. 76.

56 For more detailed FSA-Japan information see [http://www.fsa.go.jp/en/about/about03.pdf].

57 Jerry W. Markham, "A Comparative Analysis of Consolidated and Functional Regulation: Super Regulator: A Comparative Analysis of Securities and Derivatives Regulation in the United States the United Kingdom, and Japan," *Brooklyn Journal of International Law*, 28, 319, 2003, p. 20.

58 Ibid., p. 19.

59 International Monetary Fund, *Japan: Financial System Stability Assessment and Supplementary Information*, Country Report no. 03/287, Washington, September 2003, pp. 47, 65, 77.

60 Jerry W. Markham, "A Comparative Analysis of Consolidated and Functional Regulation: Super Regulator: A Comparative Analysis of Securities and Derivatives Regulation in the United States the United Kingdom, and Japan," p. 23, and International Monetary Fund, *Japan: Financial System Stability Assessment and Supplementary Information*, Country Report no. 03/287, Washington, September 2003, p. 44; David Pilling, "Regulator Drafts Plan for Japanese Bank Mergers," *Financial Times*, July 11, 2002, p. 10.

61 International Monetary Fund, *Japan: Financial System Stability Assessment and Supplementary Information*, Country Report no. 03/287, Washington, September 2003, p. 13.

62 Alexandra Nusbaum, "Investment Trust Hopes Lift Tokyo," *Financial Times*, January 29, 2000, p. 24.

63 Phred Dvorak, "Japan's Central Bank Will Buy Stocks Held by Troubled Lenders," *Wall Street Journal*, September 19, 2002, p. A-1.

64 International Monetary Fund, *Japan: 2005 Article IV Consultation — Staff Report; Staff Supplement; and Public Information Notice on the Executive Board Discussion,* IMF Country Report No. 05/273, August 2005, p. 9.

65 Hakuo Yanagisawa, "Japan's Financial Sector Reform: Reform: Progress and Challenges," address to the Financial Services Authority, September 3, 2001, [http://www. fsa.go.jp/gaiyou/gaiyoue /presen/p20010903.html].

66 For more detailed information about the Financial Supervisory Authority go to [http://www.bafin.de/cgi-bin/bafin.pl?sprache= 1&verz=0 1_About_us*0 1_Tasks_an d_Obj ectives&nofr= 1&site=0&filter=&ntick=0].

67 See CRS Report RL32354, *European Union — United States: Financial Services Action Plan's Regulatory Reform Issues*, by Walter W. Eubanks.

68 Ibid.

69 Government Accountability Office, *Financial Regulation: Industry Changes Prompt Need to Reconsider U.S. Regulatory Structure,* GAO Report GAO-05-6 1, October 6, 2004, pp. 67- 68.

70 International Monetary Fund, *Germany — 2003 Article IV Consultation Concluding Statement of the Mission*, IMF, country Report no. 3/48, July 14, 2003, p. 5, [http://www.imf.org/external/np/ms/2003/071403.htm].

71 R. Christian Bruce, "Agencies Spar Over Capital Requirements as Discord Persists on Basel II Agreement," *BNA Banking Report*, May 16, 2005. p. 1, [http://ippubs.bna.com/IP/BNA/bar.nsf/SearchAllView/09D20CE5C743FB1F85257001000A97AE?Open&highlight=BASEL,II].

72 See CRS Report RL34485, *Basel II in the United States: Progress toward a Workable Framework,* by Walter W. Eubanks and See U.S. Congress Senate Committee on Banking, Housing and Urban Affairs, *The Interagency Proposal Regarding The Basel Capital Accord,* hearing, 110th Cong., 1st sess., September 26, 2006, Available at [http://banking .pdf].

Chapter 2

FINANCIAL REGULATION: INDUSTRY TRENDS CONTINUE TO CHALLENGE THE FEDERAL REGULATORY STRUCTURE

United States Government Accountability Office

WHY GAO DID THIS STUDY

As the financial services industry has become increasingly concentrated in a number of large, internationally active firms offering an array of products and services, the adequacy of the U.S. financial regulatory system has been questioned. GAO has identified the need to modernize the financial regulatory system as a challenge to be addressed in the 21st century. This chapter, mandated by the Financial Services Regulatory Relief Act of 2006, discusses (1) measurements of regulatory costs and benefits and efforts to avoid excessive regulatory burden, (2) the challenges posed to financial regulators by trends in the industry, and (3) options to enhance the efficiency and effectiveness of the federal financial regulatory structure. GAO convened a Comptroller General's Forum (Forum) with supervisors and leading industry experts, reviewed regulatory agency policies, and summarized prior reports to meet these objectives.

WHAT GAO RECOMMENDS

GAO does not make any new recommendations in this chapter, but observes that the recommendations and options presented in prior reports remain relevant today in considering how best to improve the federal financial regulatory structure. The Chairman of the Federal Reserve and the Chairman of the National Credit Union Administration provided formal comments generally agreeing with the thrust of our report.

WHAT GAO FOUND

The inherent problems of measuring the costs and benefits of regulation make it difficult to assess the extent to which regulations may be unduly burdensome to U.S. financial services firms, particularly in comparison to firms in other countries. Additionally, it is difficult to separate the costs of complying with regulation from other costs and thus determine regulatory burden. Regulatory agencies, however, have undertaken several initiatives to reduce regulatory burden; these efforts contributed to the Financial Services Regulatory Relief Act of 2006. While noting that regulation contributes to confidence in financial institutions and markets, participants in the Forum agreed regulators have opportunities to further reduce regulatory burden and suggested regulators better measure the results of implemented regulations. GAO also recently recommended regulatory agencies consider whether and how to measure the performance of regulation during the process of promulgating the regulation and improving the communication of regulatory reviews to the public.

The current regulatory structure, with multiple agencies that oversee segments of the financial services industry, is challenged by a number of industry trends. The development of large, complex, internationally active firms whose product offerings span the jurisdiction of several agencies creates the potential for inconsistent regulatory treatment of similar products, gaps in consumer and investor protection, or duplication among regulators. Regulatory agencies have made efforts to collaborate in responding to these trends and avoid inconsistencies, gaps, and duplication. However, challenges remain; until recently, the Office of Thrift Supervision and the Securities and Exchange Commission, for instance, had not sought to resolve potentially duplicative and inconsistent regulation of several financial services conglomerates for which both agencies have jurisdiction. Finally, despite the challenges posed by the industry's dynamic environment, accountability for addressing issues that span agencies' jurisdiction is not clearly assigned. These issues have led GAO to suggest in prior work that the federal regulatory structure should be modernized.

GAO and others have recommended several options to accomplish modernization of the federal financial regulatory structure; these include consolidating certain regulatory functions as well as having a single regulator for large, complex firms. There also are potential lessons that can be learned from the experience of other nations that have restructured their financial regulators. Several Forum participants, for instance, suggested that one important lesson the United States could learn from the United Kingdom's Financial Services Authority was the value of setting principles or goals for regulators. The Department of the Treasury's recently announced plan to propose a restructured regulatory system provides an opportunity to take the first step toward modernization by providing clear and consistent goals for the regulatory agencies.

ABBREVIATIONS

AIM	Alternative Investment Market
BSA	Bank Secrecy Act
CEA	Commodity Exchange Act

CFTC	Commodity Futures Trading Commission
CRS	Congressional Research Service
CSE	consolidated supervised entity
EGRPRA	Economic Growth and Regulatory Paperwork Reduction Act of 1996
EU	European Union
FDIC	Federal Deposit Insurance Corporation
FDICIA	Federal Deposit Insurance Corporation Improvement Act
FINRA	Financial Industry Regulatory Authority
Forum	Comptroller General's Forum
FSA	United Kingdom - Financial Services Authority
Group	President's Working Group
ILC	industrial loan company
IMF	International Monetary Fund
LTCM	Long-Term Capital Management
NCUA	National Credit Union Administration
NPR	Notice of Proposed Rulemaking
OCC	Office of the Comptroller of the Currency
OTS	Office of Thrift Supervision
SEC	Securities and Exchange Commission
SRO	self-regulatory organization
Treasury	Department of the Treasury

October 12, 2007

The Honorable Christopher Dodd
Chairman
The Honorable Richard Shelby
Ranking Member
Committee on Banking, Housing, and Urban Affairs
United States Senate

The Honorable Barney Frank
Chairman
The Honorable Spencer Bachus
Ranking Member
Committee on Financial Services
House of Representatives

The financial services industry—including the banking, securities, and futures sectors—has changed significantly over the last several decades.[1] Firms today are generally fewer and larger, provide more and varied services, offer similar products, and operate in increasingly global markets. These developments have both benefits and risks for the overall U.S. economy. Despite these changes, the U.S. financial regulatory structure has largely remained the same. It is a complex system of multiple federal and state regulators as well as self-regulatory organizations (SROs) that operate largely along functional lines, even as these lines have become increasingly blurred in the industry. Regulated financial institutions have learned to operate and thrive under the existing regulatory system. However, concerns about inefficient overlaps in responsibility, undue regulatory burden, and possible gaps in oversight raise questions about whether the current structure is best suited to meet the nation's needs.

We identified a need to modernize the financial regulatory system as a challenge to be addressed in the 21st century, noting that although multiple specialized regulators bring critical skills to bear in their areas of expertise, they have difficulty identifying and responding to risks that cross industry lines.[2] We asked whether it is time to modernize the financial regulatory system to promote a more coherent and integrated structure and specify goals more clearly. Such concerns also have been recently raised by the International Monetary Fund (IMF).[3] In a statement regarding its review of U.S. economic developments, IMF concluded that rapid innovation in the U.S. financial industry had created new regulatory challenges for a system disadvantaged by its overlapping regulatory oversight. IMF stated that emphasis should be placed on strategies to improve regulatory effectiveness, such as implementing general regulatory principles or goals to ease interagency coordination and shorten reaction times to industry developments. Similarly, the Department of the Treasury has undertaken an initiative to examine the regulatory structure associated with financial institutions, partly in response to concerns that the current structure may make U.S. financial markets less competitive. Treasury expects to develop a plan by early 2008 to identify a regulatory structure with improved oversight, increased efficiency, reduced overlap, and the ability to adapt to financial market participants' constantly changing strategies and tools.

Debate about modernizing the current financial regulatory structure is not new. However, there is continuing value in reexamining the current regulatory system and structure and considering ways in which it could be more efficient and effective.

In response to a mandate in the Financial Services Regulatory Relief Act of 2006,[4] this chapter

- describes measurements of the costs and benefits of financial regulation in general and current efforts to avoid excessive regulatory burden;[5]
- describes financial industry trends and the challenges that these pose to the federal financial regulatory structure; and
- discusses various options to enhance the efficiency and effectiveness of the federal financial regulatory structure.

To meet our objectives, we convened a Comptroller General's Forum (Forum) on June 11, 2007, that brought together leading experts from the financial services industry, the regulatory agencies, and academia to discuss issues relative to our objectives. The Forum agenda covered three broad topics: (1) balancing regulatory costs and benefits, (2) financial services regulation in a dynamic environment, and (3) assessing options for enhancing the financial regulatory system. Forum participants were selected to provide perspectives from different segments of the industry and different regulatory agencies. To encourage a free exchange of information and viewpoints, no specific statements or opinions expressed by Forum participants are attributed to any participant. To meet our objectives, we also met with federal regulators to discuss our objectives and reviewed regulatory agency documents and reports. We also reviewed and summarized relevant analysis, conclusions, and recommendations from our earlier reports on financial regulation. (These reports are referenced in footnotes or noted in Related GAO Products at the end of this chapter.) We conducted our work between January 2007 and October 2007 in Chicago, Illinois, and Washington, D.C., in accordance with generally accepted government auditing standards. Appendix I provides a list of Forum participants.

RESULTS IN BRIEF

Regulators and the financial services industry face challenges measuring regulatory costs and benefits, making it difficult to assess the extent to which regulations may be unduly burdensome to U.S. firms—particularly in comparison to the amount of regulation that firms face in other countries. Most notably, it is hard to separate the costs of complying with regulation from other costs. As a result, it is difficult for regulators to determine the extent that costs to implement rules impose regulatory burden and for the industry to substantiate claims about burdensome regulation. Measuring regulatory benefits remains an even greater challenge largely because of the difficulty in quantifying benefits such as improved consumer protection or financial stability, though regulators and other groups acknowledge that financial regulation provides such benefits as an increased confidence in our financial markets and an enhanced level of consumer protection. Nevertheless, regulators have responded to concerns about specific regulatory burdens, and many provisions of the Financial Services Regulatory Relief Act of 2006 are based on regulators' identification of regulations that are outdated or unnecessarily burdensome. However, some groups still assert that regulatory burden has increased significantly over time and that regulators should do more to address such burdens. Forum participants agreed with these assertions, suggesting that regulators improve measurements of implemented regulations' results as a way to promote their own regulatory accountability. Continued efforts such as those that the bank regulatory agencies undertook in response to the Economic Growth and Regulatory Paperwork Reduction Act of 1996 (EGRPRA) could be important steps in identifying and eliminating outdated, unnecessary, and unduly burdensome regulations. We recently recommended several steps agencies should take to ensure they conduct effective and transparent reviews of regulations, including consideration of whether and how to measure the performance of a regulation during the process of promulgating the regulation and steps to improve the communication of regulatory reviews to the public. Further consideration of steps such as these could help ensure financial regulations are cost-effective.

The current regulatory structure—characterized by specialization and competition among regulators as well as charter choice—has contributed to broad and deep U.S. financial markets, but the agencies that share responsibility for financial regulation face continued challenges from financial trends including increased globalization, consolidation, and product convergence. In particular, the offering of similar financial products and services by firms subject to different regulatory regimes creates the potential for regulatory inconsistencies and regulatory gaps, among other issues. For example, in our prior work, we reported that holding companies of industrial loan companies (ILC) are overseen by regulators with different authority than holding companies of other depository institutions. As a result of differences in supervision, ILCs in a holding company structure may pose more risk of loss to the Deposit

Insurance Fund than other types of insured depository institutions in a holding company structure. The Federal Deposit Insurance Corporation (FDIC), the regulator of ILCs, has placed a moratorium on applications for the ILC charter by commercial firms to allow it and Congress to further evaluate ILC ownership and its related issues. Similarly, we previously have reported that both the Office of Thrift Supervision (OTS) and the Securities and Exchange Commission (SEC) have jurisdiction over the holding companies of several large financial services firms, but had not resolved how to clarify accountability for the supervision of these firms, creating the potential for duplicative or inconsistent regulation. Regulators have made efforts to collaborate to respond to changes in the industry to avoid inconsistencies, gaps, and duplicative activities. OTS and SEC, for instance, have begun meeting to resolve the potential for duplicative or inconsistent regulation for the holding companies where they share jurisdiction. Also, the President's Working Group (Group) provides a framework for coordinating policies and actions that cross jurisdictional lines. However, we have reported that the Group is not well suited to orchestrate a consistent set of goals or objectives that would direct the work of the different agencies because it lacks the authority to bind members to its decisions or positions. While the regulatory agencies have taken actions to work collaboratively in response to the industry's trends, continued progress in these areas would help to make our existing regulatory structure more effective.

In our prior work, we have recommended that Congress consider changes to the regulatory system to meet the challenges posed by the industry's trends and identified a number of options to accomplish this. Financial regulators today are increasingly dealing with large, complex firms that cross formerly distinct industry boundaries; however, the effects of the incremental development of our regulatory structure and the challenges that agencies face in responding to the dynamic industry environment are now more evident. The present federal financial regulatory structure, which has evolved largely as a result of periodic ad hoc responses to crises, continues to be challenged by the industry's trends of increased consolidation, conglomeration, convergence, and globalization. Today, financial services firms offering similar products may be subject to different regulatory regimes, creating the potential for inconsistent regulation. Many firms are subject to multiple regulators, creating the potential for regulatory duplication. At the same time, as our prior work has noted, no single agency has the responsibility and authority to identify and address risks that cross markets and industries. Thus, we and others previously have identified several options for consideration that, despite costs and risks, offer opportunities to enhance the efficiency and effectiveness of the regulatory system. We believe these options remain relevant today in considering how best to modernize the federal financial regulatory structure. Others also have proposed options for restructuring the federal financial regulatory system. Other nations have reorganized their regulatory systems; some have consolidated regulators into a single agency, while others have created specialized regulatory agencies that focus solely on ensuring the safety and soundness of institutions or on consumer protection. Lessons may be learned in this regard from the principles-based approach modeled by the United Kingdom, which consolidated several agencies into a single financial regulator, the Financial Services Authority (FSA). Some Forum participants noted that an important lesson from FSA's experience could be its development of clearly stated principles defining the regulator's priorities. Given the continued challenges faced by the current regulatory structure, establishing clear, consistent regulatory goals may be an important first step to improving its effectiveness.

We are not making new recommendations in this chapter, but believe that our prior recommendations to enhance the effectiveness of the current regulatory process remain relevant. We also continue to believe that the options we presented in prior work for modifying the existing regulatory structure to better meet today's financial environment remain relevant. Finally, we and others also have stressed the importance of establishing clearer, more consistent goals for financial regulation. A critical first step to modernizing the regulatory system and enhancing its ability to meet the challenges of the dynamic financial services industry includes clearly defining regulatory agencies' goals and objectives. Such goals and objectives could help establish agency priorities as well as define responsibility and accountability for identifying risks, including those that cross markets and industries. No single financial regulator is currently in a position to set these goals, and current interagency groups have not proven themselves appropriate vehicles for goal setting. As Treasury considers how best to rationalize the U.S. financial regulatory structure, it has the opportunity to work with other agencies to define clear and consistent goals and objectives. Defining these goals could provide the impetus for making progress on the design of the financial regulatory system, and thus could be an important first step in the Secretary's plan to develop a more modern, efficient oversight structure that is better able to adapt to the industry's changes.

We provided the Secretary of the Treasury and the heads of CFTC, the Federal Reserve, FDIC, NCUA, OCC, OTS, and SEC with drafts of this chapter for their comment. We received written comments from the Chairman of the Board of Governors of the Federal Reserve System and the Chairman of NCUA who generally agreed with the thrust of our report; these are reprinted in appendixes II and III. We also received technical comments from the staffs at the Treasury, the Federal Reserve, CFTC, FDIC, NCUA, OCC, OTS, and SEC that we have incorporated in the report.

Background

In the banking industry, the specific regulatory configuration depends on the type of charter the banking institution chooses. Bank charter types include

- *commercial banks*, which originally focused on the banking needs of businesses, but then over time broadened their services;
- *thrifts*, which include savings banks, savings associations, and savings and loans, were originally created to serve the needs—particularly the mortgage needs—of those not served by commercial banks;
- *credit unions*, which are member-owned cooperatives run by member- elected boards with a historic emphasis on serving people of modest means; and
- *industrial loan companies (ILCs)*, also known as industrial banks, which are state-chartered financial institutions that have grown from small, limited-purpose

institutions to a diverse industry that includes some of the nation's largest and more complex financial institutions.[6]

These charters may be obtained at the state or national level for all except ILCs, which are only chartered at the state level. State regulators charter institutions and participate in the oversight of those institutions; however, all of these institutions have a primary federal regulator if they offer federal deposit insurance. The primary federal regulators are the following:

- The Office of the Comptroller of the Currency (OCC), which charters and supervises national banks. As of December 30, 2006, there were 1,715 commercial banks with a national bank charter. These banks held the dominant share of bank assets, about $6.829 trillion.
- The Federal Reserve, which serves as the regulator for state-chartered banks that opt to be members of the Federal Reserve System. As of December 30, 2006, the Federal Reserve supervised 902 state member banks, with total assets of $1.406 trillion.
- The Federal Deposit Insurance Corporation (FDIC), which supervises all other state-chartered commercial banks with federally insured deposits, as well as federally insured state savings banks. As of December 30, 2006, there were 4,785 state-chartered banks and 435 state-chartered savings banks, with $ 1.855 trillion and $306 billion in total assets, respectively. In addition, FDIC has certain backup supervisory authority for federally insured banks and savings institutions.
- The Office of Thrift Supervision (OTS), which charters and supervises federally chartered savings institutions. As of December 30, 2006, OTS supervised 844 institutions with $1.464 trillion in total assets.
- The National Credit Union Administration (NCUA), which charters and supervises federally chartered credit unions. As of December 30, 2006, 8,362 credit unions hold $710 billion in assets.

These federal regulators have established capital requirements for the depository institutions they supervise, conduct onsite examinations and offsite monitoring to assess an institution's financial condition, and monitor and enforce compliance with banking and consumer laws. Regulators also issue regulations, take enforcement actions, and close institutions they determine to be insolvent.

The securities and futures industries are regulated under a combination of self-regulation (subject to oversight of the appropriate federal regulator) and direct oversight by the Securities and Exchange Commission (SEC) and the Commodity Futures Trading Commission (CFTC), respectively. In the securities industry, the self-regulatory organizations (SROs) have responsibility for oversight of the securities markets and their participants by establishing the standards under which their members conduct business; monitoring business conduct; and bringing disciplinary actions against their members for violating applicable federal statutes, SEC's rules, and their own rules.[7] SEC oversees SROs by inspecting their operations and reviewing their rule proposals and appeals of final disciplinary proceedings. In the futures industry, SROs include the futures exchanges and the National Futures Association. Futures SROs are responsible for establishing and enforcing rules governing member conduct and trading; providing for the prevention of market manipulation, including monitoring trading activity; ensuring that futures industry professionals meet qualifications; and examining members for financial strength and other regulatory purposes. The Commodity Futures Trading Commission (CFTC) independently monitors, among other things, exchange trading activity, large trader positions, and certain market participants' financial conditions.[8]

The U.S. regulatory system for financial services is described as "functional" so that financial products or activities generally are regulated according to their function, no matter who offers the product or participates in the activity. Broker-dealer activities, for instance, are generally subject to SEC's jurisdiction, whether the broker-dealer is a subsidiary of a bank holding company subject to Federal Reserve supervision or a subsidiary of an investment bank. The functional regulator approach is intended to provide consistency in regulation, focus regulatory restrictions on the relevant functions area, and avoid the potential need for regulatory agencies to develop expertise in all aspects of financial regulation.

Many of the largest financial legal entities are part of holding company structures—companies that hold stock in one or more subsidiaries—and conduct business and manage risks on a consolidated basis. Many of these companies are subject to consolidated supervision that provides a basis for examining the financial and operating risks faced by holding companies and the controls in place to manage those risks at a consolidated, or holding company-wide, level. Companies that own or control banks are regulated and supervised by the Federal Reserve as bank holding companies, and their nonbanking activities generally are limited to those the Federal Reserve has determined to be closely related to banking. Under the Gramm-Leach-Bliley Act, bank holding companies can qualify as financial holding companies and thereby engage in a range of financial activities broader than those permitted for "traditional" bank holding companies. Savings and loan or thrift holding companies (thrift holding companies), that own or control one or more savings associations (but not a bank) are subject to supervision by OTS and, depending upon certain circumstances, may not face the types of activities' restrictions imposed on bank holding companies. Certain holding companies that own large broker-dealers can elect to be supervised by SEC as consolidated supervised entities (CSE). SEC provides group-wide oversight of these entities unless they are determined to already be subject to "comprehensive, consolidated supervision" by another principal regulator. While holding company supervisors oversee the holding company, the appropriate functional regulator remains primarily responsible for supervising any functionally regulated subsidiary within the holding company.

In prior reports, we have noted that characteristics of the U.S. regulatory structure can have positive effects.[9] Specialization by regulatory agencies allows them to better understand the risks associated with particular activities or products. Competition among regulators helps to account for regulatory innovation, providing businesses with a method to move to regulators whose approaches better match businesses' operations. We also have noted that the system is complex, with a single large firm subject to oversight by multiple federal and state agencies, as figure 1 illustrates.

The Federal Reserve and the Department of the Treasury (Treasury) also share responsibility for maintaining financial stability. Treasury also represents the United States on international financial market issues and, in consultation with the President, also may approve special resolution options for insolvent financial institutions whose failure could threaten the stability of the financial system. Two-thirds of the Federal Reserve's Board of Governors and FDIC's Board of Directors must approve any extraordinary coverage.

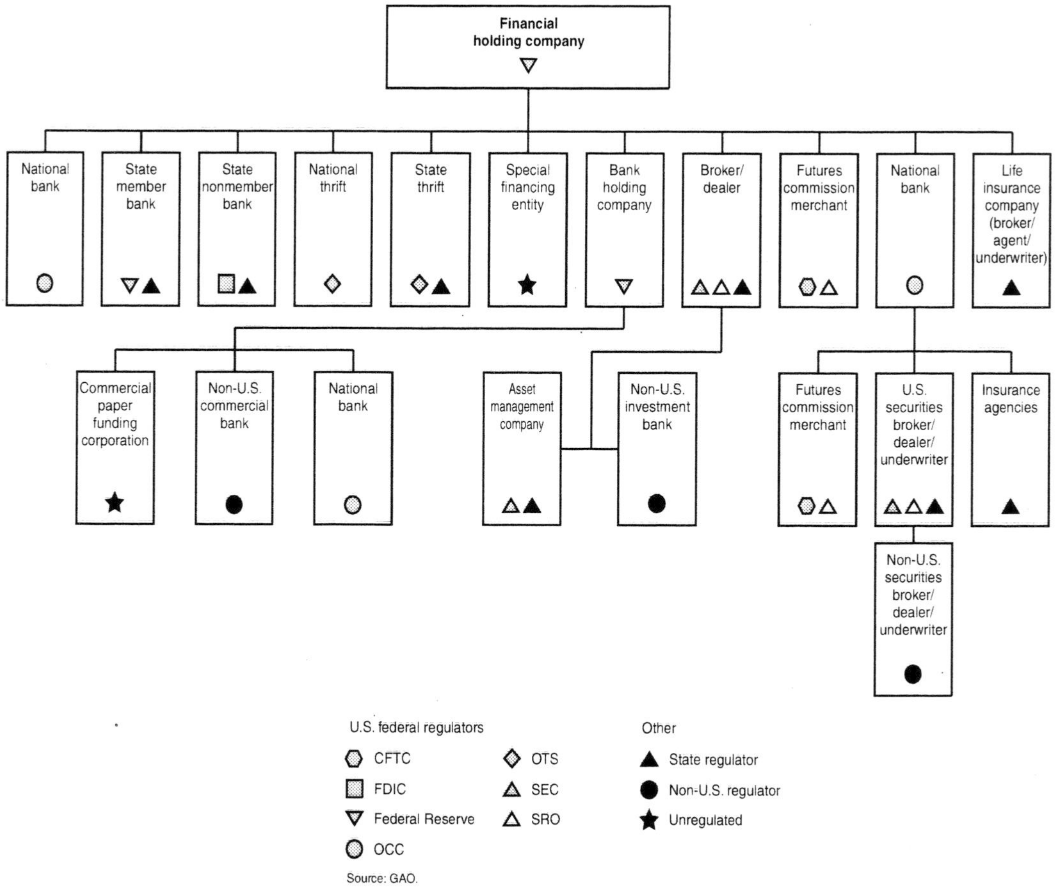

Source: GAO.

Figure 1. Federal Supervisors for a Hypothetical Financial Holding Company

MEASURING THE COSTS AND BENEFITS OF REGULATION HAS BEEN DIFFICULT, COMPLICATING EFFORTS TO REDUCE REGULATORY BURDEN

Measuring the costs and benefits of financial regulation has posed a challenge to regulators and the financial services industry. Though precise measurement remains a challenge, many claim regulation has become more burdensome over time. Regulators have responded to these concerns by reviewing existing regulations to identify ways to reduce unnecessary regulatory burdens. Such reviews have, in some cases, assisted in identifying the costs and benefits of regulation and removing unnecessary burden. However, some groups still assert regulatory burden has increased significantly over time and regulators should do more to address such burdens. Forum participants agreed with these assertions, suggesting regulators improve measurements of the results of implemented regulations as a way to promote their own regulatory accountability. We recently recommended several steps that agencies should take to ensure they conduct effective and transparent reviews of regulations, including consideration of whether and how to measure the performance of regulation during the process of promulgating the regulation and steps to improve the communication of regulatory reviews to the public.[10]

Regulators and the Financial Services Industry Face Challenges Measuring Regulatory Costs and Benefits

The difficulty of reliably estimating the costs of regulation to the industry and to the nation has long been recognized, and the benefits of regulation are generally regarded as even more difficult to measure. This situation presents challenges for regulators that attempt to estimate the anticipated costs of regulations, and also for industry to substantiate claims about regulatory burden. For example, a 1998 Federal Reserve staff study concluded that it had insufficient information to reliably estimate the total cost of regulations for commercial banks.[11]

One limitation of efforts to measure regulatory costs is the difficulty that businesses have in separating the costs of regulatory compliance from other costs related to risk management or recordkeeping. For instance, bank capital adequacy regulation provides an example of the inherent difficulty of assessing the value of regulation. Our work on the implementation of the Basel II risk-based capital framework noted that banks often could not separate out costs related directly to the implementation of the framework, as systems often served multiple purposes, such as reporting for many kinds of regulations and also for internal, risk management purposes.[12] Similarly, an analysis of financial regulation in the United Kingdom found that firms tend not to separate out costs for complying with regulations, and firms could not estimate hypothetical savings if certain regulations were removed.[13]

While regulation provides a broad assurance of the strength of financial markets, it is difficult to measure those benefits, in part because regulations seeking to ensure financial stability aim to prevent low- probability, high-cost events.

Concerns Exist that Regulation Could Hinder Market Efficiency

Recent reports by industry participants, academics, and policymakers also have suggested that regulatory burden may be lessening U.S. securities markets' viability and challenging their competitiveness.[14] A number of factors have been asserted as contributing to a perceived loss in U.S. competitiveness, with one potential factor being the litigious environment of the United States. Some industry representatives, market analysts, and academics argue that this environment creates concerns for firms about potential class action and other lawsuits that may impact their decision to engage in business in the United States. Another factor is the often limited coordination among regulators that at times results in overlapping regulatory jurisdictions and confusing regulations. Additionally, questions regarding the jurisdiction over some financial products raise doubts for firms about how such products will be regulated. For example, the U.S. Chamber of Commerce has questioned whether CFTC should have jurisdiction over securities futures products, and recommended that jurisdiction be shifted to the SEC.[15] In our work we also have noted that SEC and CFTC share overlapping jurisdiction on financial products that have the features of both securities and futures, which can inhibit market innovation by potentially causing market participants to design products based on how they might be regulated.[16] However, some argue that regulatory competition helps bring about innovation in regulatory approaches, as one Forum participant noted.

U.S. Regulators Have Reviewed Existing Regulations

U.S. regulatory agencies have undertaken several efforts to lessen regulatory burden and cost of existing regulations. Federal banking agencies have undertaken a major initiative to address the regulatory burden of depository institutions in response to the Economic Growth and Regulatory Paperwork Reduction Act of 1996 (EGRPRA). The act requires federal banking regulators to review their regulations at least once every 10 years and to identify and eliminate outdated, unnecessary, or unduly burdensome regulatory requirements, as appropriate. Agencies also are required to report to Congress on regulatory burdens that must be addressed through legislative action.[17]

Bank regulatory agencies have made changes to regulation and reporting requirements as part of the EGRPRA process. Bank agencies modernized their call report procedures, for instance,[18] and sought comments and suggestions on outdated, unnecessary, or overly burdensome regulations. In response to these comments, for example, OCC published a Notice of Proposed Rulemaking soliciting comments on proposed amendments to OCC regulations that, among other changes, would eliminate or streamline existing requirements or procedures.[19] Another outcome of the EGRPRA process was the development of proposals that were incorporated into the Financial Services Regulatory Relief Act of 2006.

Forum Participants Shared Concerns Regarding Regulatory Burden

A majority of Forum participants held the view that regulations had become more burdensome over the past decade. However, one participant noted that while some regulations may be considered burdensome to industry, they may be necessary to ensure public confidence. Others noted the importance of considering legislation's contribution to regulatory burden. In addition, some participants shared the opinion that federal regulation has hurt the competitiveness of U.S. securities markets.

Some Forum participants agreed that cost-benefit analysis presents a number of measurement challenges, primarily because some costs are easier to measure than benefits. One participant, for instance, noted the benefits from legislation or regulation could include enhanced confidence in markets, something that cannot be valued. Forum participants suggested measurement should focus on outcomes and results, and regulators should improve measurements for their own regulatory accountability. One participant noted the Bank Secrecy Act (BSA), for example, has resulted in filing many currency transaction reports and suspicious activity reports, but the benefits of such filings are sometimes unclear to banks.[20] The participant added that regulators should consider whether the BSA is providing the intended results and outcomes, considering the costs.[21]

To improve the measurement of costs and benefits, some Forum participants thought a good practice to adopt from the U.K.'s Financial Services Authority (FSA) would be its conduct of cost-benefit analyses. To assure that FSA accomplishes its regulatory goals efficiently, it is required to submit cost-benefit analyses for its proposals. In addition, FSA must report annually on its costs relative to the costs of regulation in other countries and must provide its next fiscal year budget for public comment 3 months prior to the end of the current fiscal year.

While regulators have attempted to address concerns about regulatory burden by issuing guidance, assessing the level of regulatory burden, and conducting retrospective reviews, a majority of Forum participants also believed regulatory bodies could take advantage of additional opportunities to reduce the regulatory burden placed on financial firms. One participant noted that the London Stock Exchange's Alternative Investment Market (AIM)[22] is an example of a market that has little regulation and might demonstrate how lighter regulatory approaches could be implemented. This participant also noted, however, that such approaches have been criticized for not providing adequate investor protection.

We Have Recommended Improved Review of Regulations

Retrospective reviews such as those conducted under EGRPRA and other legislation and guidance assist in assessing the effectiveness of how regulations were implemented and help identify opportunities to reduce regulatory burdens and validate regulatory cost and benefit estimates.[23] The EGRPRA process, for example, provided an opportunity for the financial industry to suggest ways to improve upon and simplify regulations applicable to federally-insured depository institutions. Regulatory agency officials reported that similar retrospective reviews have resulted in cost savings to their agencies and to regulated parties. For example, the agencies noted that modernized call report processing would decrease the cost of data collection and verification for all parties.

In a 2007 report, we recommended that agencies improve the effectiveness and transparency of retrospective regulatory reviews and identify opportunities for Congress to revise and consolidate existing requirements.[24] We found that though agencies have conducted many such reviews, the public generally remains unaware of the scope and frequency of such reviews, and agencies can be better prepared to undertake reviews by planning how they will collect relevant performance data on regulations before promulgating the regulation, or prior to the review.

Developments in a Dynamic Financial Industry Environment Pose Challenges to the Federal Financial Regulatory Structure

Strengths of the current regulatory structure—including regulatory competition, regulatory specialization, and charter choice—have contributed to the development of a strong U.S. financial system. However, the structure is not always well-suited to handle challenges and emerging issues in the financial industry. Industry developments, including the trends of consolidation and globalization, as well as legislative changes, challenge regulators to provide consistent regulatory guidance and treatment of similar firms. Further, increased convergence in product offerings and increased concentration of assets in large, complex firms pose a challenge for regulatory agencies to act consistently in responding to risks that cut across the functional lines that define the regulatory structure. While the regulatory agencies have taken action to work collaboratively in response to the industry's trends, we have noted in the past that it is difficult to collaborate within the fragmented U.S. regulatory system and concluded that the structure of the federal regulatory system should be reexamined.

Aspects of the Current Regulatory Structure Have Contributed to a Strong Financial System but also Create Challenges

The current regulatory structure has contributed to the development of U.S. financial markets and to overall economic growth and stability. However, this structure, characterized by specialization of and competition among multiple regulatory agencies, has both strengths and weaknesses. On the positive side, specialization allows regulators to better understand the risks associated with particular activities or products and to better represent the views of all segments of the industry. Moreover, regulators have developed skilled staff with specialized knowledge of particular industries that can be brought to bear during supervisory examinations. Competition among regulators helps to account for regulatory innovation by providing businesses with a choice among regulators whose approaches better match the businesses' operations. Regulated financial institutions have learned to operate and even thrive under the existing regulatory system. Banks, for example, note the benefit of having multiple charter options that serve different business needs.[25] Competition among the banking regulators, especially the Federal Reserve and OCC, is credited with prompting certain changes in regulation. These changes include the removal of prohibitions against securities firms, banks, and insurance companies operating in a single holding company structure and increased regulatory attention to the provision of loans in certain minority areas.[26]

At the same time, these very characteristics may hinder the effective and efficient oversight of large, complex, internationally active firms that compete across sectors and national boundaries. The specialized and differential oversight of holding companies by different regulators has the potential to create competitive imbalances among firms based on regulatory differences alone. Specifically, although holding companies in different sectors may offer similar services and therefore have similar risk profiles, they may not be subject to the same supervision and regulation. For example, under the new CSE rules, some firms could be subject to both SEC and OTS holding company oversight, and as OTS pointed out in its response to the CSE proposal, perhaps subject to conflicting regulatory requirements.

Key Trends Have Changed the Financial Services Industry

Legislative and industry developments have brought about four key interrelated and ongoing trends in the financial services industry:[27]

- *consolidation:* fewer firms comprise the industry than in the past;
- *conglomeration:* firms have merged or acquired one another, creating fewer, often larger firms in terms of asset size;
- *convergence:* banking, securities, and futures firms offer similar products; and
- *globalization:* firms have expanded throughout the country and the world.

The financial services industry, generally, has seen an increased concentration of assets in the largest firms, combined with a decrease in the overall number of firms. This trend is most dramatic in the banking sector of the financial services industry. During the 10-year period between 1996 and 2006, banking institutions merged or acquired each other to such an extent that 24 percent fewer institutions existed in 2006 than 10 years earlier (decreasing from 11,480 to 8,683 institutions). At the same time, the share of banking assets held by the largest 25 banks grew from about 34 percent to about 58 percent (see figure 2.).

Small institutions, such as small credit unions and state-chartered banks, are the most numerous, though the number of all institutions under the various charters has decreased over time.[28] Consolidation has been pronounced in national banks. The number of national banks has decreased by 37 percent, from 2,726 to 1,715, and their assets increased nearly three-fold, from $2.5 trillion to $6.8 trillion (see figure 3). The increase in assets from 1996 through the end of 2006 has been significant for other institutions as well, with assets at least doubling among state-chartered commercial banks that are not members of the Federal Reserve (from $925 billion to $1.9 trillion), federally chartered savings banks (from $614 billion to $1.3 trillion), and credit unions (from $327 billion to $710 billion).

The securities and futures segments also have seen substantial growth in volume. Since 1996, assets among securities firms have increased about 70 percent—from about $1.8 trillion to about $5.9 trillion, according to the Securities Industry and Financial Markets Association.[29] The securities industry has long been concentrated, with the assets of the largest 10 firms exceeding 50 percent since at least 1996.[30] Similarly, the annual volume of active trading in futures contracts increased from about 499 million contracts to more than 2.5 billion between 1996 and 2006, according to the CFTC.

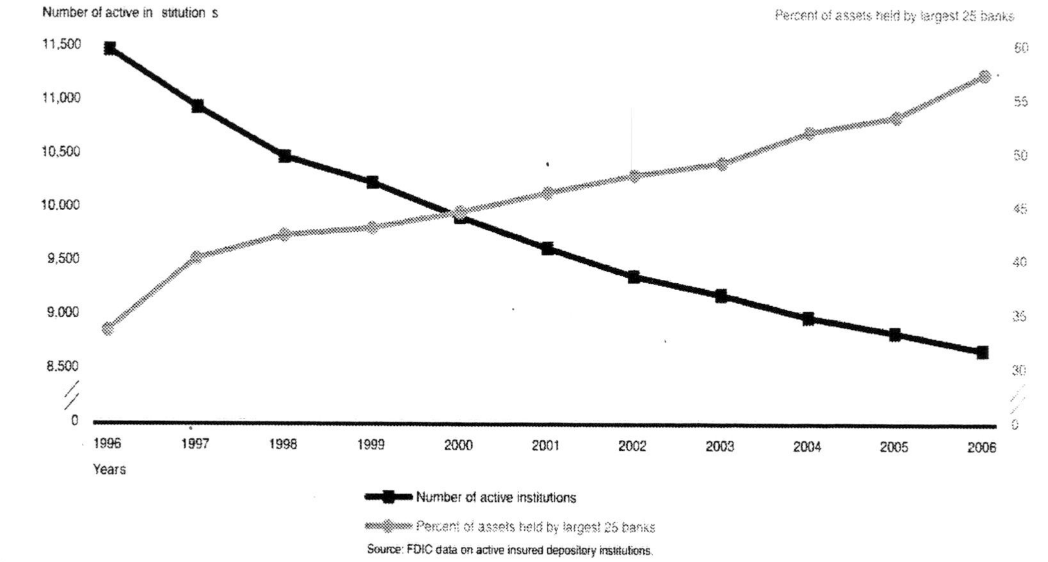

Source: GAO analysis based on data from FDIC and NCUA.

Figure 2. Percent of Assets Held by Largest 25 Banks and Number of Active Banking Institutions, 1996-2006

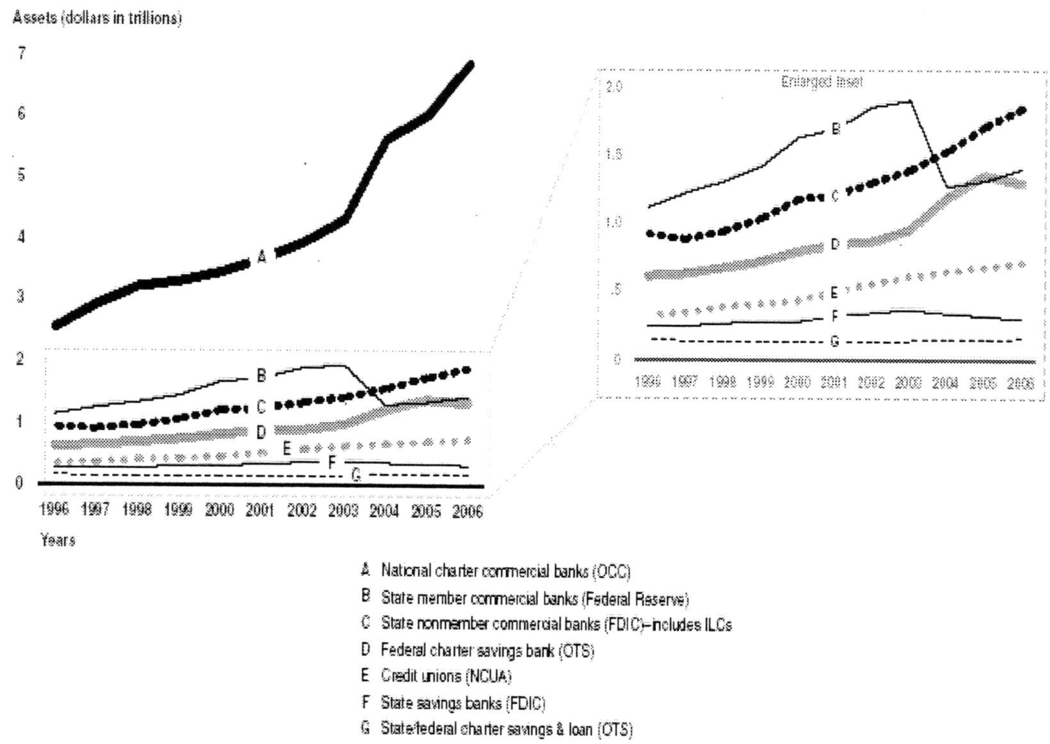

Source: GAO analysis based on data from FDIC and NCUA.

Figure 3. Changes in Assets by Bank Charter, 1996-2006

The conglomeration of firms and convergence of products offered by firms across sectors increasingly have come to characterize the large players in the industry. With regard to increased conglomeration, a research report by International Monetary Fund (IMF) staff—based on a worldwide sample of the largest 500 financial services firms in terms of assets—shows that the percentage of U.S. financial institutions in the sample engaged to some significant degree in at least two of the functional sectors of banking, securities, and insurance increased from 42 percent in 1995 to 61.5 percent in 2000. In addition, the conglomerates included in the IMF review held 73 percent of the assets of all of the U.S. firms included in the sample.[31]

As a result of conglomeration, financial institutions have converged in their products, increasingly offering products that are less distinct than in the past. For example, banks, broker-dealers, and investment companies all offer variable annuities. In addition, these institutions offer accounts or services that are legally distinct but function in similar ways, such as checking accounts, cash management accounts, and money market mutual funds.[32]

Banks and securities firms have greatly extended their reach throughout the world, comprising an industry that has global operations. Such international presence has brought about links among markets, as evidenced by recent negative impacts on German and French banks as a result of subprime mortgage defaults in the United States.[33] Increasingly, non-U.S. operations also form a substantial percentage of revenues for U.S.-based financial services firms. For example, Goldman Sachs reported to SEC that in the first half of 2007, it had earned the majority of its revenues (over 50 percent) from non-U.S. operations.[34] Similarly, Citigroup reported that about 44 percent of its income came from regions other than the United States.[35] U.S.-based financial services firms have also increased their operational presence in other countries over time, with some firms booking most of their credit derivative trades, for example, in major markets such as London.[36]

Recent Legislative Changes Have Affected the Financial Services Industry

The financial services industry and the manner in which it is regulated have changed in recent decades as a result of legislative action. The legislation both responded and contributed to the industry trends. For example, while banking and securities activities had generally been separated in the United States after the Glass-Steagall Act of 1933, the Gramm-Leach-Bliley Act of 1999 eased many of the restrictions limiting the ability of banks and securities firms to affiliate with one another; some restrictions, however, had been gradually eased as a result of regulatory interpretations of prior law.

As figure 4 indicates, changes in legislation have affected business practices of the financial services industry as well as its regulatory oversight. In many cases, legislation responded to a crisis. The Financial Institutions Reform, Recovery, and Enforcement Act of 1989 and the Federal Deposit Insurance Corporation Improvement Act (FDICIA) of 1991 responded, in large part, to the savings and loan crisis of that period. FDICIA, for instance, mandated that the agencies take "prompt corrective action" when a bank's capital falls below specified thresholds; this responded to concerns that regulatory forbearance with troubled institutions was excessive and contributed to further problems.

In addition, legislation over the past two decades has created new reporting requirements for firms, such as disclosures required by the Home Mortgage Disclosure Act and enhanced antiterrorism and antimoney-laundering requirements, such as those imposed by the USA Patriot Act.

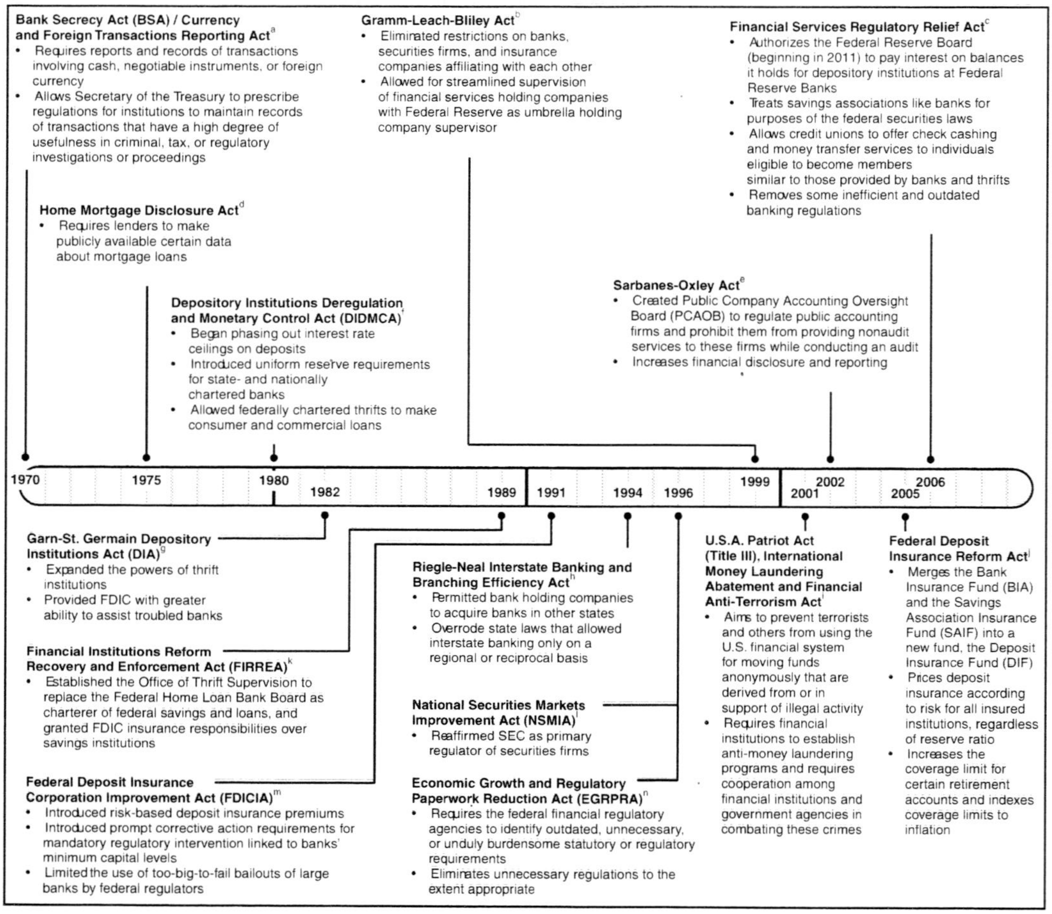

Source: GAO.

[a] Pub. L. No. 91-508, Titles I, II, 84 Stat. 1114, 1118 (1970).

[b] Pub. L. No. 106-102, 113 Stat. 1338 (1999).

[c] Pub. L. No. 109-351, 120 Stat. 1966 (2006).

[d] Pub. L. No. 94-200, Title III, 89 Stat. 1124, 1125 (1975).

[e] Pub. L. No. 107-204, 116 Stat. 745 (2002).

[f] Pub. L. No. 96-221, 94 Stat. 132 (1980).

[g] Pub. L. No. 97-320, 96 Stat. 1469 (1982).

[h] Pub. L. No. 103-328, 108 Stat. 2338 (1994).

[i] Pub. L. No. 107-56, Title III, 15 Stat. 272, 296 (2001).

[j] Pub. L. No. 109-171, Title II, 120 Stat. 4, 9 (2005).

[k] Pub. L. No. 101-73, 103 Stat. 183 (1989).

[l] Pub. L. No. 104-290, 110 Stat. 3416 (1996).

[m] Pub. L. No. 102-242, 105 Stat. 2236 (1991).

[n] Pub. L. No. 104-208, Title II, Div. A, 110 Stat. 3009-394 (1996).

Figure 4. Selected Legislation Resulting in Financial Regulatory Changes

These laws, however, have not led to comprehensive changes in the federal financial regulatory structure. For example, the landmark Gramm-Leach-Bliley Act in some ways recognized the blurring of distinctions among banking, securities, and insurance activities that had already happened in the marketplace and codified regulatory decisions that had been made to deal with these industry changes. While recognizing industry and regulatory changes, that act changed neither the number of regulatory agencies nor, in most cases, the primary objectives and responsibilities of the existing agencies.

Recent Industry Changes Demonstrate the Challenges Confronting Financial Regulators

The industry's trends, coupled with legislative changes, challenge regulatory agencies to provide adequate regulatory oversight while ensuring that regulation does not place any segment of the industry at a disadvantage relative to the others. The current structure—with its multiple regulators and charters—is further challenged by the need to recognize sector differences and simultaneously provide similar regulatory treatment for similar products. Regulatory agencies do collaborate to ensure consistent treatment of similar activities across institutional charters and legal entities, as well as in consolidated supervision of large, complex organizations. However, our prior work involving (1) consolidated supervision of holding companies, (2) the ILC charter, (3) U.S. capital adequacy regulation, (4) charter choice and OCC preemption rules, and (5) the regulation of securities and futures markets found instances where regulatory differences could lead to unequal treatment of firms.

Consolidated Supervision of Holding Companies

Consolidated supervision[37]—holding company supervision at the top tier or ultimate holding company in a financial enterprise—has become more important in light of changes in the financial services industry, particularly with respect to the increased importance of enterprise risk management of large, complex financial services firms. The Gramm-Leach-Bliley Act recognized the blurring of distinctions among the banking, securities and insurance activities happening in the marketplace, and recognized consolidated supervision as a basis for regulators to oversee the risks of financial services firms on the same level that the firms manage those risks. In March 2007, we reported that many large U.S. financial institutions were being supervised on a consolidated basis and that this was consistent with international standards that focus on having regulators familiar with the organizational structure, risk management and controls, and capital adequacy of these enterprises.[38]

In this prior work, however, we found some evidence of duplication and inconsistency when different agencies are responsible for consolidated and primary supervision, suggesting that opportunities remain for enhanced collaboration to promote greater consistency.[39] For example, we found that while the Federal Reserve and OCC have and generally follow procedures to resolve differences, a large, complex banking organization initially received conflicting information from the Federal Reserve, its consolidated supervisor, and OCC, its primary bank supervisor, about the firm's business continuity provisions. Also, SEC and OTS both have consolidated supervisory authority for some of the same firms but we found they did not have an effective mechanism for collaborating to prevent duplication and ensure consistency. In response, the Director of OTS said that he would take steps to develop an effective mechanism for OTS and SEC to work together.

In order to ensure that consolidated supervisors, specifically the Federal Reserve, SEC, and OTS, are promoting consistency with primary bank and other supervisors and not duplicating efforts, we recommended in March 2007 that these agencies identify additional ways to more effectively collaborate with primary bank and functional supervisors (e.g., developing appropriate mechanisms to better define responsibilities and to monitor, evaluate, and report jointly on results).[40] To take advantage of opportunities to promote better accountability and limit the potential for duplication and regulatory gaps, we recommended that these agencies foster more systematic collaboration among themselves to promote supervisory consistency, particularly for firms that provide similar services. In particular, we recommended that OTS and SEC clarify accountability when the agencies both had jurisdiction over a single company. Systematic collaboration would help to limit duplication, ensure that all regulatory areas are effectively covered, and ensure that resources are focused most effectively on the greatest risks across the regulatory system.

ILC Holding Company Regulation

In 2005 we reported that the parent companies of ILCs were not being overseen at the consolidated level by bank supervisors with clear authority for consolidated supervision.[41] ILCs typically are owned or controlled by a holding company that also may own other entities, and thus pose risks to the deposit insurance fund that are similar to those presented by other parents of depository institutions. However, FDIC, the primary bank supervisor for ILCs, has less extensive authority to supervise ILC holding companies than the Federal Reserve or OTS, the consolidated supervisors of bank and thrift holding companies, respectively. In addition, the parents of some ILCs—because they are exempt from the Bank Holding Company Act—are able to mix banking and commerce to a greater extent than the parents of other insured depository institutions.[42] Because of these inconsistencies, we (and the FDIC Office of the Inspector General) concluded that ILCs in a holding company structure may pose more risk to the deposit insurance fund than other types of insured depository institutions operating in a holding company. We recommended that Congress consider (1) options that would better ensure supervisors of institutions with similar risks have similar authorities and (2) the advantages and disadvantages of a greater mixing of banking and commerce by ILCs or other financial institutions. In July 2006, FDIC announced a moratorium on ILC applications from commercial entities for 6 months. On February 5, 2007, the agency extended the moratorium for another year.[43]

Basel II Implementation

Efforts to revise capital adequacy regulations for U.S. banks and bank holding companies also highlight the challenges regulatory agencies have in treating institutions consistently while also respecting their differences. Current capital adequacy regulations are based on a 1988 international accord to establish a common framework and reduce competitive inequalities among international banks. Advances in risk management strategies and other developments since 1988, however, have prompted an effort through the Basel Committee on Banking Supervision to present a new framework—commonly called Basel II—that would reflect these developments.

Applying Basel II in the United States has raised serious concerns, however. Because each federal regulator oversees a different set of institutions and has different perspectives and goals, reaching consensus on some issues in developing the Basel II framework has been difficult even though all of the agencies generally agree that limitations in the current Basel I framework have rendered it increasingly inadequate for supervising the capital adequacy of the largest, most complex banks. For example, officials from FDIC have been concerned about the use of banks' risk-based capital models under Basel II because, while these models have been used for internal risk assessment and management for years, with the exception of certain market risk models, they are relatively unproven as a regulatory capital tool, and questions remain about the reliability of data underlying the models. To address some of these concerns, agencies have proposed a number of safeguards in the proposed Basel II rule. Officials from the Federal Reserve and OCC—as the regulators of the vast majority of core banks that would be required to adopt Basel II's "advanced approach"— acknowledged data limitations and the uncertain impact on capital requirements, but highlighted the limitations of Basel I, the increased risk sensitivity of Basel II, the advances in risk management at large banks, the safeguards to ensure capital adequacy, and regulator experience in reviewing economic capital models as reasons to proceed with implementing Basel II. Further, regulatory agencies noted concerns about potential competitive inequities between large and small banks in the United States, if small banks are required to hold more regulatory capital than large banks for some similar risks. Finally, U.S. banks implementing Basel II's advanced approach have expressed concerns that the U.S. leverage requirement would put them at a competitive disadvantage against international financial institutions that do not face such a requirement.[44]

On September 25, 2006, the regulators issued a joint Notice of Proposed Rulemaking (NPR) that proposed a new risk-based capital adequacy framework that would require some and permit other qualifying banks to use an internal ratings-based approach to calculate regulatory credit risk capital requirements and advanced measurement approaches to calculate regulatory operational risk capital requirements. According to the NPR, the framework is intended to produce more risk-sensitive capital requirements than currently used by the agencies. The framework also seeks to build upon improvements to risk assessment approaches adopted by a number of large banks over the last decade. However, concern remained that applying different capital adequacy regulations to different institutions, even though it is intended to respect differences among institutions, may lead to competitive inequities. In our report, we made several recommendations to the agencies to improve the transparency of the process of developing new regulations.[45] On July 20, 2007, the agencies announced an agreement regarding implementation of Basel II and to finalize rules implementing the advanced approaches for computing large banks' risk-based capital requirements expeditiously.

OCC Preemption and Charter Choice

Bank regulatory agencies and others have argued that charter choice, allowing for differences in the regulation of financial institutions, is a central element in promoting an efficient U.S. financial services industry. This choice permits institutions to not only select the charter that best corresponds to their business plans and organization but also to protect themselves against arbitrary regulation. Differences in regulation reflect, at least in part, differences between the types of charters. In turn, regulatory competition has prompted changes to modernize the regulatory structure and allow financial institutions to offer a diverse range of products and services to meet the needs of their customers. However, such diversity challenges regulatory agencies to ensure supervisory and regulatory differences are based on legitimate differences in business plans and intended markets among the institutions under supervision and not an attempt to give one type of institution a competitive advantage over others.

The recent debate regarding OCC's interpretation of its authority to preempt state laws brought particular attention to the question of regulatory consistency, charter choice, and safety and soundness. In January 2004, OCC issued two final rules that are jointly referred to as the preemption rules. The "bank activities" rule addressed the applicability of state laws to national banking activities, while the "visitorial powers" rule set forth OCC's view of its authority to inspect, examine, supervise, and regulate national banks and their operating subsidiaries. The rules addressed OCC's authority to preempt state laws that applied to operating subsidiaries of national banks if those operating subsidiaries were conducting banking activities permitted for the national bank itself. However, the rules do not fully resolve uncertainties about the applicability of state consumer protection laws, particularly those aimed at preventing unfair and deceptive acts and practices. National banks are subject to federal consumer protection laws, including the Federal Trade Commission Act's prohibition of unfair or deceptive acts or practices. OCC supervises national banks and helps to enforce their compliance with these federal requirements. Opponents of OCC's position stated such preemption would weaken consumer protections and the rules could undermine the dual banking system, because state-chartered banks would have an incentive to change their charters from state to federal since national banks do not have to comply with state laws that apply to banking activities and, to the extent that compliance with federal law is less costly or burdensome than state regulation, the federal charter provides for lower regulatory costs and easier access to markets.[46] Supporters of the rules asserted that providing consistent regulation for national banks, rather than differing state regulatory regimes, was necessary to ensure efficient nationwide operation of national banks. Recently, the Supreme Court upheld OCC authority under the National Bank Act to preempt state regulation of the mortgage lending activities of a national bank's operating subsidiary.[47]

In our review of OCC's preemption rulemaking, we recommended that the Comptroller of the Currency clarify the characteristics of state consumer protection laws that would make them subject to federal preemption. OCC responded that the Consumer Financial Protection Forum, chaired by the U.S. Department of the Treasury, was established to bring federal and state regulators together to focus exclusively on consumer protection issues and to provide a permanent forum for communication on those issues. OCC believes this will provide an opportunity for federal and state regulators to better understand their differing perspectives, but what effect the Consumer Financial Protection Forum will have remains to be determined.

SEC and CFTC Joint Jurisdiction over Certain Products

Securities and futures markets, regulated by SEC and CFTC respectively, have become increasingly interconnected, raising the question whether separate regulatory agencies over these markets remain appropriate. SEC has authority over securities trading and the securities markets, whose primary purpose historically has been to facilitate capital formation. CFTC has authority over futures trading and the futures markets, which have primarily been used for risk management purposes. However, distinction between a financial product as a security or a future has become increasingly difficult as more and more products are developed that combine characteristics of both securities and futures. Derivatives— including security-based futures and options as well as traditional commodity-based contracts—have grown dramatically in recent years.[48] There is concern that the split in regulatory responsibility between SEC and CFTC could result in uncertainty about regulatory jurisdiction over some types of derivative products and possibly encourage companies to structure new products and activities so they avoid oversight completely.

We have long reported that the differences in U.S. securities and futures laws and markets will continue to require both SEC's and CFTC's regulatory staff to have some specialized expertise.[49] However, the two agencies also have had to work together to clarify their joint jurisdiction over certain products, such as futures on single stocks and certain stock indexes. Concerns that restrictions in a 1981 agreement between CFTC and SEC to prevent such trading on futures exchanges may have limited investor choice led to calls to repeal the restrictions. These calls were countered by concerns about doing so without first resolving applicable differences between securities and commodities laws and regulations, including the lack of comparable insider trading restrictions and consumer protection requirements. We recommended that CFTC and SEC work together and with Congress to develop and implement an appropriate legal and regulatory framework for removing the restrictions.[50] In 2000, CFTC and SEC reached agreement to jointly regulate single stock futures under a framework aimed at promoting competition, maintaining market integrity, and protecting customers. In turn, Congress codified the agreement in the Commodity Futures Modernization Act of 2000.

Regulators Have Often Collaborated to Respond to Regulatory Challenges but More Could be Done

Under the current structure, financial regulatory agencies often have collaborated to achieve their goals. For example, in 2007, we reported on a joint regulatory initiative of bank and securities regulators that recently facilitated the monitoring of industry-wide progress on reducing confirmation backlogs in the regulation of over-the-counter credit derivatives.[51] In 2006, we reported that in an effort to establish greater consistency in their examination procedures and oversight directed at preventing, detecting, and prosecuting money laundering, the federal banking regulators, with participation from the Financial Crimes Enforcement Network, jointly developed and issued an interagency examination procedures manual describing the risk assessments for Bank Secrecy Act (BSA) examinations.[52] To further strengthen BSA oversight, the agencies said that they were committed to ongoing interagency coordination. The bank regulatory agencies and NCUA also participate in the Federal Financial Institutions Examination Council, established in 1979 as a formal interagency communication vehicle for prescribing uniform supervisory standards.[53] A representative of state banking authorities was added to this council as a full voting member by the Financial Services Regulatory Relief Act of 2006. FDIC, the Federal Reserve, and OCC also work collaboratively under the Shared National Credit Program (a joint review of large, syndicated loans shared by banks that may have different supervisors) and the Interagency Country Exposure Review Committee (a joint determination of the level of risk for credit exposures to various countries). Moreover, both the Comptroller of the Currency and the Director of OTS are members of the FDIC Board of Directors.

More broadly, federal financial regulators have been involved in interagency efforts, including the President's Working Group, which provides a framework for coordinating policies and actions that cross agency jurisdictional lines.[54] We have reported, however, that the Group is not well suited to orchestrate a consistent set of goals or objectives that would direct the work of the different agencies. We noted that agency officials involved with the Group were "generally adverse to any formalization of the group and said that it functions well as an informal coordinating body."[55]

While the agencies do exchange information, they have opportunities to improve collaboration. We have noted in the past that it is difficult to collaborate within the fragmented U.S. regulatory system and have recommended that Congress modernize or consolidate the regulatory system. However, we previously have reported that under the current system, agencies have opportunities to collaborate more systematically and thus ensure that institutions operating under the oversight of multiple financial supervisors receive consistent guidance and face minimal supervisory burden. In our consolidated supervision report, we made recommendations to the Federal Reserve, OTS, and SEC to improve efforts to collaborate and increase consistency in their consolidated supervision program. In addition, we recommended that agencies foster more systematic collaboration among their agencies to promote supervisory consistency, particularly for firms that provide similar services.[56] In particular, we recommended that OTS and SEC clarify accountability for holding companies that operate under both agencies' jurisdictions. (The agencies have reported subsequent actions to improve their programs in these regards.)

Accountability for Identifying and Responding to Risks that Span Financial Sectors Is Not Clearly Defined

Because our regulatory structure relies on having clear-cut boundaries between the "functional" areas, industry changes that have caused those boundaries to blur have placed strains on the regulatory framework, and accountability for addressing risks that cross boundaries is not clearly defined. While diversification across activities and locations may have lowered the risks faced by some large, complex, internationally active firms, understanding and overseeing them also has become a much more complex undertaking, requiring staff who can evaluate the risk portfolio of these institutions and their management systems and performance. Regulators must be able to ensure effective risk management without needlessly restraining risk taking, which would hinder economic growth. Similarly, because firms are taking on similar risks across "functional" areas, to understand the risks of a given institution or those that span institutions or industries, regulators need a more complete picture of the risk portfolio of the financial services industry as a whole, both in the United States and abroad.

As we have discussed above, some of the means by which U.S. regulators collaborate across sectors do not provide for the systematic sharing of information, making it more difficult for regulators to identify emerging threats to financial stability. These means also do not allow for a satisfactory assessment of risks that cross traditional regulatory and industry boundaries and therefore may inhibit the ability to detect and contain certain financial crises, as can be seen in the following:

- With regard to the President's Working Group, we reported in 2000 that although it has served as a mechanism to share information during unfolding crises, its activities generally have not included such matters as routine surveillance of risks that cross markets or of information sharing that is specific enough to help identify potential crises.[57] The Group has served as an informal mechanism for coordination and cooperation rather than as a mechanism to ensure accountability for issues that span agency jurisdiction.
- In reviewing the near collapse of Long-Term Capital Management (LTCM)—one of the largest U.S. hedge funds—in 1998, we reported that regulators continued to focus on individual firms and markets but failed to address interrelationships across industries; accountability for those relationships was not clearly defined. Thus, federal financial regulators did not identify the extent of weaknesses in bank, securities, and futures firm risk management practices until after LTCM's near collapse and had not sufficiently considered the systemic threats that can arise from unregulated entities.[58]
- In reviewing responses to the events of September 11, 2001, we reported that the multiple agency structure of U.S. financial services regulation has slowed the development of a strategy that would ensure continuity of business for financial markets in the event of a terrorist attack.[59]
- In a recent review of interagency communication regarding enforcement actions taken by the regulatory agencies against individuals and firms, we reported that while information sharing among financial regulators is a key defense against fraud and market abuses, regulators do not have ready access to all relevant data related to regulatory enforcement actions taken against individuals or firms. We also reported that many financial regulators do not share relevant consumer complaint data amongst themselves on certain hybrid products such as variable annuities (products that contain characteristics of both securities and insurance products) in a routine, systematic fashion, compounding the problem that consumers may have in identifying the relevant regulator.[60]

Through its supervision of bank and financial holding companies, the Federal Reserve has oversight responsibility for a substantial share of the financial services industry. The scope of its oversight, however, is limited to bank and financial holding companies. While each agency develops its own strategic plan for meeting its mission, no government agency has the authority to identify and address issues in the financial system as a whole, and monitor the ability of regulators to meet their objectives on an ongoing basis.[61] We repeatedly have noted that regulators could do more to share information and monitor risks across markets or "functional" areas to identify potential systemic crises and limit opportunities for fraud and abuse.[62]

From an overall perspective the system is not proactive, but instead reacts in a piecemeal, ad hoc fashion—often when there is a crisis. During a crisis, or in anticipation of one, no one has the authority and there is no formal cooperative mechanism to conduct risk analyses, prioritize tasks, or allocate resources across agencies, although the Office of Management and Budget may perform some of these tasks for agencies funded by federal appropriations. Several Forum participants, for instance, suggested that Congress establish an agency with authority to set regulatory standards and goals and to hold regulators accountable to those goals.

The federal financial regulatory agencies face challenges posed by the dynamic financial environment: the industry's trends of consolidation, conglomeration, convergence, and globalization have created an environment that differs substantially from the prevailing environment when agencies were formed and their goals set by legislation. In particular, the fact that different agencies have jurisdiction over large, complex firms that offer similar services to their customers creates the potential for inconsistent and inequitable treatment. Differences, even subtle ones, among the agencies' goals exacerbate the potential for inconsistency.

Several Forum participants noted that subtle differences among agency goals can be significant. Further, despite the changes posed by the industry's dynamic environment, clear accountability for addressing issues that span agencies' jurisdiction is not clearly assigned in the current system. These issues have led us to suggest that modernizing the federal financial regulatory system is a key challenge facing the United States in the 21st century.

OPTIONS TO CHANGE THE FEDERAL FINANCIAL REGULATORY STRUCTURE

In our previous work, we suggested options for Congress to consider to modernize the current regulatory system. Additionally, others have recommended changes, frequently intended to simplify the complex multiagency structure. The financial regulatory structure, however, has remained largely the same despite changes in the financial services industry. Forum participants and others have suggested that some lessons could be learned from the principles-based approach to regulation of the United Kingdom's Financial Services Authority (FSA). However, participants also noted that the lessons should be considered in light of the differences between the United States and the United Kingdom and the limited experience of FSA, particularly the fact that it had not dealt, at the time of the Forum, with a significant economic crisis or downturn. Defining clear and consistent goals for regulatory agencies would be a significant step toward modernizing the regulatory structure.

Modernizing the Financial Regulatory System Remains a Challenge

As early as 1994, we voiced our support for modernizing the federal financial regulatory structure. More recently, we provided various options for Congress to consider, including

- consolidating the regulatory structure within the "functional" areas;
- moving to a regulatory structure based on regulation by objective (a "twin peaks" model);
- combining all financial regulators into a single entity; or
- creating or authorizing a single entity to oversee all large, complex, internationally active firms, while leaving the rest of the structure in place.

Each of these options would provide potential improvements, as well as some risks and costs. Consolidating the regulatory structure within "functional" areas, such as banking and securities, would provide a central point of communication for a sector's issues and could reduce barriers to communication and coordination among the regulatory agencies; it also could remove opportunities for regulatory experimentation and the other positive aspects of regulatory competition. A "twin peaks model" would involve setting up one safety and soundness regulatory entity and one conduct-of-business regulatory entity charged with ensuring compliance with the full range of conduct-of-business issues, including consumer and investor protection, disclosure, money laundering, and some governance issues. On the positive side, this could ensure that conduct-of-business issues are not subordinated to safety and soundness issues, as some fear. However, this structure would not facilitate regulators' understanding of linkages between safety and soundness and conduct-of-business, such as a financial services firm's reputational risk. A single regulator, like FSA, would have the ability to evaluate such linkages, but ensuring the accountability of such a large agency to consumers or industry would be difficult. Finally, a single agency charged with oversight of large, complex firms could be able to provide consistent regulatory treatment and to identify and respond to issues that cross current regulatory agency boundaries. However, it might be difficult to find and maintain an appropriate balance between the interests of the large, internationally active firms and smaller entities; this option, further, might add another agency to a regulatory system that already has many agencies.[63]

IMF noted these options in suggesting that the United States review the rationalization for its financial regulation.

As we previously have noted, the specifics of a regulatory structure, including the number of regulatory agencies and roles assigned to each, may not be the critical determinant in whether a regulatory system is successful. The skills of the people working in the regulatory system, the clarity of its objectives, its independence, and its management systems are also critical to the success of financial regulation.[64]

Others also have proposed changes to modernize the financial regulatory system, including the following:

- 1994 Treasury proposal.[65] This proposal would have realigned the federal banking agencies by core policy functions—that is, bank supervision and regulation function, central bank function, and deposit insurance function. Generally, this proposal would have combined OCC, OTS, and certain functions of the Federal Reserve and FDIC into a new independent agency, the Federal Banking Commission, that would have been responsible for bank supervision and regulation. FDIC would have continued to be responsible for administering federal deposit insurance, and the Federal Reserve would have retained central bank responsibilities for monetary policy, liquidity lending, and the payments system. Although FDIC and the Federal Reserve would have lost most bank supervisory rule-making powers, each would have been allowed access to all information of the new agency, as well as retain limited secondary or backup enforcement authority. In addition, the Federal Reserve would be authorized to examine a cross section of large and small banking organizations jointly with the new agency. FDIC would have continued to oversee activities of state banks and thrifts that could pose risks to the insurance funds and to resolve failures of insured banks.

- H.R. 1227 (1993).[66] This proposal would have consolidated OCC and OTS in an independent Federal Bank Agency and aligned responsibilities among the new and existing agencies. It also would have reduced the multiplicity of regulators to which a single banking organization could be subject while avoiding the concentration of regulatory power of a single federal agency. The role of the Federal Financial Institution Examination Council would have been strengthened; it would have seen to the uniformity of examinations, regulation, and supervision among the three remaining supervisors. According to a Congressional Research Service (CRS) analysis, this proposal would have put the Federal Reserve in charge of more than 40 percent of banking organization assets, with the rest divided between the new agency and a reorganized FDIC.[67]
- 1994 LaWare proposal.[68] The LaWare proposal was outlined in congressional testimony but never presented as a formal legislative proposal, according to Federal Reserve officials. It called for a division of responsibilities defined by charter class and a merging of OCC and OTS responsibilities. The two primary agencies under the proposal would have been an independent Federal Banking Commission and the Federal Reserve, which would have supervised all independent state banks and depository institutions in any holding company whose lead institution was a state-chartered bank. The new agency would have supervised all independent national banks and thrifts and depository institutions in any banking organization whose lead institution was a national bank or thrift. FDIC would not have examined financially healthy institutions, but would have been authorized to join in examination of problem banking institutions. Based on estimates of assets of commercial banks and thrifts performed by CRS, the LaWare proposal would have put the new agency in charge of more commercial bank assets than the Federal Reserve.
- 2002 FDIC Chairman proposal. Donald E. Powell, then Chairman of the FDIC, proposed to design a new regulatory system that would reflect the modern financial services marketplace. Three federal financial services regulators would carry out federal supervision: one would be responsible for regulating the banking industry, another for the securities industry, and a third for insurance companies that choose a federal charter.
- Similarly, proposals have been made to restructure futures and securities regulation. In particular, proposals have been made to consolidate SEC and CFTC, partly in response to increasing convergence in new financial instrument and trading strategies of the securities and futures markets.

Some Lessons May Be Learned from the United Kingdom's FSA Model which Emphasizes a Principles-based Approach to Regulation

Beginning in 1997, the United Kingdom consolidated its financial services regulatory structure, combining nine different regulatory bodies, including SROs, into the FSA. While FSA is the sole supervisor for all financial services, other government agencies, especially the Bank of England and Her Majesty's Treasury, still play some role in the regulation and supervision of financial services.[69]

FSA government officials and experts on the model cited important changes in the financial services industry as some of the reasons for consolidating the regulatory bodies that oversee banking, securities, and insurance activities. These included the blurring of the distinctions between different kinds of financial services businesses, and the growth of large, conglomerate, financial services firms that allocate capital and manage risk on a groupwide basis. Other reasons for consolidating included some recognition of regulatory weaknesses in certain areas and enhancing the United Kingdom's power in the European Union[70] and other international deliberations.[71]

A number of participants in the Forum believed that lessons can be learned from the FSA's single regulator model. Specifically, some participants noted that FSA's establishment and use of regulatory goals through its principles-based approach to regulation may help to improve the effectiveness of the U.S. regulatory structure. In particular, several participants suggested adopting a principles-based approach to prudential regulation.

According to FSA, principles-based regulation means, where possible, moving away from dictating industry behavior through detailed, prescriptive rules and supervisory actions describing how firms should operate their business. Instead, the FSA established 11 high-level principles that give firms the responsibility to decide how best to align their business objectives and processes with regulatory outcomes that have been specified.

Some Forum participants noted that in the United States, such principles or goals would work best if established for regulators rather than for the industry since rules provide a safe harbor effect that principles for industry behavior would not provide. Specifically, one participant noted that the litigious business environment in the United States makes specificity in rules essential so that firms know explicitly what behavior is acceptable in the market. Similarly, consumers and investors of financial products in the United States may feel most comfortable with an industry regulated by rules since they may provide greater assurance that violators will be prosecuted. Some participants said principles would be more appropriate in guiding prudential or safety and soundness regulation than they would be for consumer protection or conduct-of-business regulation. Another participant stated that principles-based regulation may provide some benefits, but benefits may not result in cost savings and must be considered carefully in relation to the U.S. financial regulatory system. In fact, most Forum participants stated that a move toward principles-based regulation in the United States would have a small or moderate impact on lowering regulatory costs. In addition, some participants cautioned against wholesale adoption of the FSA's model of principles-based regulation noting that the UK's regulatory system had not yet been tested by an economic downturn or the failure of a large institution at the time of the Forum. Finally, one Forum participant noted that the FSA's focus on regulatory outcomes would be a good practice to adopt in the United States.

According to CFTC officials, the agency currently uses a principles-based approach to supervising the futures industry. Under the Commodity Exchange Act (CEA), exchanges and clearing houses must adhere to a set of statutory "core principles." According to CFTC, the agency may set out acceptable practices that serve as safe-harbors for the industry's compliance with each principle. Conversely, the CEA allows for the industry and SROs to formulate their own acceptable practices and submit them to the CFTC for approval. CFTC officials noted that, with a few exceptions, there are no longer prescriptive regulations that dictate exclusive means of compliance; rather, exchanges have the choice of following

CFTC-approved acceptable practices or adopting their own measures for complying with the overarching principle.

Clear, Consistent Regulatory Goals Are Important Steps to Improve Regulatory Effectiveness

In addition to suggesting options to modernize the federal financial regulatory structure, our prior work also has identified the importance of clear and consistent goals for financial regulation. Such goals would facilitate consideration of options to modernize the regulatory structure. In 1996, we identified the following four goals:[72]

1. Consolidated and comprehensive oversight, with coordinated regulation and supervision of individual components. The Basel Committee, for example, indicates in its core principles, that "an essential element of banking supervision is that supervisors supervise the banking group on a consolidated basis, adequately monitoring and, as appropriate, applying prudential norms to all aspects of the business conducted by the group worldwide."[73] Regulators would rely upon functional regulators for information and supervision of individual components, but remain responsible for ascertaining the safety and soundness of the consolidated organization as a whole.
2. Independence from undue political pressure, balanced by appropriate accountability and adequate congressional oversight. Effective regulatory oversight would recognize the need to guard against undue political influence by incorporating appropriate checks and balances.
3. Consistent rules, consistently applied for similar activities. Effective regulatory oversight would ensure that institutions conducting the same lines of business or offering equivalent products are generally subject to similar rules, standards, or guidelines for those lines of business or products.
4. Enhanced efficiency and reduced regulatory burden. By establishing consolidated, comprehensive, and coordinated oversight and applying consistent rules across similar activities, inefficiencies such as duplication of effort and regulatory burden caused by reporting similar data to multiple regulators, could be eliminated or reduced.

A review of our work suggests three additional goals that would also be important to improve regulatory effectiveness:

1. Transparency in rule making. Transparency in rule making in an environment where multiple regulators bring multiple goals and perspectives would entail the maximum possible disclosure regarding the intended goals of proposed regulations, the basis for the selection of the regulatory approach, and planned evaluation of the implemented regulation. This would help reduce industry uncertainty about, and possible opposition to, proposed rules and their impact on the industry. Transparency also would help to ensure consistent expectations of regulators and the industry.[74]

2. Commitment to consumer and investor protection. Currently, consumer protection (including consumers as investors) is administered by a variety of agencies and can result in differential regulation and the inequitable treatment of firms competing in the same market. In addition, consumers can suffer if they receive different levels of protection when they purchase different products and services from different types of financial firms. Equal treatment and equal access to credit also are important objectives.[75]
3. Ensuring safety and soundness. Ensuring a safe and sound banking system and promoting financial system stability require a balance between the need for effective regulatory oversight and the possibility that too much oversight could hinder competition. Fulfilling this goal also requires developing a system that limits the extension of the federal safety net in order to encourage market as well as regulatory discipline.[76]

Other organizations have noted the importance of clearly specified regulatory goals for regulatory effectiveness. The Basel Committee on Banking Supervision developed 25 core principles for effective banking supervision that have been used by countries as a benchmark for assessing the quality of their supervisory systems and for identifying a baseline level of sound supervisory practices. The core principles are a framework of minimum standards for sound supervisory practices and are considered universally applicable.[77] The first of the principles states that an effective system of banking supervision will have clear responsibilities and objectives for each authority involved in the supervision of banks.

In August 2007, IMF issued a report regarding the findings of its consultation with the United States as part of its mission to review U.S. economic developments.[78] IMF concluded that while the U.S. economy continues to show remarkable dynamism and resilience, it faced important challenges, such as the need to maintain a robust financial system. IMF found that the current structure's multiple federal and state regulators overseeing the evolving financial market system may limit regulatory effectiveness and slow responses to pressing issues. Therefore, IMF suggested the United States increase the use of general principles or goals to guide financial regulation. According to IMF, general regulatory goals may ease interagency coordination and shorten reaction times to industry developments.

Treasury Has Announced Plans to Consider Regulatory Structure Modernization

The Secretary of the Treasury recently announced an action plan that will consider reforms to modernize the U.S. financial regulatory structure as part of a plan to maintain the global leadership of U.S. capital markets. According to Treasury's press release, the plan seeks a modern regulatory structure with improved oversight, increased efficiency, reduced overlap, and the ability to adapt to market participants' constantly changing strategies and tools.[79] Treasury officials noted they recognize that designing such a system is a long-term endeavor. They said, however, they will seek to propose first steps that would begin the process. Treasury intends to publish the result of its study in early 2008.

APPENDIX I: PARTICIPANTS IN THE JUNE 11, 2007, COMPTROLLER GENERAL'S FORUM

Moderator	Title	Organization
David M. Walker	Comptroller General	U.S. Government Accountability Office
Participant		
Wayne Abernathy	Executive Director	American Bankers Association
Scott Albinson	Managing Director	J.P. Morgan Chase
Konrad Alt	Managing Director	Promontory Financial Group
John Bowman	Deputy Director and Chief Counsel	Office of Thrift Supervision
Richard Carnell	Associate Professor of Law	Fordham University School of Law
Gerald Corrigan	Managing Director	Goldman, Sachs & Co.
John Damgard	President	Futures Industry Association
Roger Ferguson	Chairman	Swiss Re America Holding Corporation
Peter Fisher	Chairman	BlackRock Asia
Jeffrey Gillespie	Deputy Chief Counsel	Office of the Comptroller of the Currency
Robert Glauber	Visiting Professor	Harvard Law School
Carrie Hunt	Sr. Counsel & Director, Regulatory Affairs	National Association of Federal Credit Unions
Marc Lackritz	President and CEO	Securities Industry & Financial Markets Association
Walter Lukken	Acting Chairman	Commodity Futures Trading Commission
Dave Marquis	Director, Examination & Insurance	National Credit Union Administration
Michael Menzies	Vice Chair	Independent Community Bankers of America
Art Murton	Director, Insurance and Research	Federal Deposit Insurance Corporation
Vincent Reinhart	Director, Division of Monetary Affairs	Board of Governors of the Federal Reserve System
Thomas Russo	Vice Chair and Chief Legal Officer	Lehman Brothers
Mary Schapiro	Chairman and CEO	NASD
William Seidman	Chief Commentator	CNBC
Erik Sirri	Director, Market Regulation	Securities and Exchange Commission
Mike Stevens	Sr. Vice President, Regulatory Policy	Conference of State Bank Supervisors
Peter Wallison	Senior Fellow	American Enterprise Institute
Julie Williams	First Senior Deputy Comptroller & Chief Counsel	Office of the Comptroller of the Currency

Note: Organizational affiliation for identification purposes only.

Appendix II: Comments from the Chairman of the Board of Governors of the Federal Reserve System

BOARD OF GOVERNORS
OF THE
FEDERAL RESERVE SYSTEM
WASHINGTON, D. C. 20551

BEN S. BERNANKE
CHAIRMAN

September 28, 2007

Mr. Richard J. Hillman
Managing Director
Financial Markets and Community Investment
Government Accountability Office
Washington, D.C. 20548

Dear Mr. Hillman:

The Federal Reserve appreciates the opportunity to comment on a draft of the GAO's report on the regulatory structure for financial services and trends in the financial services industry and (GAO-08-32). The report draws on several reports previously prepared by the GAO as well as the perspectives of participants in a forum hosted by the Comptroller General on June 11, 2007. This forum, in which the Federal Reserve was pleased to participate, included representatives of various financial services regulatory authorities, financial services organizations and others.

As your report notes, the current regulatory structure for financial services in the United States is somewhat complex. This is due in part to Congress' decision, which was reviewed and reaffirmed in the Gramm-Leach Bliley Act of 1999, to build on the well established, "functional" regulatory structures in place for the banking, securities and commodity sectors. This framework recognizes that the different financial services sectors are governed by differing statutory requirements, builds on the expertise of the relevant agency or agencies in each sector, and helps ensure that regulatory requirements and burdens remain tailored to the relevant sectors. Importantly, the current framework also provides for firms that control an insured depository institution to be subject to consolidated or "umbrella" supervision by a Federal agency.[1] As your report notes, the current regulatory framework has contributed to the development of U.S. financial markets and overall economic growth and stability.

We agree that it is useful to periodically review ways of enhancing this regulatory framework to determine if, in light of the ever-changing financial services marketplace, modifications would allow the system to achieve its fundamental goals more effectively, efficiently and consistently. Any potential changes should be carefully

[1] Your report also recognizes that the corporate owners of industrial loan companies (ILCs) currently are not subject to the same consolidated supervisory framework as bank holding companies and that, due to these differences, ILCs in a holding company structure may pose more risk to the deposit insurance fund.

Richard J. Hillman
Page 2

evaluated and consistent with the core public policy objectives of financial regulation and supervision.

As I have noted previously, these objectives in the broadest sense are financial stability, investor and consumer protection, and market integrity. On a slightly more granular level, achieving these objectives requires laws, regulations and coordinated actions to protect the safety and soundness of depository institutions that have access to the Federal safety net (deposit insurance and access to the Federal Reserve's discount window and payments systems); promote financial innovation, evolution and competition; limit the potential for explicit or implicit expansion of the Federal safety net; promote market discipline; and provide consumers of financial products and services appropriate protections.

Recent market events highlight the importance of financial stability, the critical role of the Federal Reserve in protecting against financial crisis and systemic risks, and the important synergies between the Federal Reserve's supervisory and financial stability responsibilities. The Federal Reserve's supervision and regulation of banking organizations provide the Federal Reserve with information, expertise and powers that are highly valuable in carrying out our responsibilities for deterring and managing financial crises, overseeing the payments system, acting as a liquidity provider through the discount window and conducting monetary policy.

We also agree that changes in the financial services marketplace make it even more important for firms that control an insured depository institution to be overseen by a Federal agency on a consolidated or group-wide basis. As your report notes, the Federal Reserve oversees a substantial share of the financial services industry in its role as consolidated supervisor for all bank holding companies (including financial holding companies formed under the Gramm-Leach-Bliley Act). As the GAO previously has recognized, the Federal Reserve has a well-developed, systematic and risk-focused program for the supervision of bank holding companies on a consolidated basis.

In its role as consolidated or "umbrella" supervisor for bank holding companies, the Federal Reserve collaborates extensively with other bank supervisors and functional regulators. We have worked hard to establish the requisite information sharing agreements and protocols that make systematic collaboration possible and rely, to the fullest extent possible, on the examination and other supervisory work conducted by the primary bank and functional supervisors of a bank holding company's subsidiaries in assessing the risks of the organization as a whole. Through these efforts, as well as through our participation in the Federal Financial Institutions Examination Council and the President's Working Group on Financial Markets, we seek to advance the important goals of providing consistent supervision to similarly situated organizations in a manner that promotes financial stability, market efficiency, consumer protection and the other goals of Federal supervision, while at the same time respecting the individual statutory

Richard J. Hillman
Page 3

missions and responsibilities of all involved agencies.[2] I'm pleased to note that we recently instituted a variety of changes to the Federal Reserve's Quality Management Framework for Reserve Banks to further enhance the consistency in our supervisory processes and products.[3] The Federal Reserve will continue to look for opportunities to enhance our supervisory program for banking organizations and to collaborate with other agencies and Congress to bring greater consistency to the supervision of organizations that control an insured depository institution.

Federal Reserve staff separately has provided GAO staff with technical and correcting comments on the draft report. We hope that these comments were helpful.

Sincerely,

cc: James M. McDermott, GAO

---

[2] The draft report notes one instance where a bank holding company informed the GAO that it initially had received conflicting views from the Federal Reserve and the Office of the Comptroller of the Currency ("OCC"), the primary supervisor of the holding company's lead bank subsidiary, concerning the adequacy of the organization's business continuity plans. However, in that case, the Federal Reserve and OCC worked cooperatively to develop a uniform view regarding this important aspect of the organization's risk management systems and controls. This consistent view was formally communicated in writing by both agencies to the organization, whose senior management concurred with these findings.

[3] See Revised Guidelines for Reserve Bank Quality Management Frameworks, AD Letter 07-23/CA Admin Letter 07-11 (Aug. 30, 2007).

Appendix III: Comments from the Chairman of the National Credit Union Administration

National Credit Union Administration

Office of the Chairman

September 25, 2007

United States Government Accountability Office
James McDermott
Assistant Director, Financial Markets
And Community Investment
Washington, D.C. 20548

Dear Mr. McDermott:

I am responding to your September 11, 2007 letter, which contained the U.S. Government Accountability Office's (GAO) draft report entitled Financial Regulation: Industry Trends Continue to Challenge the Federal Regulatory Structure (GAO-08-32). We originally provided written comments to GAO in April 2007 prior to the Comptroller General's Forum held in June 2007 on this subject matter and also met with GAO staff on September 5, 2007.

We appreciate the opportunity to comment on industry trends given the current federal regulatory structure in the United States. We do not have any additional comments than those already provided both verbally and in writing to GAO.

If you have any additional questions, please contact me.

Sincerely,

JoAnn Johnson
Chairman

1775 Duke Street—Alexandria, VA 22314-3428—703-518-6300—703-518-6319-Fax

Related GAO Products

Credit Unions: Greater Transparency Needed on Who Credit Unions Serve and on Senior Executive Compensation Arrangements. GAO-07-29. Washington, D.C.: November 30, 2006.

Industrial Loan Corporations: Recent Asset Growth and Commercial Interest Highlight Differences in Regulatory Authority. GAO-06-961T. Washington, D.C.: July 12, 2006.

Bank Secrecy Act: Opportunities Exist for FinCEN and the Banking Regulators to further Strengthen the Framework for Consistent BSA Oversight. GAO-06-386. Washington, D.C.: April 28, 2006.

Sarbanes-Oxley Act: Consideration of Key Principles Needed in Addressing Implementation for Smaller Public Companies. GAO-06-361. Washington, D.C.: April 13, 2006.

Mutual Fund Industry: SEC's Revised Examination Approach Offers Potential Benefits, but Significant Oversight Challenges Remain. GAO- 05-415. Washington, D.C.: August 17, 2005.

Mutual Fund Trading Abuses: Lessons Can Be Learned from SEC Not Having Detected Violations at an Earlier Stage. GAO-05-313. Washington, D.C.: April 20, 2005.

Credit Unions: Financial Condition Has Improved, but Opportunities Exist to Enhance Oversight and Share Insurance Management. GAO-04- 91. Washington, D.C.: October 27, 2003.

Securities Markets: Competition and Multiple Regulators Heighten Concerns about Self-Regulation. GAO-02-362. Washington, D.C.: May 3, 2002.

Large Bank Mergers: Fair Lending Review Could be Enhanced with Better Coordination. GAO/GGD-00-16, Washington, D.C.: November 3, 1999.

Bank Oversight Structure: U.S. and Foreign Experience May Offer Lessons for Modernizing U.S. Structure. GAO/GGD-97-23. Washington, D.C.: November 20, 1996.

End Notes

[1] The scope of our work includes regulatory oversight of the banking, securities, and futures industry sectors by the federal government. The federal financial regulators in the scope of our work are: the Federal Reserve, Federal Deposit Insurance Corporation (FDIC), Office of the Comptroller of the Currency (OCC), Office of Thrift Supervision (OTS), National Credit Union Administration (NCUA), Securities and Exchange Commission (SEC), and Commodity Futures Trading Commission (CFTC). The scope of our work excludes government-sponsored enterprises such as Fannie Mae and Freddie Mac; state financial regulatory agencies, including those in the insurance sector; the securities and futures industry SROs, and the Public Company Accounting Oversight Board.

[2] GAO, *21st Century Challenges: Reexamining the Base of the Federal Government*, GAO-05-325SP (Washington, D.C.: February 2005).

[3] International Monetary Fund, *United States: 2007 Article IV Consultation—Staff Report: Staff Statement; and Public Information Notice on the Executive Board Discussion*, IMF Country Report No. 07/264 (Washington, D.C., August 2007).

[4] Financial Services Regulatory Relief Act of 2006, Pub. L. No. 109-35 1, § 1002, 120 Stat. 1966, 2009-2010 (Oct. 13, 2006).

[5] By "costs and benefits of financial regulation in general," we mean to include the measurement of the costs and benefits of financial regulation to firms, regulators, and the overall economy.

[6] For more information on ILCs, see GAO, *Industrial Loan Corporations: Recent Asset Growth and Commercial Interest Highlight Differences in Regulatory Authority*, GAO-05-621 (Washington, D.C.: Sept. 15, 2005).

[7] Recently, the two largest securities industry SROs merged into one SRO known as the Financial Industry Regulatory Authority (FINRA) which is responsible for overseeing nearly 5,100 brokerage firms.

[8] For more information on securities and banking regulators, see GAO, *Financial Regulation: Industry Changes Prompt Need to Reconsider U.S. Regulatory Structure*, GAO-05-61 (Washington D.C.: Oct. 6, 2004).

[9] See GAO-05-61, 9.

[10] GAO, *Reexamining Regulations: Opportunities Exist to Improve Effectiveness and Transparency of Retrospective Reviews*, GAO-07-791 (Washington, D.C., Jul. 16, 2007).

[11] Gregory Elliehausen, "The Cost of Bank Regulation: A Review of the Evidence," Federal Reserve Staff Study. Washington, D.C., April 1998, 29. Earlier, we concluded that industry estimates of regulatory compliance

costs for banks were not reliable because of methodological deficiencies. See GAO, *Regulatory Burden: Recent Studies, Industry Issues, and Agency Initiatives*, GAO/GGD-94-28 (Washington, D.C.: Dec. 13, 1993).

[12] GAO, *Risk-Based Capital: Bank Regulators Need to Improve Transparency and Overcome Impediments to Finalizing the Proposed Basel II Framework*, GAO-07-253 (Washington, D.C.: Feb. 2007).

[13] Deloitte, *The Cost of Regulation Study*, A report commissioned by the Financial Services Authority and the Financial Services Practitioner Panel, (London, June 28, 2006).

[14] U.S. Chamber of Commerce, *Report and Recommendations of the Commission on the Regulation of U.S. Capital Markets in the 21st Century*, March 2007; McKinsey and Company, *Sustaining New York's and the US' Global Financial Services Leadership*, a report commissioned by New York City Mayor Michael Bloomberg and New York Senator Charles Schumer. January 22, 2007; Interim *Report of the Committee on Capital Markets Regulation*, November 30, 2006.

[15] U.S. Chamber of Commerce, *Report and Recommendations of the Commission on the Regulation of U.S. Capital Markets in the 21st Century*, March 2007.

[16] GAO, *Financial Market Regulation: Benefits and Risks of Merging SEC and CFTC*, GAO/T-GGD-95-153 (Washington, D.C.: May 3, 1995).

[17] As of October 5, 2007, this chapter had not been released.

[18] Call reports provide financial and structural information, such as ownership, for FDIC- insured depository institutions.

[19] 72 Fed. Reg. 36550 (July 3, 2007).

[20] We currently have ongoing work in this area to review the resources required for banks to file such reports.

[21] Agencies accomplish this task, in part, by conducting what GAO has referred to as "retrospective reviews" to determine the effectiveness of a regulation and its implementation. See GAO, *Reexamining Regulations: Opportunities Exist to Improve Effectiveness and Transparency of Retrospective Reviews*, GAO-07-791 (Washington, D.C.: July 2007).

[22] The London Stock Exchange created AIM to offer smaller companies from throughout the world and in any industry the opportunity to list on its exchange and be subject to less regulation. Listing requirements do not require particular financial track records, a trading history, or minimum requirements for size or number of shareholders. Companies listed on AIM today represent many sizes and industries.

[23] Section 3 of the Regulatory Flexibility Act of 1980 (Pub. L. No. 96-354, 94 Stat. 1164, 1169 (1980) (codified at 5 U.S.C. § 610) requires agencies to periodically review all rules issued by the agency, within 10 years of their adoption as final rules, that have or will have a "significant economic impact upon a substantial number of small entities." The purpose of these reviews is to determine whether such rules should be continued without change, or should be amended or rescinded, consistent with the stated objectives of applicable statutes, to minimize any significant economic impact of the rules upon a substantial number of such small entities. These reviews are referred to as Section 610 reviews.

[24] GAO-07-791.

[25] Charter choice is influenced by many factors, including the size and complexity of banking operations, an institution's business needs, and regulatory expertise tailored to the scale of the bank's operations. See GAO, *OCC Preemption Rules: OCC Should Further Clarify the Applicability of State Consumer Protection Laws to National Banks*, GAO-06-387 (Washington, D.C.: Apr. 28, 2006), 25-28.

[26] GAO-05-61, 114.

[27] These trends are discussed in greater detail in GAO-05-61, ch. 2.

[28] The number of ILCs actually grew during the period 1996-2006; however, they represent a very small percent of total deposits in the banking industry; insured deposits in ILCs represented less than 3 percent of the total estimated deposits in 2006.

[29] Assets, though an imperfect measure of increased growth in the securities industry, tend to be more stable than revenues and show a clearer picture of the size of the industry over time. This figure includes total assets and not assets under management. Revenues, another measure commonly used to reflect the growth of the securities industry, increased by about 61 percent over this same period from about $172 billion to $437 billion.

[30] GAO-05-61, 46-47.

[31] Gianni DeNicolo, Philip Bartholomew, Jahanara Zaman, and Mary Zephirin, "Bank Consolidation, Internationalization, and Conglomeration: Trends and Implications for Financial Risk" (IMF Working Paper 03/158, Washington, D.C., July 2003).

[32] GAO-05-61.

[33] IKB Deutsche Industriebank, PNB Paribas, and other foreign banks experienced losses due to defaults on subprime mortgages in the United States, according to news reports.

[34] According to SEC filings, 51.3 percent of Goldman Sachs revenues in the first half of 2007 were earned in Asia, Europe, the Middle East, and Africa. Revenues earned in the Americas were 48.7 percent, most of which was earned in the United States.

[35] Citigroup, Form 10-K for 2006, filed with SEC; p. 5.

[36] GAO, *Credit Derivatives: Confirmation Backlogs Increased Dealers' Operational Risks, but Were Successfully Addressed after Joint Regulatory Action*, GAO-07-716 (Washington, D.C.: June 13, 2007).

[37] For enterprises engaged in commercial activities, consolidated supervision also may refer to supervision of the enterprise consolidated at the highest-level holding company engaged in financial activities. For foreign banking firms that operate in the United States without a U.S. holding company, consolidated supervision may refer to the oversight of all U.S. activities of the foreign firm.

[38] GAO, *Financial Market Regulation: Agencies Engaged in Consolidated Supervision Can Strengthen Performance Measurement and Collaboration*, GAO-07-154 (Washington, D.C.: Mar. 15, 2007).

[39] GAO-07-154, 39, 48-51.

[40] GAO, *Financial Market Regulation: Agencies Engaged in Consolidated Supervision Can Strengthen Performance Measurement and Collaboration*, GAO-07-154 (Washington, D.C.: March 15, 2007).

[41] See GAO-05-621. In most respects, ILCs may engage in the same activities as other depository institutions insured by the FDIC and thus may offer a full range of loans, including consumer, commercial and residential real estate, small business, and subprime. ILCs are also subject to the same federal safety and soundness safeguards and consumer protection laws that apply to other FDIC-insured institutions.

[42] GAO found that nonfinancial, commercial firms in the automobile, retail, and energy industries, among others, own ILCs, many of which directly supported their parent's commercial activities.

[43] 72 Fed. Reg. 5290 (Feb. 5, 2007).

[44] In addition to the risk-based capital requirement, U.S. banks must also satisfy a leverage requirement that defines a minimum level for a simple ratio of specified components of total capital (those defined as Tier I under current rules) to on-balance sheet assets. See GAO-07-253, 32 ff.

[45] See GAO-07-253, 77-79.

[46] GAO, *OCC Preemption Rules: OCC Should Further Clarify the Applicability of State Consumer Protection Laws to National Banks*, GAO-06-387 (Washington, D.C.: Apr. 28, 2006).

[47] Watters v. Wachovia, N.A., 127 S. Ct. 1559 (Apr. 17, 2007).

[48] For example, since their introduction in the early 1990s, credit derivatives surpassed a notional amount of $34 trillion at year-end 2006. See GAO-07-716.

[49] See, for example, GAO, *CFTC/SEC Enforcement Programs: Status and Potential Impact of a Merger*, GAO/T-GGD-96-36 (Washington, D.C.: Oct. 25, 1995).

[50] GAO, *CFTC and SEC: Issues Related to the Shad-Johnson Jurisdictional Accord*, GAO/GGD-00-89 (Washington, D.C.: Apr. 6, 2000).

[51] GAO-07-716.

[52] GAO, *Bank Secrecy Act: Opportunities Exist for FinCEN and the Banking Regulators to Further Strengthen the Framework for Consistent BSA Oversight*, GAO-06-386 (Washington, D.C.: Apr. 28, 2006).

[53] See GAO-05-61, 97-98.

[54] See GAO, *Fincncial Regulatory Coordination: The Role and Functioning of the President's Working Group*, GAO/GGD-00-46 (Washington, D.C.: Jan. 2000).

[55] GAO/GGD-04-46, 3.

[56] GAO-07-154.

[57] GAO/GGD-00-46.

[58] GAO, *Long-Term Capital Management: Regulators Need to Focus Greater Attention on Systemic Risk*, GAO/GGD-00-3, (Washington, D.C.: Oct. 29, 1999).

[59] GAO, *Potential Terrorist Attacks: Additional Actions Needed to Better Prepare Critical Financial Market Participants*, GAO-03-251 (Washington, D.C.: Feb. 12, 2003).

[60] GAO, *Better Information Sharing among Financial Services Regulators Could Improve Protections for Consumers*, GAO-04-882R (Washington, D.C.: June 29, 2004).

[61] We have noted limitations on effectively planning strategies that cut across regulatory agencies. See GAO-05-61.

[62] GAO-05-61.

[63] GAO-05-61.

[64] GAO-05-61.

[65] This proposal was outlined in the statement of the Honorable Lloyd Bentsen, Secretary of the Treasury, before the Committee on Banking, Housing, and Urban Affairs of the U.S. Senate (Mar. 1, 1994).

[66] The Bank Regulatory Consolidation and Reform Act of 1993, H.R. 1227, 103rd Cong. (1993).

[67] CRS, *Bank Regulatory Agency Consolidation Proposals: A Structural Analysis* (Washington, D.C., Mar. 18, 1994).

[68] This proposal was outlined in the statement of Alan Greenspan, Chairman, Board of Governors of the Federal Reserve System, before the Committee on Banking, Housing, and Urban Affairs of the U.S. Senate (Mar. 2, 1994).

[69] While FSA is responsible for supervision of financial entities, the Bank of England retains primary responsibility for the overall stability of the financial system. It retains lender-oflast-resort responsibilities but must consult with the Treasury if taxpayers are at risk. High- level representatives from the three agencies meet monthly to discuss issues of mutual concern. See GAO-05-61, 67.

[70] The European Union (EU) is a treaty-based organization of European countries in which countries cede some of their sovereignty so that decisions on specific matters of joint interest can be made democratically at the European level. GAO-05-61, 62.

[71] In 1996, Japan also consolidated and modified its financial services regulatory structure in response to persistent problems in that sector. A single regulator, the Financial Services Agency (Japan-FSA), is responsible for supervising the entire financial services industry. Since its creation, Japan-FSA has overseen the mergers of several large banks and has reported progress in addressing the issue of nonperforming loans held by Japanese banks. In the review of Japan-FSA issued in 2003, however, IMF raised questions about the independence and enforcement powers of the agency.

[72] GAO, *Bank Oversight: Fundamental Principles for Modernizing the U.S. Structure,* GAO/T-GGD-96-117 (Washington, D.C.: May 2, 1996).

[73] Basel Committee on Banking Supervision, *Core Principles for Effective Bank Supervision.* (Basel, Switzerland, October 2006), 5.

[74] See, GAO-07-791.

[75] GAO, *OCC Preemption Rulemaking: Opportunities Existed to Enhance the Consultative Efforts and Better Document the Rulemaking Process,* GAO-06-8 (Washington, D.C.: Oct. 17, 2005).

[76] See GAO-05-61.

[77] The Basel Committee's core principles for effective banking supervision are conceived as a voluntary framework of minimum standards for sound supervisory practices; national authorities are free to put in place supplementary measures that they deem necessary to achieve effective supervision in their jurisdictions. In 2006, the Committee revised the core principles, in part, to enhance consistency between the core principles and the corresponding standards for securities and insurance. While the Committee recognized there may be legitimate reasons for differences in core principles within each sector, the changes recognized the importance of consistency across sectors.

[78] IMF undertakes missions, in most cases to member countries, as part of regular (usually annual) consultations under article IV of IMF's Articles of Agreement, in the context of a request to use IMF resources (borrow from IMF), as part of discussions of staff-monitored programs, and as part of other staff reviews of economic developments.

[79] Department of the Treasury, *Paulson Announces Next Steps to Bolster U.S. Markets' Global Competitiveness.* (Washington, D.C., June 27, 2007.)

In: Modernizing Financial Regulation
Editor: Lawrence P. Cowell
ISBN: 978-1-60741-442-1

Chapter 3

FINANCIAL REGULATION: A FRAMEWORK FOR CRAFTING AND ASSESSING PROPOSALS TO MODERNIZE THE OUTDATED U.S. FINANCIAL REGULATORY SYSTEM

United States Government Accountability Office

WHY GAO DID THIS STUDY

The United States and other countries are in the midst of the worst financial crisis in more than 75 years. While much of the attention of policymakers understandably has been focused on taking short-term steps to address the immediate nature of the crisis, these events have served to strikingly demonstrate that the current U.S. financial regulatory system is in need of significant reform.

To help policymakers better understand existing problems with the financial regulatory system and craft and evaluate reform proposals, this chapter (1) describes the origins of the current financial regulatory system, (2) describes various market developments and changes that have created challenges for the current system, and (3) presents an evaluation framework that can be used by Congress and others to shape potential regulatory reform efforts. To do this work, GAO synthesized existing GAO work and other studies and met with dozens of representatives of financial regulatory agencies, industry associations, consumer advocacy organizations, and others. Twenty-nine regulators, industry associations, and consumer groups also reviewed a draft of this chapter and provided valuable input that was incorporated as appropriate. In general, reviewers commented that the report represented an important and thorough review of the issues related to regulatory reform.

WHAT GAO FOUND

The current U.S. financial regulatory system has relied on a fragmented and complex arrangement of federal and state regulators—put into place over the past 150 years—that has not kept pace with major developments in financial markets and products in recent decades. As the nation finds itself in the midst of one of the worst financial crises ever, the regulatory system increasingly appears to be ill-suited to meet the nation's needs in the 21st century. Today, responsibilities for overseeing the financial services industry are shared among almost a dozen federal banking, securities, futures, and other regulatory agencies, numerous self-regulatory organizations, and hundreds of state financial regulatory agencies. Much of this structure has developed as the result of statutory and regulatory changes that were often implemented in response to financial crises or significant developments in the financial services sector. For example, the Federal Reserve System was created in 1913 in response to financial panics and instability around the turn of the century, and much of the remaining structure for bank and securities regulation was created as the result of the Great Depression turmoil of the 1920s and 1930s.

Several key changes in financial markets and products in recent decades have highlighted significant limitations and gaps in the existing regulatory system.

- First, regulators have struggled, and often failed, to mitigate the systemic risks posed by large and interconnected financial conglomerates and to ensure they adequately manage their risks. The portion of firms operating as conglomerates that cross financial sectors of banking, securities, and insurance increased significantly in recent years, but none of the regulators is tasked with assessing the risks posed across the entire financial system.
- Second, regulators have had to address problems in financial markets resulting from the activities of large and sometimes less-regulated market participants—such as nonbank mortgage lenders, hedge funds, and credit rating agencies—some of which play significant roles in today's financial markets.
- Third, the increasing prevalence of new and more complex investment products has challenged regulators and investors, and consumers have faced difficulty understanding new and increasingly complex retail mortgage and credit products. Regulators failed to adequately oversee the sale of mortgage products that posed risks to consumers and the stability of the financial system.
- Fourth, standard setters for accounting and financial regulators have faced growing challenges in ensuring that accounting and audit standards appropriately respond to financial market developments, and in addressing challenges arising from the global convergence of accounting and auditing standards.
- Finally, despite the increasingly global aspects of financial markets, the current fragmented U.S. regulatory structure has complicated some efforts to coordinate internationally with other regulators.

As a result of significant market developments in recent decades that have outpaced a fragmented and outdated regulatory structure, significant reforms to the U.S. regulatory system are critically and urgently needed. The current system has important weaknesses that, if not addressed, will continue to expose the nation's financial system to serious risks. As early as 1994, GAO identified the need to examine the federal financial regulatory structure, including the need to address the risks from new unregulated products. Since then, GAO has described various options for Congress to consider, each of which provides potential improvements, as well as some risks and potential costs. This chapter offers a framework for crafting and evaluating regulatory reform proposals; it consists of the following nine characteristics that should be reflected in any new regulatory system. By applying the elements of this framework, the relative strengths and weaknesses of any reform proposal should be better revealed, and policymakers should be able to focus on identifying trade-offs and balancing competing goals. Similarly, the framework could be used to craft proposals, or to identify aspects to be added to existing proposals to make them more effective and appropriate for addressing the limitations of the current system.

Characteristic		Description
✓	**Clearly defined regulatory goals**	Goals should be clearly articulated and relevant, so that regulators can effectively carry out their missions and be held accountable. Key issues include considering the benefits of re-examining the goals of financial regulation to gain needed consensus and making explicit a set of pdated comprehensive and cohesive goals that reflect today's environment.
✓	**Appropriately comprehensive**	Financial regulations should cover all activities that pose risks or are otherwise important to meeting regulatory goals and should ensure that appropriate determinations are made about how extensive such regulations should be, considering that some activities may require less regulation than others. Key issues include identifying risk-based criteria, such as a product's or institution's potential to create systemic problems, for determining the appropriate level of oversight for financial activities and institutions, including closing gaps that contributed to the current crisis.
✓	**Systemwide focus**	Mechanisms should be included for identifying, monitoring, and managing risks to the financial system regardless of the source of the risk. Given that no regulator is currently tasked with this, key issues include determining how to effectively monitor market developments to identify potential risks; the degree, if any, to which regulatory intervention might be required; and who should hold such responsibilities.
✓	**Flexible and adaptable**	A regulatory system that is flexible and forward looking allows regulators to readily adapt to market innovations and changes. Key issues include identifying and acting on emerging risks in a timely way without hindering innovation.
✓	**Efficient and effective**	Effective and efficient oversight should be developed, including eliminating overlapping federal regulatory missions where appropriate, and minimizing regulatory burden without sacrificing effective oversight. Any changes to the system should be continually focused on improving the effectiveness of the financial regulatory system. Key issues include determining opportunities for consolidation given the large number of overlapping participants now, identifying the appropriate role of states and self-regulation, and ensuring a smooth transition to any new system.

Table (Continued)

Characteristic		Description
✓	**Consistent consumer and investor protection**	Consumer and investor protection should be included as part of the regulatory mission to ensure that market participants receive consistent, useful information, as well as legal protections for similar financial products and services, including disclosures, sales practice standards, and suitability requirements. Key issues include determining what amount, if any, of consolidation of responsibility may be necessary to streamline consumer protection activities across the financial services industry.
✓	**Regulators provided with independence, prominence, authority, and accountability**	Regulators should have independence from inappropriate influence, as well as prominence and authority to carry out and enforce statutory missions, and be clearly accountable for meeting regulatory goals. With regulators with varying levels of prominence and funding schemes now, key issues include how to appropriately structure and fund agencies to ensure that each one's structure sufficiently achieves these characteristics.
✓	**Consistent financial oversight**	Similar institutions, products, risks, and services should be subject to consistent regulation, oversight, and transparency, which should help minimize negative competitive outcomes while harmonizing oversight, both within the United States and internationally. Key issues include identifying activities that pose similar risks, and streamlining regulatory activities to achieve consistency.
✓	**Minimal taxpayer exposure**	A regulatory system should foster financial markets that are resilient enough to absorb failures and thereby limit the need for federal intervention and limit taxpayers' exposure to financial risk. Key issues include identifying safeguards to prevent systemic crises and minimizing moral hazard.

Source: GAO.

ABBREVIATIONS

BFCU	Bureau of Federal Credit Unions
CDO	collateralized debt obligation
CEC	Commodity Exchange Commission
CFTC	Commodity Futures Trading Commission
CSE	Consolidated Supervised Entity
FASB	Financial Accounting Standards Board
FDIC	Federal Deposit Insurance Corporation
FHFA	Federal Housing Finance Agency
FHFB	Federal Housing Finance Board
FHLBB	Federal Home Loan Bank Board
FRS	Federal Reserve System
FSLIC	Federal Savings and Loan Insurance Corporation
FTC	Federal Trade Commission
GFA	Grain Futures Administration
GLBA	Gramm-Leach-Bliley Act of 1999

GSE	government-sponsored enterprise
IMF	International Monetary Fund
LTCM	Long Term Capital Management
NAIC	National Association of Insurance Commissioners
NCUA	National Credit Union Administration
NRSRO	nationally recognized statistical rating organization
OCC	Office of the Comptroller of the Currency
OFHEO	Office of Federal Housing Enterprise Oversight
OTC	over-the-counter
OTS	Office of Thrift Supervision
PCAOB	Public Company Accounting Oversight Board
SEC	Securities and Exchange Commission
SRO	self-regulatory organization

January 8, 2009
Congressional Addressees

The United States is in the midst of the worst financial crisis in more than 75 years. In recent months, federal officials have taken unprecedented steps to stem the unraveling of the financial services sector by committing trillions of dollars of taxpayer funds to rescue financial institutions and restore order to credit markets, including the creation of a $700 billion program that has been used so far to inject money into struggling institutions in an attempt to stabilize markets.[1] This current crisis largely stems from defaults on U.S. subprime mortgage loans, many of which were packaged and sold as securities to buyers in the United States and around the world. With financial institutions from many countries participating in these activities, the resulting turmoil has afflicted financial markets globally and has spurred coordinated action by world leaders in an attempt to protect savings and restore the health of the markets. While much of policymakers' attention understandably has been focused on taking short-term steps to address the immediate nature of the crisis, these events have served to strikingly demonstrate that the current U.S. financial regulatory system is in need of significant reform.[2]

The current U.S. regulatory system has relied on a fragmented and complex arrangement of federal and state regulators—put into place over the past 150 years—that has not kept pace with the major developments that have occurred in financial markets and products in recent decades. In particular, the current system was not designed to adequately oversee today's large and interconnected financial institutions, whose activities pose new risks to the institutions themselves as well as risk to the broader financial system—called systemic risk, which is the risk that an event could broadly effect the financial system rather than just one or a few institutions. In addition, not all financial activities and institutions fall under the direct purview of financial regulators, and market innovations have led to the creation of new and sometimes very complex products that were never envisioned as the current regulatory system developed. In light of the recent turmoil in financial markets, the current financial regulatory system increasingly appears to be ill-suited to meet the nation's needs in the 21st century.

As the administration and Congress continue to take actions to address the immediate financial crisis, determining how to create a regulatory system that reflects new market realities is a key step to reducing the likelihood that the U.S. will experience another financial crisis similar to the current one. As a result, considerable debate is under way over whether and how the current regulatory system should be changed, including calls for consolidating regulatory agencies, broadening certain regulators' authorities, or subjecting certain products or entities to more regulation. For example, in March 2008, the Department of the Treasury (Treasury) proposed significant financial regulatory reforms in its "Blueprint for a Modernized Financial Regulatory Structure," and other federal regulatory officials and industry groups have also put forth reform proposals.[3] Under the Emergency Economic Stabilization Act, Treasury is required to submit to Congress by April 30, 2009, a report with recommendations on "the current state of the financial markets and the regulatory system."[4] As these and other proposals are developed or evaluated, it will be important to carefully consider their advantages and disadvantages and long-term implications.

To help policymakers weigh the various proposals and consider ways in which the current regulatory system could be made more effective and efficient, we prepared this chapter under the authority of the Comptroller General. Specifically, our report (1) describes the origins of the current financial regulatory system, (2) describes various market developments and changes that have raised challenges for the current system, and (3) presents an evaluation framework that can be used by Congress and others to craft or evaluate potential regulatory reform efforts going forward. This chapter's primary focus is on discussing how various market developments have revealed gaps and limitations in the existing regulatory system. Although drawing on examples of events from the current crisis, we do not attempt to identify all of the potential weaknesses in the actions of regulators that had authority over the institutions and products involved.

To address these objectives, we synthesized existing GAO work on challenges to the U.S. financial regulatory structure and on criteria for developing and strengthening effective regulatory structures.[5] We also reviewed existing studies, government documents, and other research for illustrations of how current and past financial market events have exposed inadequacies in our existing financial regulatory system and for suggestions for regulatory reform. In a series of forums, we discussed these developments and the elements of a potential framework for an effective regulatory system with groups of financial regulators of banking, securities, futures, insurance, and housing markets; representatives of financial services industry associations and individual financial institutions; and with selected consumer advocacy organizations, academics, and other experts in financial markets issues. The work upon which this chapter is based was conducted in accordance with generally accepted government auditing standards. Those standards require that we plan and perform the audit to obtain sufficient, appropriate evidence to provide a reasonable basis for our findings and conclusions based on our audit objectives. We believe that the evidence obtained provides a reasonable basis for our findings and conclusions based on our audit objectives. This work was conducted between April 2008 and December 2008. A more extensive discussion of our scope and methodology appears in appendix I.

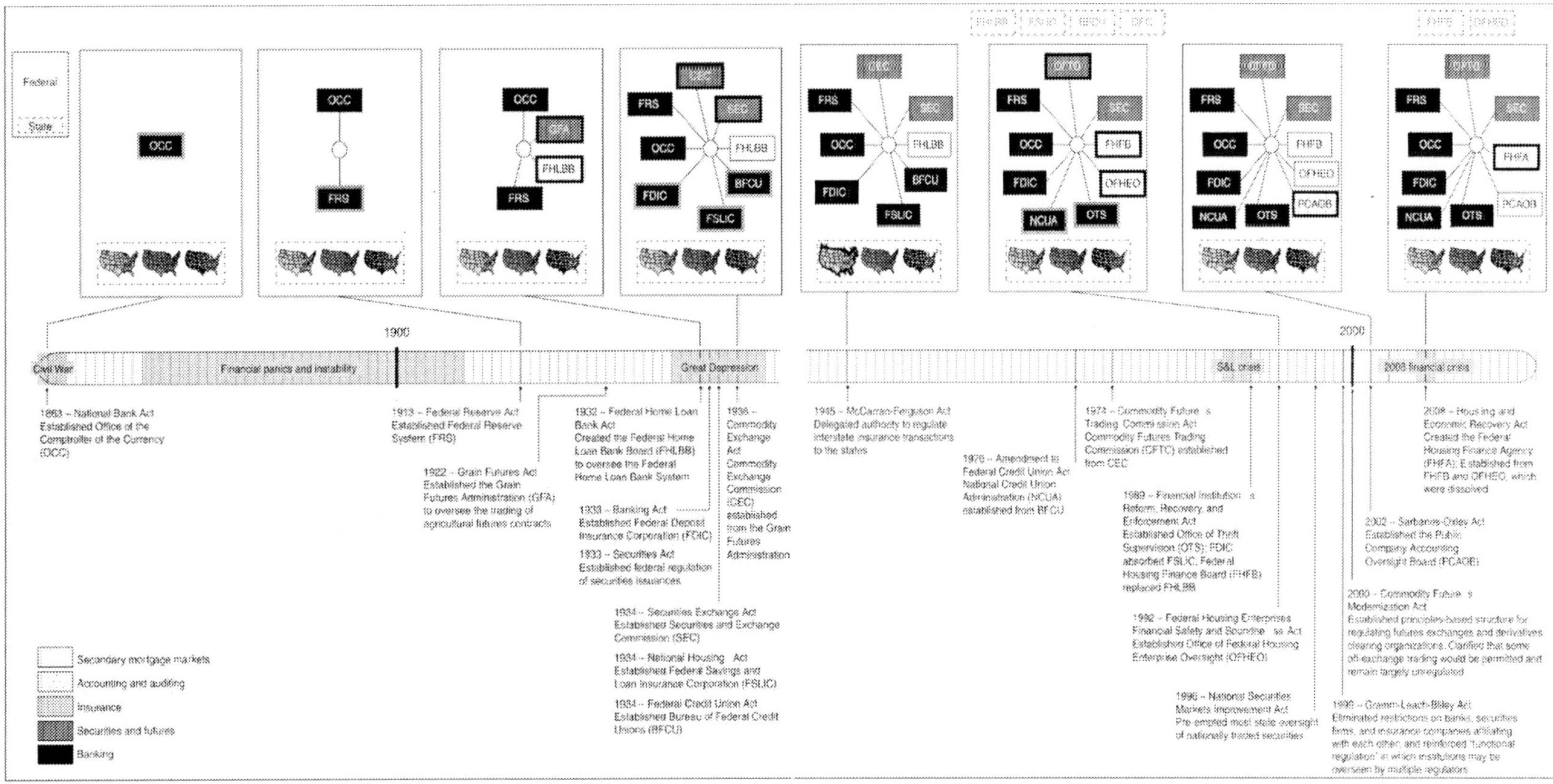

Source: GAO.

Figure 1. Formation of U.S. Financial Regulatory System (1863-2008)

BACKGROUND

While providing many benefits to our economy and citizens' lives, financial services activities can also cause harm if left unsupervised. As a result, the United States and many other countries have found that regulating financial markets, institutions, and products is more efficient and effective than leaving the fairness and integrity of these activities to be ensured solely by market participants themselves.

The federal laws related to financial regulation set forth specific authorities and responsibilities for regulators, although these authorities typically do not contain provisions explicitly linking such responsibilities to overall goals of financial regulation. Nevertheless, financial regulation generally has sought to achieve four broad goals:

- *Ensure adequate consumer protections.* Because financial institutions' incentives to maximize profits can in some cases lead to sales of unsuitable or fraudulent financial products, or unfair or deceptive acts or practices, U.S. regulators take steps to address informational disadvantages that consumers and investors may face, ensure consumers and investors have sufficient information to make appropriate decisions, and oversee business conduct and sales practices to prevent fraud and abuse.

- *Ensure the integrity and fairness of markets.* Because some market participants could seek to manipulate markets to obtain unfair gains in a way that is not easily detectable by other participants, U.S. regulators set rules for and monitor markets and their participants to prevent fraud and manipulation, limit problems in asset pricing, and ensure efficient market activity.

- *Monitor the safety and soundness of institutions.* Because markets sometimes lead financial institutions to take on excessive risks that can have significant negative impacts on consumers, investors, and taxpayers, regulators oversee risk-taking activities to promote the safety and soundness of financial institutions.

- *Act to ensure the stability of the overall financial system.* Because shocks to the system or the actions of financial institutions can lead to instability in the broader financial system, regulators act to reduce systemic risk in various ways, such as by providing emergency funding to troubled financial institutions.

Although these goals have traditionally been their primary focus, financial regulators are also often tasked with achieving other goals as they carry out their activities. These can include promoting economic growth, capital formation, and competition in our financial markets. Regulators have also taken actions with an eye toward ensuring the competitiveness of regulated U.S. financial institutions with those in other sectors or with others around the world. In other cases, financial institutions may be required by law or regulation to foster social policy objectives such as fair access to credit and increased home ownership.

In general, these goals are reflected in statutes, regulations, and administrative actions, such as rulemakings or guidance, by financial institution supervisors. Laws and regulatory agency policies can set a greater priority on some roles and missions than others. Regulators are usually responsible for multiple regulatory goals and often prioritize them differently. For example, state and federal bank regulators generally focus on the safety and soundness of depository institutions; federal securities and futures regulators focus on the integrity of markets, and the adequacy of information provided to investors; and state securities regulators primarily address consumer protection. State insurance regulators focus on the ability of insurance firms to meet their commitments to the insured.

The degrees to which regulators oversee institutions, markets, or products also vary depending upon, among other things, the regulatory approach Congress has fashioned for different sectors of the financial industry. For example, some institutions, such as banks, are subject to comprehensive regulation to ensure their safety and soundness. Among other things, they are subject to examinations and limitations on the types of activities they may conduct. Other institutions conducting financial activities are less regulated, such as by only having to register with regulators or by having less extensive disclosure requirements. Moreover, some markets, such as those for many over-the-counter derivatives markets, as well as activities within those markets, are not subject to oversight regulation at all.

Today's Financial Regulatory System Was Built over More Than a Century, Largely in Response to Crises or Market Developments

As a result of 150 years of changes in financial regulation in the United States, the regulatory system has become complex and fragmented. (See figure 1.) Our regulatory system has multiple financial regulatory bodies, including five federal and multiple state agencies that oversee depository institutions. Securities activities are overseen by federal and state government entities, as well as by private sector organizations performing self-regulatory functions. Futures trading is overseen by a federal regulator and also by industry self-regulatory organizations. Insurance activities are primarily regulated at the state level with little federal involvement.

Overall, responsibilities for overseeing the financial services industry are shared among almost a dozen federal banking, securities, futures, and other regulatory agencies, numerous self-regulatory organizations (SRO), and hundreds of state financial regulatory agencies. The following sections describe how regulation evolved in various sectors, including banking, securities, thrifts, credit unions, futures, insurance, secondary mortgage markets, and other financial institutions. The accounting and auditing environment for financial institutions, and the role of the Gramm-LeachBliley Act in financial regulation, are also discussed.

Banking

Since the early days of our nation, banks have allowed citizens to store their savings and used these funds to make loans to spur business development. Until the middle of the 1800s, banks were chartered by states and state regulators supervised their activities, which primarily consisted of taking deposits and issuing currency. However, the existence of multiple currencies issued by different banks, some of which were more highly valued than others, created difficulties for the smooth functioning of economic activity. In an effort to finance the nation's Civil War debt and reduce financial uncertainty, Congress passed the National Bank Act of 1863, which provided for issuance of a single national currency. This act also created the Office of the Comptroller of the Currency (OCC), which was to oversee the national currency and improve banking system efficiency by granting banks national charters to operate and conducting oversight to ensure the sound operations of these banks. As of 2007, of the more than 16,000 depository institutions subject to federal regulation in the United States, OCC was responsible for chartering, regulating, and supervising nearly 1,700 commercial banks with national charters.

In the years surrounding 1900, the United States experienced troubled economic conditions and several financial panics, including various instances of bank runs as depositors attempted to withdraw their funds from banks whose financial conditions had deteriorated. To improve the liquidity of the U.S. banking sector and reduce the potential for such panics and runs, Congress passed the Federal Reserve Act of 1913. This act created the Federal Reserve System, which consists of the Board of Governors of the Federal Reserve System (Federal Reserve), and 12 Federal Reserve Banks, which are congressionally chartered semiprivate entities that undertake a range of actions on behalf of the Federal Reserve, including supervision of banks and bank holding companies, and lending to troubled banks. The Federal Reserve was given responsibility to act as the federal supervisory agency for state-chartered banks—banks authorized to do business under charters issued by states—that are members of the Federal Reserve System.[6] In addition to supervising and regulating bank and financial holding companies and nearly 900 state- chartered banks, the Federal Reserve also develops and implements national monetary policy, and provides financial services to depository institutions, the U.S. government, and foreign official institutions, including playing a major role in operating the nation's payments system.

Several significant changes to the U.S. financial regulatory system again were made as a result of the turbulent economic conditions in the late 1920s and 1930s. In response to numerous bank failures resulting in the severe contraction of economic activity of the Great Depression, the Banking Act of 1933 created the Federal Deposit Insurance Corporation (FDIC), which administers a federal program to insure the deposits of participating banks. Subsequently, FDIC's deposit insurance authority expanded to include thrifts.[7] Additionally, FDIC provides primary federal oversight of any insured state-chartered banks that are not members of the Federal Reserve System, and it serves as the primary federal regulator for over 5,200 state-chartered institutions. Finally, FDIC has backup examination and enforcement authority over all of the institutions it insures in order to mitigate losses to the deposit insurance funds.

Securities

Prior to the 1930s, securities markets were overseen by various state securities regulatory bodies and the securities exchanges themselves. In the aftermath of the stock market crash of 1929, the Securities Exchange Act of 1934 created a new federal agency, the Securities and Exchange Commission (SEC) and gave it authority to register and oversee securities broker-dealers, as well as securities exchanges, to strengthen securities oversight and address inconsistent state securities rules.[8] In addition to regulation by SEC and state agencies, securities markets and the broker-dealers that accept and execute customer orders in these markets continue to be regulated by SROs, including those of the exchanges and the Financial Industry Regulatory Authority, that are funded by the participants in the industry. Among other things, these SROs establish rules and conduct examinations related to market integrity and investor protection. SEC also registers and oversees investment companies and advisers, approves rules for the industry, and conducts examinations of broker-dealers and mutual funds. State securities regulators—represented by the North American Securities Administrators Association—are generally responsible for registering certain securities products and, along with SEC, investigating securities fraud.[9] SEC is also responsible for overseeing the financial reporting and disclosures that companies issuing securities must make under U.S. securities laws. SEC was also authorized to issue and oversee U.S. accounting standards for entities subject to its jurisdiction, but has delegated the creation of accounting standards to a private-sector organization, the Financial Accounting Standards Board, which establishes generally accepted accounting principles.

Thrifts and Credit Unions

The economic turmoil of the 1930s also prompted the creation of federal regulators for other types of depository institutions, including thrifts and credit unions.[10] These institutions previously had been subject to oversight only by state authorities. However, the Home Owners' Loan Act of 1933 empowered the newly created Federal Home Loan Bank Board to charter and regulate federal thrifts, and the Federal Credit Union Act of 1934 created the Bureau of Federal Credit Unions to charter and supervise credit unions.[11] Congress amended the Federal Credit Union Act in 1970 to establish the National Credit Union Administration (NCUA), which is responsible for chartering and supervising over 5,000 federally chartered credit unions, as well as insuring deposits in these and more than 3,000 state-chartered credit unions.[12] Oversight of these state-chartered credit unions is managed by 47 state regulatory agencies, represented by the National Association of State Credit Union Supervisors.[13]

From 1980 to 1990, over 1,000 thrifts failed at a cost of about $100 billion to the federal deposit insurance funds. In response, the Financial Institutions Reform, Recovery, and Enforcement Act of 1989 abolished the Federal Home Loan Bank Board and, among other things, established the Office of Thrift Supervision (OTS) to improve thrift oversight.[14] OTS charters about 750 federal thrifts and oversees these and about 70 state- chartered thrifts, as well as savings and loan holding companies.[15]

Futures

Oversight of the trading of futures contracts, which allow their purchasers to buy or sell a specific quantity of a commodity for delivery in the future, has also changed over the years in response to changes in the marketplace. Under the Grain Futures Act of 1922, the trading of futures contracts was overseen by the Grain Futures Administration, an office within the Department of Agriculture, reflecting the nature of the products for which futures contracts were traded.[16] However, futures contracts were later created for nonagricultural commodities, such as energy products like oil and natural gas, metals such as gold and silver, and financial products such as Treasury bonds and foreign currencies. In 1974, a new independent federal agency, the Commodity Futures Trading Commission (CFTC), was created to oversee the trading of futures contracts.[17] Like SEC, CFTC relies on SROs, including the futures exchanges and the National Futures Association, to establish and enforce rules governing member behavior. In 2000, the Commodity Futures Modernization Act of 2000 established a principles-based structure for the regulation of futures exchanges and derivatives clearing organizations, and clarified that some off-exchange derivatives trading—and in particular trading on facilities only accessible to large, sophisticated traders—was permitted and would be largely unregulated or exempt from regulation.[18]

Insurance

Unlike most other financial services, insurance activities traditionally have been regulated at the state level. In 1944, a U.S. Supreme Court decision determined that the insurance industry was subject to interstate commerce laws, which could then have allowed for federal regulation, but Congress passed the McCarran-Ferguson Act in 1945 to explicitly return insurance regulation to the states.[19] As a result, as many as 55 state, territorial, or other local jurisdiction authorities oversee insurance activities in the United States, although state regulations and other activities are often coordinated nationally by the National Association of Insurance Commissioners (NAIC).[20]

Secondary Mortgage Markets

The recent financial crisis in the credit and housing markets has prompted the creation of a new, unified federal financial regulatory oversight agency, the Federal Housing Finance Agency (FHFA), to oversee the government-sponsored enterprises (GSE) Fannie Mae, Freddie Mac, and the Federal Home Loan Banks.[21] Fannie Mae and Freddie Mac are private, federally chartered companies created by Congress to, among other things, provide liquidity to home mortgage markets by purchasing mortgage loans, thus enabling lenders to make additional loans. The system of 12 Federal Home Loan Banks provides funding to support housing finance and economic development.[22] Until enactment of the Housing and Economic Recovery Act of 2008, Fannie Mae and Freddie Mac had been overseen since 1992 by the Office of Federal Housing Enterprise Oversight (OFHEO), an agency within the Department of Housing and Urban Development, and the Federal Home Loan Banks were subject to supervision by the Federal Housing Finance Board (FHFB), an independent regulatory agency.[23] OFHEO regulated Fannie Mae and Freddie Mac on matters of safety and soundness, while HUD regulated their mission-related activities. FHFB served as the safety and soundness and mission regulator of the Federal Home Loan Banks. In July 2008, the Housing and Economic Recovery Act of 2008 created FHFA to establish more effective and more consistent oversight of the three housing GSEs—Fannie Mae, Freddie Mac, and the Federal Home Loan Banks. With respect to Fannie Mae and Freddie Mac, the law gives

FHFA such new regulatory authorities as the power to regulate the retained mortgage portfolios, to set more stringent capital standards, and to place a failing entity in receivership. In addition, the law provides FHFA with funding outside the annual appropriations process. The law also combined the regulatory authorities for all the housing GSEs that were previously distributed among OFHEO, FHFB, and the Department of Housing and Urban Development. In September 2008, Fannie Mae and Freddie Mac were placed in conservatorship, with FHFA serving as the conservator under powers provided in the 2008 act. Treasury also created a backstop lending facility for the Federal Home Loan Banks, should they decide to use it. In November 2008, the Federal Reserve announced plans to purchase mortgage-backed securities guaranteed by Fannie Mae and Freddie Mac on the open market.

Gramm-Leach-Bliley

Changes in the types of financial activities permitted for depository institutions and their affiliates have also shaped the financial regulatory system over time. Under the Glass-Steagall provisions of the Banking Act of 1933, financial institutions were prohibited from simultaneously offering commercial and investment banking services. However, in the Gramm-Leach-Bliley Act of 1999 (GLBA), Congress permitted financial institutions to fully engage in both types of activities and, in addition, provided a regulatory process allowing for the approval of new types of financial activity.[24] Under GLBA, qualifying financial institutions are permitted to engage in banking, securities, insurance, and other financial activities. When these activities are conducted within the same bank holding company structure, they remain subject to regulation by "functional regulators," which are the federal authorities having jurisdiction over specific financial products or services, such as SEC or CFTC. As a result, multiple regulators now oversee different business lines within a single institution. For example, broker-dealer activities are generally regulated by SEC even if they are conducted within a large financial conglomerate that is subject to the Bank Holding Company Act, which is administered by the Federal Reserve. The functional regulator approach was intended to provide consistency in regulation, focus regulatory restrictions on the relevant functional area, and avoid the potential need for regulatory agencies to develop expertise in all aspects of financial regulation.

Accounting and Auditing

In addition to the creation of various regulators over time, the accounting and auditing environment for financial institutions and market participants—a key component of financial oversight—has also seen substantial change. In the early 2000s, various companies with publicly traded securities were found to have issued materially misleading financial statements. These companies included Enron and WorldCom, both of which filed for bankruptcy. When the actual financial conditions of these companies became known, their auditors were called into question, and one of the largest, Arthur Andersen, was dissolved after the Department of Justice filed criminal charges related to its audits of Enron. As a result of these and other corporate financial reporting and auditing scandals, the Sarbanes-Oxley Act of 2002 was enacted.[25] Among other things, Sarbanes-Oxley expanded public company reporting and disclosure requirements and established new ethical and corporate responsibility requirements for public company executives, boards of directors, and independent auditors. The act also created a new independent public company audit regulator, the Public Company Accounting Oversight Board, to oversee the activities of public accounting firms. The activities of this board are, in turn, overseen by SEC.

Other Financial Institutions

Some entities that provide financial services are not regulated by any of the existing federal financial regulatory bodies. For example, entities such as mortgage brokers, automobile finance companies, and payday lenders that are not bank subsidiaries or affiliates primarily are subject to state oversight, with the Federal Trade Commission acting as the primary federal agency responsible for enforcing their compliance with federal consumer protection laws.

Changes in Financial Institutions and Their Products Have Significantly Challenged the U.S. Financial Regulatory System

Several key developments in financial markets and products in the past few decades have significantly challenged the existing financial regulatory structure. (See figure 2.) First, the last 30 years have seen waves of mergers among financial institutions within and across sectors, such that the United States, while still having large numbers of financial institutions, also has several very large globally active financial conglomerates that engage in a wide range of activities that have become increasingly interconnected. Regulating these large conglomerates has proven challenging, particularly in overseeing their risk management activities on a consolidated basis and in identifying and mitigating the systemic risks they pose. A second development has been the emergence of large and sometimes less-regulated market participants, such as hedge funds and credit rating agencies, which now play key roles in our financial markets. Third, the development of new and complex products and services has challenged regulators' abilities to ensure that institutions are adequately identifying and acting to mitigate risks arising from these new activities and that investors and consumers are adequately informed of the risks. In light of these developments, ensuring that U.S. accounting standards have kept pace has also proved difficult, and the impending transition to conform to international accounting standards is likely to create additional challenges.[26] Finally, despite the increasingly global aspects of financial markets, the current fragmented U.S. regulatory structure has complicated some efforts to coordinate internationally with other regulators.

Developments in financial markets and products		Examples of how developments have challenged the regulatory system
	Emergence of large, complex, globally active, interconnected financial conglomerates	Regulators sometimes lack sufficient authority, tools, or capabilities to oversee and mitigate risks.
		Identifying, preventing, mitigating, and resolving systemic crises has become more difficult.
	Less-regulated entities have come to play increasingly critical roles in financial system	Nonbank lenders and a new private-label securitization market played significant roles in the subprime mortgage crisis that led to broader market turmoil.
		Activities of hedge funds have posed systemic risks.
		Overreliance on credit ratings of mortgage-backed products contributed to the recent turmoil in financial markets.
		Financial institutions' use of off-balance sheet entities led to ineffective risk disclosure and exacerbated recent market instability.
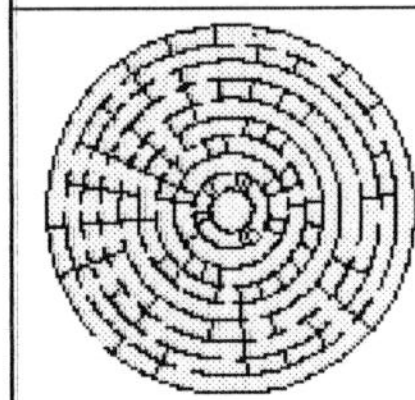	New and complex products that pose challenges to financial stability and investor and consumer understanding of risks.	Complex structured finance products have made it difficult for institutions and their regulators to manage associated risks.
		Growth in complex and less-regulated over-the-counter derivatives markets have created systemic risks and revealed market infrastructure weaknesses.
		Investors have faced difficulty understanding complex investment products, either because they failed to seek out necessary information or were misled by improper sales practices.
		Consumers have faced difficulty understanding mortgages and credit cards with new and increasingly complicated features, due in part to limitations in consumer disclosures and financial literacy efforts.
		Accounting and auditing entities have faced challenges in trying to ensure that accounting and financial reporting requirements appropriately meet the needs of investors and other financial market participants.
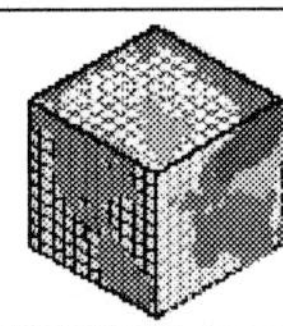	Financial markets have become increasingly global in nature, and regulators have had to coordinate their efforts internationally.	Standard setters and regulators also face new challenges in dealing with global convergence of accounting and auditing standards.
		Fragmented U.S. regulatory structure has complicated some efforts to coordinate internationally with other regulators, such as negotiations on Basel II and certain insurance matters.

Sources: GAO (analysis); Art Explosion (images).

Figure 2: Key Developments and Resulting Challenges That Have Hindered the Effectiveness of the Financial Regulatory System

Conglomeration and Increased Interconnectedness in Financial Markets Have Created Difficulties for a Regulatory System That Lacks a Systemwide Focus

Overseeing large financial conglomerates that have emerged in recent decades has proven challenging, particularly in regulating their consolidated risk management practices and in identifying and mitigating the systemic risks they pose. These systemically important institutions in many cases have tens of thousands or more customers and extensive financial linkages with each other through loans, derivatives contracts, or trading positions with other financial institutions or businesses. The activities of these large financial institutions, as we have seen by recent events, can pose significant systemic risks to other market participants and the economy as a whole, but the regulatory system was not prepared to adequately anticipate and prevent such risks.

Largely as the result of waves of mergers and consolidations, the number of financial institutions today has declined. However, the remaining institutions are generally larger and more complex, provide more and varied services, offer similar products, and operate in increasingly global markets. Among the most significant of these changes has been the emergence and growth of large financial conglomerates or universal banks that offer a wide range of products that cut across the traditional financial sectors of banking, securities, and insurance. A 2003 IMF study highlighted this emerging trend. Based on a worldwide sample of the top 500 financial services firms in assets, the study found that the percentage of the largest financial institutions in the United States that are conglomerates— financial institutions having substantial operations in more than one of the sectors (banking, securities, and insurance)—increased from 42 percent of the U.S. financial institutions in the sample in 1995 to 62 percent in 2000.[27] This new environment contrasts with that of the past in which banks primarily conducted traditional banking activities such as deposit taking and lending; securities broker-dealers were largely focused on brokerage and underwriting activities; and insurance firms offered a more limited set of insurance products. In a report that analyzed the regulatory structures of various countries, The Group of Thirty noted that the last 25 years have been a period of enormous transformation in the financial services sector, with a marked shift from firms engaging in distinct banking, securities, and insurance businesses to one in which more integrated financial services conglomerates offer a broad range of financial products across the globe. These fundamental changes in the nature of the financial service markets around the world have exposed the shortcomings of financial regulatory models, some of which have not been adapted to the changes in business structures.[28]

While posing challenges to regulators, these changes have resulted in some benefits in the United States financial services industry. For example, the ability of financial institutions to offer products of varying types increased the options available to consumers for investing their savings and preparing for their retirement. Conglomeration has also made it more convenient for consumers to conduct their financial activities by providing opportunities for one-stop shopping for most or all of their needs, and by promoting the cross-selling of new innovative products of which consumers may otherwise not have been aware.

However, the rise of large financial conglomerates has also posed risks that our current financial regulatory system does not directly address. First, although the activities of these large interconnected financial institutions often cross traditional sector boundaries, financial regulators under the current U.S. regulatory system did not always have full authority or sufficient tools and capabilities to adequately oversee the risks that these financial institutions posed to themselves and other institutions. As we noted in a 2007 report, the activities of the Federal Reserve, SEC, and OTS to conduct consolidated supervision of many of the largest U.S. financial institutions were not as efficient and effective as needed because these agencies were not collaborating more systematically.[29] In addition, the recent market crisis has revealed significant problems with certain aspects of these regulators' oversight of financial conglomerates. For example, some of the top investment banks were subject to voluntary and limited oversight at the holding-company level—the level of the institution that generally managed its overall risks—as part of SEC's Consolidated Supervised Entity (CSE) Program. SEC's program was created in 2004 as a way for global investment bank conglomerates that lack a supervisor under law to voluntarily submit to regulation.[30] This supervision, which could include SEC examinations of the parent companies' and affiliates' operations and monitoring of their capital levels, enabled the CSEs to qualify for alternative capital rules in exchange for consenting to supervision at the holding company level. Being subject to consolidated supervision was perceived as necessary for these financial institutions to continue operating in Europe under changes implemented by the European Union in 2005.[31]

Collapse of the Investment Bank Model

Until 2008, the largest U.S. investment banks all generally had similar structures that were characterized by a publicly traded holding company with a U.S. broker-dealer subsidiary. Each of these firms typically had a large number of affiliates, including certain special-purpose U.S.-regulated banks, banking and securities subsidiaries regulated in foreign jurisdictions, and unregulated subsidiaries in the United States and abroad, including those used for over-the-counter derivatives transactions. Each of these firms was also involved with mortgage activities to varying degrees, including originating loans, purchasing loans from others, and creating mortgage-backed securities sold to investors. However, unlike their commercial bank counterparts that had access to large, relatively stable deposit bases to fund part of their operations, investment banks were more dependent on short-term wholesale funding markets, such as the repurchase or "repo" market that involves placing securities (i.e., U.S. Treasury bonds) with another party in exchange for cash for a short time and agreeing to buy back the securities at the end of that period. As their mortgage-related losses increased in the recent turmoil, these institutions encountered increasing difficulties in obtaining sufficient funding in these wholesale credit markets. Although in March 2008, the Federal Reserve extended to the remaining institutions funding that had previously only been available to banks, investors' doubts about the viability of these investment banks resulted in each of the top five firms either filing for bankruptcy, being sold to other institutions, or converting themselves into bank or financial holding companies.

However, according to a September 2008 report by SEC's Inspector General, this supervisory program failed to effectively oversee these institutions for several reasons, including the lack of an effective mechanism for ensuring that these entities maintained sufficient capital. In comparison to commercial bank conglomerates, these investment banks were holding much less capital in relation to the activities exposing them to financial risk. For example, at the end of 2007, the five largest investment banks had assets to equity capital leverage ratios of between 26 and 34 to 1—meaning that for every dollar of capital capable of absorbing losses, these institutions held between $26 and $34 of assets subject to loss. In contrast, the largest commercial bank conglomerates, which were subject to different regulatory capital requirements, tended to be significantly less leveraged, with the average leverage ratio of the top five largest U.S. bank conglomerates at the end of 2007 only about 13 to 1. Moreover, because the program SEC used to oversee these investment bank conglomerates was voluntary, it had no authority to compel these institutions to address any problems that may have been identified. Instead, SEC's only means for coercing an institution to take corrective actions was to disqualify an institution from CSE status. SEC also lacked the ability to provide emergency funding for these investment bank conglomerates in a similar way that the Federal Reserve could for commercial banks. As a result, these CSE firms, whose activities resulted in their being significant and systemically important participants with vast interconnections with other financial institutions, were more vulnerable to market disruptions that could create risks to the overall financial system, but not all were subject to full and consistent oversight by a supervisor with adequate authority and resources. For example, one of the ways that the bankruptcy filing of Lehman Brothers affected other institutions was that 25 money market fund advisers had to act to protect their investors against losses arising from their investments in that company's debt, with at least one of these funds having to be liquidated and distributed to its investors.

Following the sale of Bear Stearns to JPMorgan Chase, the Lehman bankruptcy filing, and the sale of Merrill Lynch to Bank of America, the remaining CSEs opted to become bank holding companies subject to Federal Reserve oversight. SEC suspended its CSE program and the Chairman stated that "the last six months have made it abundantly clear that voluntary regulation does not work."[32]

Recent events have also highlighted difficulties faced by the Federal Reserve and OTS in their roles in overseeing risk management at large financial and thrift holding companies, respectively. In June 2008 testimony, a Federal Reserve official acknowledged such supervisory lessons, noting that under the current U.S. regulatory structure consisting of multiple supervisory agencies, challenges can arise in assessing risk profiles of large, complex financial institutions operating across financial sectors, particularly given the growth in the use of sophisticated financial products that can generate risks across various legal entities. He also noted that recent events have highlighted the importance of enterprisewide risk management, noting that supervisors need to understand risks across a consolidated entity and assess the risk management tools being applied across the financial institution.[33] Our own work had raised concerns over the adequacy of supervision of these large financial conglomerates. For example, one of the large entities that OTS oversaw was the insurance conglomerate AIG, which was subject to a government takeover necessitated by financial difficulties the firm experienced as the result of OTC derivatives activities related to mortgages. In a 2007 report, we expressed concerns over the appropriateness of having OTS oversee diverse global financial institutions given the size of the agency relative to the institutions for which it was responsible.[34] We had also noted that although OTS oversaw a number of holding companies that are primarily in the insurance business, including AIG, it had only one specialist in this area as of March 2007.[35] An OTS official noted, however, that functional regulation established by GrammLeach-Bliley avoided the need for regulatory agencies to develop expertise in all aspects of financial regulation.

Second, the emergence of these large institutions with financial obligations with thousands of other entities has revealed that the existing U.S. regulatory system is not well-equipped for identifying and addressing risks across the financial system as a whole. In the current environment, with multiple regulators primarily responsible for just individual institutions or markets, no one regulator is tasked with assessing the risks posed across the entire financial system by a few institutions or by the collective activities of the industry. For example, multiple factors contributed to the subprime mortgage crisis, and many market participants played a role in these events, including mortgage brokers, real estate professionals, lenders, borrowers, securities underwriters, investors, rating agencies and others. The collective activities of these entities, rather than one particular institution, likely all contributed to the overall market collapse. In particular, the securitization process created incentives throughout the chain of participants to emphasize loan volume over loan quality, which likely contributed to the problem as lenders sold loans on the secondary market, passing risks on to investors. Similarly, once financial institutions began to fail and the full extent of the financial crisis began to become clear, no formal mechanism existed to monitor market trends and potentially stop or help mitigate the fallout from these events. Ad hoc actions by the Department of the Treasury, the Federal Reserve, other members of the President's Working Group on Financial Markets, and FDIC were aimed at helping to mitigate the fallout once events began to unfold.[36] However, even given this ad hoc coordination, our past work has repeatedly identified limitations of the current U.S. federal regulatory structure to adequately coordinate and share information to monitor risks across markets or "functional" areas to identify potential systemic crises.[37] Whether a greater focus on systemwide risks would have fully prevented the recent financial crises is unclear, but it is reasonable to conclude that such a mechanism would have had better prospects of identifying the breadth of the problem earlier and been better positioned to stem or soften the extent of the market fallout.

Existing Regulatory System Failed to Adequately Address Problems Associated with Less-Regulated Entities That Played Significant Roles in the U.S. Financial System

A second dramatic development in U.S. financial markets in recent decades has been the increasingly critical roles played by less-regulated entities. In the past, consumers of financial products generally dealt with entities such as banks, broker-dealers, and insurance companies that were regulated by a federal or state regulator. However, in the last few decades, various entities—nonbank lenders, hedge funds, credit rating agencies, and special-purpose investment entities—that are not always subject to full regulation by such authorities have become important participants in our financial services markets. These unregulated or less-regulated entities can provide substantial benefits by supplying information or allowing financial institutions to better meet demands of consumers, investors or shareholders but pose challenges to regulators that do not fully or cannot oversee their activities.

Activities of Nonbank Mortgage Lenders Played a Significant Role in Mortgage Crisis but Were Not Adequately Addressed by Existing Regulatory System

The role of nonbank mortgage lenders in the recent financial collapse provides an example of a gap in our financial regulatory system resulting from activities of institutions that were generally subject to little or no direct oversight by federal regulators.[38] The significant participation by these nonbank lenders in the subprime mortgage market—which targeted products with riskier features to borrowers with limited or poor credit history—contributed to a dramatic loosening in underwriting standards leading up to the crisis. In recent years, nonbank lenders came to represent a large share of the consumer lending market, including for subprime mortgages. Specifically, as shown in figure 3, of the top 25 originators of subprime and other nonprime loans in 2006 (which accounted for more than 90 percent of the dollar volume of all such originations), all but 4 were nonbank lenders, accounting for 81 percent of origination by dollar volume.[39]

Although these lenders were subject to certain federal consumer protection and fair lending laws, they were generally not subject to the same routine monitoring and oversight by federal agencies that their bank counterparts were. From 2003 to 2006, subprime lending grew from about 9 percent to 24 percent of mortgage originations (excluding home equity loans), and Alt-A lending (nonprime loans considered less risky than subprime) grew from about 2 percent to almost 16 percent, according to data from the trade publication *Inside Mortgage Finance*. The resulting sharp rise in defaults and foreclosures that occurred as subprime and other homeowners were unable to make mortgage payments led to the collapse of the subprime mortgage market and set off a series of events that led to today's financial turmoil.

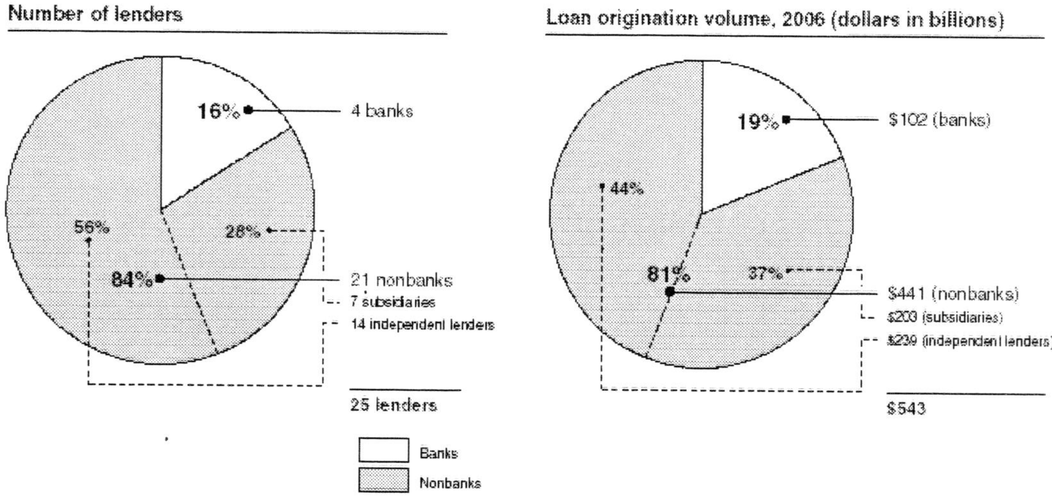

Source: GAO.

Figure 3. Status of Top 25 Subprime and Nonprime Mortgage Lenders (2006)

In previous reports, we noted concerns that existed about some of these less-regulated nonbank lenders and recommended that federal regulators actively monitor their activities.[40] For example, in a 2004 report, we reported that some of these nonbank lenders had been the targets of notable federal and state enforcement actions involving abusive lending. As a result, we recommended to Congress that the Federal Reserve should be given a greater role in monitoring the activities of some nonbank mortgage lenders that are subsidiaries of bank holding companies that the Federal Reserve regulates. Only recently, in the wake of the subprime mortgage crisis, the Federal Reserve began a pilot program in conjunction with OTS and the Conference of State Bank Supervisors to monitor the activities of nonbank subsidiaries of holding companies, with the states conducting examinations of independent state-licensed lenders. Nevertheless, other nonbank lenders continue to operate under less rigorous federal oversight and remain an example of the risks posed by less-regulated institutions in our financial regulatory system.

The increased role in recent years of investment banks securitizing and selling mortgage loans to investors further illustrates gaps in the regulatory system resulting from less-regulated institutions. Until recently, GSEs Fannie Mae and Freddie Mac were responsible for the vast majority of mortgage loan securitization. The securitization of loans that did not meet the GSEs' congressionally imposed loan limits or regulator-approved quality standards—such as jumbo loans that exceeded maximum loan limits and subprime loans—was undertaken by investment firms that were subject to little or no standards to ensure safe and sound practices in connection with the purchase or securitization of loans. As the volume of subprime lending grew dramatically from around 2003 through 2006, investment firms took over the substantial share of the mortgage securitization market. As shown in figure 4, this channel of mortgage funding—known as the private label mortgage-backed securities market— grew rapidly and in 2005 surpassed the combined market share of the GSEs and Ginnie Mae—a government corporation that guarantees mortgage-backed securities. As the volume of subprime loans increased, a rapidly growing share was packaged into private label securities, reaching 75 percent in 2006, according to the Federal Reserve Bank of San Francisco.

As shown in figure .4, this growth allowed private label securities to become approximately 55 percent of all mortgage-backed security issuance by 2005. This development serves as yet another example of how a less-regulated part of the market, private label securitization, played a significant role in fostering risky subprime mortgage lending, exposing a gap in the financial regulatory structure.

The role of mortgage brokers in the sale of mortgage products in recent years has also been a key focus of attention of policymakers. In past work, we noted that the role of mortgage brokers grew in the years leading up to the current crisis. By one estimate, the number of brokerages rose from about 30,000 firms in 2000 to 53,000 firms in 2004. In 2005, brokers accounted for about 60 percent of originations in the subprime market (compared with about 25 percent in the prime market).[41] In 2008, in the wake of the subprime mortgage crisis, Congress enacted the Secure and Fair Enforcement for Mortgage Licensing Act, as part of the Housing and Economic Recovery Act, to require enhanced licensing and registration of mortgage brokers.[42]

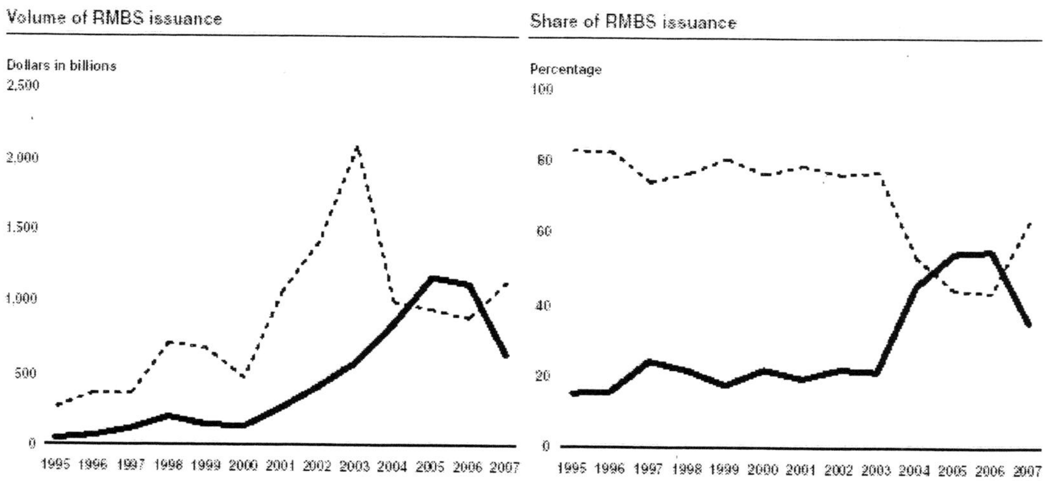

Source: GAO analysis of data from Inside Mortgage Finance.

Figure 4. Growth in Proportion of Private Label Securitization in the Mortgage-Backed Securities Market, in Dollars and Percentage of Dollar Volume (1995-2007)

Activities of Hedge Funds Can Pose Systemic Risks not Recognized by Regulatory System

Hedge funds, which are professionally managed investment funds for institutional and wealthy investors, have become significant participants in many important financial markets. For example, hedge funds often assume risks that other more regulated institutions are unwilling or unable to assume, and therefore generally are recognized as benefiting markets by enhancing liquidity, promoting market efficiency, spurring financial innovation, and helping to reallocate financial risk. But hedge funds receive less-direct oversight than other major market participants such as mutual funds, another type of investment fund that manages pools of assets on behalf of investors.[43] Hedge funds generally are structured and operated in a manner that enables them to qualify for exemptions from certain federal securities laws and regulations.[44] Because their participants are presumed to be sophisticated and therefore not require the full protection offered by the securities laws, hedge funds have not generally been subject to direct regulation. Therefore, hedge funds are not subject to regulatory capital requirements, are not restricted by regulation in their choice of investment strategies, and are not limited by regulation in their use of leverage. By soliciting participation in their funds from only certain large institutions and wealthy individuals and refraining from advertising to the general public, hedge funds are not required to meet the registration and disclosure requirements of the Securities Act of 1933 or the Securities Exchange Act of 1934, such as providing their investors with detailed prospectuses on the activities that their fund will undertake using investors' proceeds.[45] Hedge fund managers that trade on futures exchanges and that have U.S. investors are required to register with CFTC and are subject to periodic reporting, recordkeeping, and disclosure requirements of their futures activities, unless they notify the Commission that they qualify for an exemption from registration.[46]

The activities of many, but not all, hedge funds have recently become subject to greater oversight from SEC, although the rule requiring certain hedge fund advisers to register as investment advisers was recently vacated by a federal appeals court. In December 2004, SEC amended its rules to require certain hedge fund advisers that had been exempt from registering with SEC as investment advisers under its "private adviser" exemption to register as investment advisers.[47] In August 2006, SEC estimated that over 2,500 hedge fund advisers were registered with the agency, although what percentage of all hedge fund advisers active in the United States that this represents is not known. Registered hedge fund advisers are subject to the same requirements as all other registered investment advisers, including providing current information to both SEC and investors about their business practices and disciplinary history, maintaining required books and records, and being subject to periodic SEC examinations. Some questions exist over the extent of SEC's authority over these funds. In June 2006, the U.S. Court of Appeals for the District of Columbia overturned SEC's amended rule, concluding that the rule was arbitrary because it departed, without reasonable justification, from SEC's long-standing interpretation of the term "client" in the private adviser exemption as referring to the hedge fund itself, and not to the individual investors in the fund.[48] However, according to SEC, most hedge fund advisers that previously registered have chosen to retain their registered status as of April 2007.

Although many hedge fund advisers are now subject to some SEC oversight, some financial regulators and market participants remain concerned that hedge funds' activities can create systemic risk by threatening the soundness of other regulated entities and asset markets. Hedge funds have important connections to the financial markets, including significant business relationships with the largest regulated commercial banks and broker-dealers. They act as trading counterparties with many of these institutions and constitute in many markets a significant portion of trading activity, from stocks to distressed debt and credit derivatives.[49]

The far-reaching consequences of potential hedge fund failures first became apparent in 1998. The hedge fund Long Term Capital Management (LTCM) experienced large losses related to the considerable positions— estimated to be as large as $100 billion—it had taken in various sovereign debt and other markets, and regulators coordinated with market participants to prevent a disorderly collapse that could have led to financial problems among LTCM's lenders and counterparties and potentially to the rest of the financial system.[50] No taxpayer funds were used as part of this effort; instead, the various large financial institutions with large exposures to this hedge fund agreed to provide additional funding of $3.6 billion until the fund could be dissolved in an orderly way. Since LTCM, other hedge funds have experienced near collapses or failures, including two funds owned by Bear Stearns, but these events have not had as significant impact on the broader financial markets as LTCM.

Also, since LTCM's near collapse, investors, creditors, and counterparties have increased their efforts to impose market discipline on hedge funds. According to regulators and market participants, creditors and counterparties have been conducting more extensive due diligence and monitoring risk exposures to their hedge fund clients. In addition, hedge fund advisers have improved disclosure and become more transparent about their operations, including their risk-management practices. However, we reported in 2008 that some regulators continue to be concerned that the counterparty credit risk created when regulated financial institutions transact with hedge funds can be a primary channel for potentially creating systemic risk.[51]

Credit Rating Agency Activities Also Illustrate the Failure of the Regulatory System to Address Risks Posed by Less-Regulated Entities

Similar to hedge funds, credit rating agencies have come to play a critical role in financial markets, but until recently they received little regulatory oversight. While not acting as direct participants in financial markets, credit ratings are widely used by investors for distinguishing the creditworthiness of bonds and other securities. Additionally, credit ratings are used in local, federal, and international laws and regulations as a benchmark for permissible investments by banks, pension funds, and other institutional investors. Leading up to the recent crisis, some investors had come to rely heavily on ratings in lieu of conducting independent assessments on the quality of assets. This overreliance on credit ratings of subprime mortgage-backed securities and other structured credit products contributed to the recent turmoil in financial markets. As these securities started to incur losses, it became clear that their ratings did not adequately reflect the risk that these products ultimately posed. According to the trade publication *Inside B&C Lending*, the three major credit rating agencies have each downgraded more than half of the subprime mortgage-backed securities they originally rated between 2005 and 2007.

However, despite the critical nature of these rating agencies in our financial system, the existing regulatory system failed to adequately foresee and manage their role in recent events. Until recently, credit rating agencies received little direct oversight and thus faced no explicit requirements to provide information to investors about how to understand and appropriately use ratings, or to provide data on the accuracy of their ratings over time that would allow investors to assess their quality. In addition, concerns have been raised over whether the way in which credit rating agencies are compensated by the issuers of the securities that they rate affects the quality of the ratings awarded. In a July 2008 report, SEC noted multiple weaknesses in the management of these conflicts of interest, including instances where analysts expressed concerns over fees and other business interests when issuing ratings and reviewing ratings criteria.[52] However, until 2006, no legislation had established statutory regulatory authority or disclosure requirements over credit rating agencies.[53] Then, to improve the quality of ratings in response to events such as the failures of Enron and Worldcom—which highlighted the limitations of credit ratings in identifying companies' financial strength— Congress passed the Credit Rating Agency Reform Act of 2006, which established limited SEC oversight, requiring their registration and certain recordkeeping and reporting requirements.[54]

Since the financial crisis began, regulators have taken steps to address the important role of rating agencies in the financial system. In December 2008, in response to the subprime mortgage crisis and resulting credit market strains, SEC adopted final rule amendments and proposed new rule amendments that would impose additional requirements on nationally recognized statistical rating organizations in order to address concerns raised about the policies and procedures for, transparency of, and potential conflicts of interest relating to ratings. Determining the most appropriate government role in overseeing credit rating activities is difficult. For example, SEC has expressed concerns that too much government intervention—such as regulatory requirements of credit ratings for certain investments or examining the underlying methodology of ratings—would unintentionally provide an unofficial "seal of approval" on the ratings and therefore be counterproductive to reducing overreliance on ratings. Whatever the solution, it is clear that the current regulatory system did not properly recognize and address the risks associated with the important role these entities played.

Regulatory System Failed to Identify Risks Associated with Special-Purpose Entities

The use by financial institutions of special-purpose entities provides another example of how less-regulated aspects of financial markets came to play increasingly important roles in recent years, creating challenges for regulators in overseeing risks at their regulated institutions. Many financial institutions created and transferred assets to these entities as part of securitizations for mortgages or to hold other assets and produce fee income for the institution that created it—known as the sponsor. For example, after new capital requirements were adopted in the late 1980s, some large banks began creating these entities to hold assets for which they would have been required to hold more capital against if the assets were held within their institutions. As a result, these entities are also known as off-balance sheet entities because they generally are structured in such a way that their assets and liabilities are not required to be consolidated and reported as part of the overall balance sheet of the sponsoring financial institution that created them. The amount of assets accumulated in these entities resulted in them becoming significant market participants in the last few years. For example, one large commercial bank reported that its off-balance sheet entities totaled more than $1 trillion in assets at the end of 2007.

CREDIT RATINGS AND THE FINANCIAL CRISIS

Traditionally, products receiving the highest credit ratings, such as AAA, were a small set of corporate and sovereign bonds that were deemed to be the safest and most stable debt investments. However, credit rating agencies assigned similarly high credit ratings to many of the newer mortgage-related products even though these products did not have the same characteristics as previously highly rated securities. As a result of these ratings, institutions were able to successfully market many of these products, including to other financial firms and institutional investors in the United States and around the world. Ratings were seen to provide a common measure of credit risk across all debt products, allowing structured credit products that lacked an active secondary market to be valued against similarly rated products with available prices. Starting in mid-2007, increasing defaults on residential mortgages, particularly those for subprime borrowers, led to a widespread, rapid, and severe series of downgrades by rating agencies on subprime-related structured credit products. These downgrades undermined confidence in the quality of ratings on these and related products. Along with increasing defaults, the uncertainty over credit ratings led to a sharp repricing of assets across the financial system and contributed to large writedowns in the market value of assets by banks and other financial institutions. This contributed to the unwillingness of many market participants to transact with each other due to concerns over the actual value of assets and the financial condition of other financial institutions.

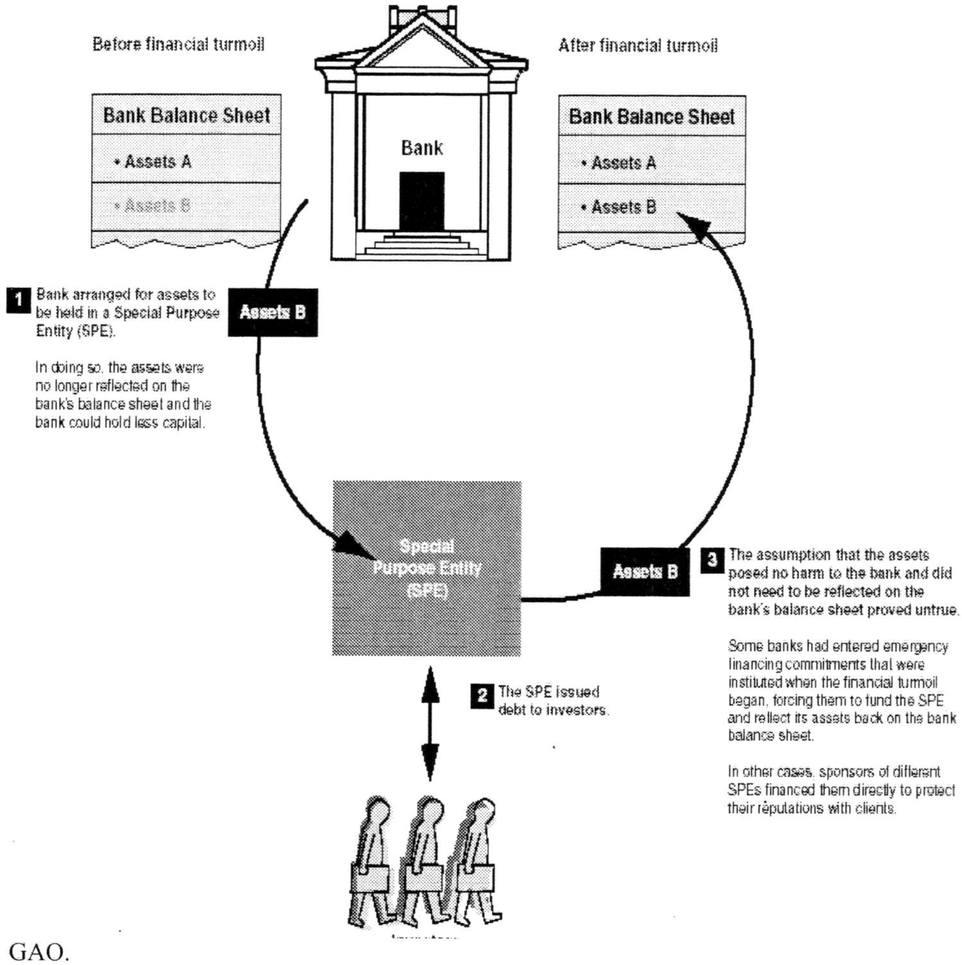

Source: GAO.

Figure 5. Example of an Off-Balance Sheet Entity

Some of these off-balance sheet entities were structured in a way that left them vulnerable to market disruptions. For example, some financial institutions created entities known as asset-backed commercial paper conduits that would purchase various assets, including mortgage-related securities, financial institution debt, and receivables from industrial businesses. To obtain the funds to purchase these assets, these special- purpose vehicles often borrowed using shorter-term instruments, such as commercial paper and medium-term notes. The difference between the interest paid to the commercial paper or note holders and the income earned on the entity's assets produced fee and other income for the sponsoring institution. However, these structures carried the risk that the entity would find it difficult or costly to renew its debt financing under less-favorable market conditions.

Although structured as off-balance sheet entities, when the turmoil in the markets began in 2007, many financial institutions that had created these entities had to take back the loans and securities in certain types of these off-balance sheet entities. (See figure 5.)

In general, banks stepped in to finance the assets held by these entities when they were unable to refinance their expiring debt due to market concerns over the quality of the assets. In some cases, off-balance sheet entities relied on emergency financing commitments that many sponsoring banks had extended to these entities. In other cases, financial institutions supported troubled off-balance sheet entities to protect their reputations with clients even when no explicit requirement to do so existed. This, in turn, contributed to the reluctance of banks to lend as they had to fund additional troubled assets on their balance sheets. Thus, although the use of these entities seemingly had removed the risk of these assets from these institutions, their inability to obtain financing resulted in the ownership, risks, and losses of these entities' assets coming back into many of the sponsoring financial institutions.

According to a 2008 IMF study, financial institutions' use of off-balance sheet entities made it difficult for regulators, as well as investors, to fully understand the associated risks of such activities. In response to these developments, regulators and others have begun to reassess the appropriateness of the regulatory and accounting treatment for these entities. In January 2008, SEC asked the Financial Accounting Standards Board (FASB), which establishes U.S. financial accounting and reporting standards, to consider further improvements to the accounting and disclosure for off-balance sheet transactions involving securitization. FASB and the International Accounting Standards Board both have initiated projects to improve the criteria for determining when financial assets and related liabilities that institutions transfer to special-purpose entities should be included on the institutions' own balance sheets— known as consolidation—and to enhance related disclosures. As part of this effort, FASB issued proposed standards that would eliminate a widely used accounting exception for off-balance sheet entities, introduce a new accounting model for determining whether special-purpose entities should be consolidated that is less reliant on mathematical calculations and more closely aligned with international standards, and require additional disclosures about institutions' involvement with certain special-purpose entities. On December 18, 2008, the International Accounting Standards Board also issued a proposed standard on consolidation of special- purpose entities and related risk disclosures. In addition, in April 2008, the Basel Committee on Banking Supervision announced new measures to capture off-balance sheet exposures more effectively.

Nevertheless, this serves as another example of the failure of the existing regulatory system to recognize the problems with less-regulated entities and take steps to address them before they escalate. Existing accounting and disclosure standards had not required banks to extensively disclose their holdings in off-balance sheet entities and allowed for very low capital requirements. As a March 2008 study by the President's Working Group on Financial Markets noted, before the recent market turmoil, supervisory authorities did not insist on appropriate disclosures of firms' potential exposure to off-balance sheet entities.

New and Complex Financial Products and Services Also Revealed Limitations in the Regulatory Structure

Another development that has revealed limitations in the current regulatory structure has been the proliferation of more complex financial products. Although posing challenges, these new products also have provided certain benefits to financial markets and consumers. For example, the creation of securitized products such as mortgage-backed securities increased the liquidity of credit markets by providing additional funds to lenders and a wider range of investment returns to investors with excess funds. Other useful product innovations included OTC derivatives, such as currency options, which provide a purchaser the right to buy a specified quantity of a currency at some future date, and interest rate swaps, which allow one party to exchange a stream of fixed interest rate payments for a stream of variable interest rate payments. These products help market participants hedge their risks or stabilize their cash flows. Alternative mortgage products, such as interest-only loans, originally were used by a limited subset of the population, mainly wealthy borrowers, to obtain more convenient financing for home purchases. Despite these advantages, the complexity and expanded use of new products has made it difficult for the current regulatory system to oversee risk management at institutions and adequately protect individual consumers and investors.

New Complex Securitized Products Have Created Difficulties for Institutions and Regulators in Valuing and Assessing Their Risks

Collateralized debt obligations (CDO) are one of the new products that proliferated and created challenges for financial institutions and regulators. In a basic CDO, a group of loans or debt securities are pooled and securities are then issued in different tranches that vary in risk and return depending on how the underlying cash flows produced by the pooled assets are allocated. If some of the underlying assets defaulted, the more junior tranches—and thus riskier ones—would absorb these losses first before the more senior, less-risky tranches. Purchasers of these CDO securities included insurance companies, mutual funds, commercial and investment banks, and pension funds. Many CDOs in recent years largely consisted of mortgage-backed securities, including subprime mortgage- backed securities.

Although CDOs have existed since the 1980s, recent changes in the underlying asset mix of these products led to increased risk that was poorly understood by the financial institutions involved in these investments. CDOs had consisted of simple securities like corporate bonds or loans, but more recently have included subprime mortgage-backed securities, and in some cases even lower-rated classes of other equally complex CDOs. Some of these CDOs included investments in 100 or more asset-backed securities, each of which had its own large pool of loans and specific payment structures.[55] A large share of the total value of the securities issued were rated AA or AAA—designating them as very safe investments and unlikely to default—by the credit rating agencies. In part because of their seemingly high returns in light of their rated risk, demand for these new CDOs grew rapidly and on a large scale. Between 2004 and 2007, nearly all adjustable-rate subprime mortgages were packaged into mortgage-backed securities, a large portion of which were structured into CDOs.

As housing prices in the United States softened in the last 2 years, default and foreclosure rates on the mortgages underlying many CDOs rose and the credit rating agencies downgraded many CDO ratings, causing investors to become unwilling to purchase these products in the same quantities or at the prices previously paid. Many financial institutions, including large commercial and investment banks, struggled to realize the size of their exposure to subprime credit risk. Many of these institutions appeared to have underestimated the amount of risk and potential losses that they could face from creating and investing in these products. Reductions in the value of subprime-backed CDOs have contributed to reported losses by financial institutions totaling more than $750 billion globally, as of

September 2008, according to the International Monetary Fund, which estimates that total losses on global holdings of U.S. loans and securities could reach $1.4 trillion.

Several factors could explain why institutions—and regulators—did not effectively monitor and limit the risk that CDOs represented. Products like CDOs have risk characteristics that differ from traditional investments. First, the variation and complexity of the CDO structures and the underlying assets they contain often make estimating potential losses and determining accurate values for these products more difficult than for traditional securities. Second, although aggregating multiple assets into these structures can diversify and thus reduce the overall risk of the securities issued from them, their exposure to the overall housing market downturn made investors reluctant to purchase even the safest tranches, which produced large valuation losses for the holders of even the highest-rated CDO securities.[56] Finally, Federal Reserve staff noted that an additional reason these securities performed worse than expected was that rating agencies and investors did not believe that housing prices could have fallen as significantly as they have.

The lack of historical performance data for these new instruments also presented challenges in estimating the potential value of these securities. For example, the Senior Supervisors Group—a body comprising senior financial supervisors from France, Germany, Switzerland, the United Kingdom, and the United States—reported that some financial institutions substituted price and other data associated with traditional corporate debt in their loss estimation models for similarly rated CDO debt, which did not have sufficient historical data.[57] As a report by a group of senior representatives of financial regulators and institutions has noted, the absence of historical information on the performance of CDOs created uncertainty around the standard risk-management tools used by financial institutions.[58] Further, structured products such as CDOs may lack an active and liquid market, as in the recent period of market stress, forcing participants to look for other sources of valuation information when market prices are not readily available. For instance, market participants often turned to internal models and other methods to value these products, which raised concerns about the consistency and accuracy of the resulting valuation information.

Growth in OTC Derivatives Markets, Which Feature Complex Products That Are Not Regulated, Raised Regulator Concerns about Systemic Risk and Weak Market Infrastructure

The rapid growth in OTC derivatives—or derivatives contracts that are traded outside of regulated exchanges—is another example of how the emergence of large markets for increasingly complex products has challenged our financial regulatory system. OTC derivatives, which began trading in the 1980s, have developed into markets with an estimated notional value—which is the amount underlying a financial derivatives contract—of about $596 trillion, as of December 2007, according to the Bank for International Settlements.[59] OTC derivatives transactions are generally not subject to regulation by SEC, CFTC, or any other U.S. financial regulator and in particular are not subject to similar disclosure and other requirements that are in place for most securities and exchange- traded futures products. Institutions that conduct derivatives transactions may be subject to oversight of their lines of business by their regulators. For example, commercial banks that deal in OTC derivatives are subject to full examinations by their respective regulators. On the other hand, investment banks generally conducted their OTC derivatives activities in affiliates or subsidiaries that traditionally—since most OTC derivatives are not securities—were not subject to direct oversight by SEC, although SEC did review how the largest investment banks that were subject to its CSE program were managing the risk of such activities.

Although OTC derivatives and their markets are not directly regulated, the risk exposures that these products created among regulated financial institutions can be sometimes large enough to raise systemic risk concerns among regulators. For example, Bear Stearns, the investment bank that experienced financial difficulties as the result of its mortgage-backed securities activities, was also one of the largest OTC derivatives dealers. According to regulators, one of the primary reasons the Federal Reserve, which otherwise had no regulatory authority over this securities firm, facilitated the sale of Bear Stearns rather than let it go bankrupt was to avoid a potentially large systemic problem because of the firm's large OTC derivatives obligations. More than a decade ago, we reported that the large financial interconnections between derivatives dealers posed risk to the financial system and recommended that Congress and financial regulators take action to ensure that the largest firms participating in the OTC derivatives markets be subject to similar regulatory oversight and requirements.[60]

The market for one type of OTC derivative—credit default swaps—had grown so large that regulators became concerned about its potential to create systemic risks to regulated financial institutions. Credit default swaps are contracts that act as a type of insurance, or a way to hedge risks, against default or another type of credit event associated with a security such as a corporate bond. One party in the contract—the seller of protection—agrees, in return for a periodic fee, to compensate the other party—the protection buyer—if the bond or other underlying entity defaults or another specified credit event occurs. In recent years, the size of the market for credit default swaps (in terms of the notional amount of outstanding contracts) has increased almost tenfold from just over $6 trillion in 2004 to almost $58 trillion at the end of 2007, according to the Bank for International Settlements.

As this market has grown, regulators increasingly have become concerned about the adequacy of the infrastructure in place for clearing and settling these contracts, especially the ability to quickly resolve contracts in the event of a large market participant failure. For example, in September 2008, concerns over the effects that a potential bankruptcy of AIG—which was a large seller of credit default swaps—would have on this firm's swap counterparties contributed to a decision by the Federal Reserve to lend the firm up to $85 billion.[61] The Federal Reserve expressed concern at the time that a disorderly failure of AIG could add to already significant levels of financial market fragility and lead to substantially higher borrowing costs, reduced household wealth, and materially weaker economic performance. As with other OTC derivatives, credit default swaps are not regulated as products, but many of the large U.S. and internationally regulated financial institutions act as dealers. Despite the credit default market's rapid growth, as recently as 2005 the processing of transactions was still paper-based and decentralized. Regulators have put forth efforts over the years to strengthen clearing and settlement mechanisms. For example, in September 2005, the Federal Reserve Bank of New York began working with dealers and market participants to strengthen arrangements for clearing and settling these swap transactions. Regulators began focusing on reducing a large backlog of unconfirmed trades, which can inhibit market participants' ability to manage their risks if errors are not found quickly or if uncertainty exists about how other institutions would be affected by the failure of a firm with which they hold credit default swap contracts. Regulators continue to monitor dealers' progress on these efforts to reduce operational risk arising from these products, and recently have begun holding discussions with the largest credit derivatives dealers and other entities, including certain exchanges, regarding the need to establish a centralized clearing facility, which could reduce the risk of any one dealer's failure to the overall system. In November 2008, the President's Working Group on Financial Markets announced policy objectives to guide efforts to address challenges associated with OTC derivatives, including recommendations to enhance the market infrastructure for credit default swaps. However, as of December 2008, no such entity had begun operations.

New Complex Products Have Also Created Challenges for Regulators in Ensuring Adequate Investor and Consumer Protection

The regulations requiring that investors receive adequate information about the risks of financial assets being marketed to them are also being challenged by the development of some of these new and complex products. For some of the new products that have been created, market participants sometimes had difficulty obtaining clear and accurate information on the value of these assets, their risks, and other key information. In some cases, investors did not perform needed due diligence to fully understand the risks associated with their investment. In other cases, investors have claimed they were misled by broker-dealers about the advantages and disadvantages of products. For example, investors for municipal governments in Australia have accused Lehman Brothers of misleading them regarding the risks of CDOs. As another example, the treasurer of Orange County who oversaw investments leading to the county's 1994 bankruptcy claimed to have relied on the advice of a large securities firm for his decision to pursue leveraged investments in complex structured products. Finally, a number of financial institutions—including Bank of America, Wachovia, Merrill Lynch, and UBS—have recently settled SEC allegations that these institutions misled investors in selling auction-rate securities, which are bonds for which the interest rates are regularly reset through auctions. In one case, Bank of America, in October 2008, reached a settlement in principle in response to SEC charges that it made misrepresentations to thousands of businesses, charities, and institutional investors when it told them that the products were safe and highly liquid cash and money market alternative investments.

Similarly, the introduction and expansion of increasingly complicated retail products to new and broader consumer populations has also raised challenges for regulators in ensuring that consumers are adequately protected. Consumers face growing difficulty in understanding the relative advantages and disadvantages of products such as mortgages and credit cards with new and increasingly complicated features, in part because of limitations on the part of regulatory agencies to improve consumer disclosures and financial literacy. For example, in the last few years many borrowers likely did not understand the risks associated with taking out their loans, especially in the event that housing prices would not continue to increase at the rate at which they had been in recent years. In particular, a significant majority of subprime borrowers from 2003 to 2006 took out adjustable-rate mortgages whose interest rates were fixed for the first 2 or 3 years but then adjusted to often much higher interest rates and correspondingly higher mortgage payments. In addition, many borrowers took out loans with interest-only features that resulted in significant increases in mortgage payments later in the loan. The combination of reduced underwriting standards and a slowdown in house price appreciation led many borrowers to default on their mortgages.

Alternative mortgage products such as interest-only or payment option loans, which allow borrowers to defer repayment of principal and possibly part of the interest for the first few years of the loan, grew in popularity and expanded greatly in recent years. From 2003 through 2005, originations of these types of mortgage products grew threefold, from less than 10 percent of residential mortgage originations to about 30 percent. For many years, lenders had primarily marketed these products to wealthy and financially sophisticated borrowers as financial management tools. However, lenders increasingly marketed alternative mortgage products as affordability products that enabled a wider spectrum of borrowers to purchase homes they might not have been able to afford using a conventional fixed-rate mortgage. Lenders also increased the variety of such products offered after interest rates rose and adjustable rate mortgages became less attractive to borrowers.

In past work, we found that most of the disclosures for alternative mortgage products that we reviewed did not always fully or effectively explain the risks associated with these products and lacked information on some important loan features.[62] Some evidence suggests more generally that existing mortgage disclosures were inadequate, a problem that is likely to grow with the increased complexity of products. A 2007 Federal Trade Commission report found that both prime and subprime borrowers failed to understand key loan terms when viewing current disclosures.[63] In addition, some market observers have been critical of regulators' oversight of these products and whether products with such complex features were appropriate for some of the borrowers to which they were marketed. For example, some were critical of the Federal Reserve for not acting more quickly to use its authority under the 1994 Home Ownership and Equity Protection Act to prohibit unfair or deceptive acts or practices in the mortgage market. Although the Federal Reserve took steps in 2001 to ban some practices, such as engaging in a pattern or practice of refinancing certain high-cost loans when it is not in the borrower's interest, it did not act again until 2008, when it banned additional products and practices, such as certain loans with limited documentation. In a 2007 testimony, a Federal Reserve official noted that writing such rules is difficult, particularly since determinations of unfairness or deception depend heavily on the facts of an individual case.[64]

Efforts by regulators to respond to the increased risks associated with new mortgage products also have sometimes been slowed in part because of the need for five federal regulators to coordinate their response. In late 2005, regulators began crafting regulatory guidance to strengthen lending practices and improve disclosures for loans that start with relatively low payments but leave borrowers vulnerable to much higher ones later. The regulators completed their first set of such standards in September 2006, with respect to the disclosure of risks associated with nontraditional mortgage products, and a second set, applicable to subprime mortgage loans, in June 2007.[65] Some industry observers and consumer advocacy groups have criticized the length of time it took for regulators to issue these changes, noting that the second set of guidance was released well after many subprime lenders had already gone out of business.

As variations in the types of credit card products and terms have proliferated, consumers also have faced difficulty understanding the rates and terms of their credit card accounts. Credit card rate and fee disclosures have not always been effective at clearly conveying associated charges and fees, creating challenges to informed financial decision making. Although credit card issuers are required to provide cardholders with information aimed at facilitating informed use of credit, these disclosures have serious weaknesses that likely reduce consumers' ability to understand the costs of using credit cards. Because the pricing of credit cards is not generally subject to federal regulation, these disclosures are the primary federal consumer protection mechanism against inaccurate and unfair credit card practices. However, we reported in 2006 that the disclosures in materials provided by four of the largest credit card issuers were too complicated for many consumers to understand. Following our report, Federal Reserve staff began using consumer testing to involve them to a greater extent in the preparation of potentially new and revised disclosures, and in May 2007, issued proposed changes to credit card disclosure requirements. Nonetheless, the Federal Reserve recognizes the challenge of presenting the information that consumers may need to understand the costs of their cards in a clear way, given the increasingly complicated terms of credit card products.[66] In December 2008, the Federal Reserve, OTS, and NCUA finalized rules to ban various unfair credit card practices, such as allocating payments in a way that unfairly maximizes interest charges.

The expansion of new and more complex products also raises challenges for regulators in addressing financial literacy. We have also noted in past work that even a relatively clear and transparent system of disclosures may be of limited use to borrowers who lack sophistication about financial matters.[67] In response to increasing evidence that many Americans are lacking in financial literacy, the federal government has taken steps to expand financial education efforts. However, attempts by the Financial Literacy and Education Commission to coordinate federal financial literacy efforts have sometimes proven difficult due, in part, to the need to reach consensus among its 20 participating federal agencies, which have different missions and perspectives. Moreover, the commission's staff and funding resources are relatively small, and it has no legal authority to require agencies to redirect their resources or take other actions.[68]

Increased Complexity and Other Factors Have Challenged Accounting Standard Setters and Regulators

As new and increasingly complex financial products have become more common, FASB and SEC have also faced challenges in trying to ensure that accounting and financial reporting requirements appropriately meet the needs of investors and other financial market participants.[69] The development and widespread use of increasingly complex financial products has heightened the importance of having effective accounting and financial reporting requirements that provide interested parties with information that can help them identify and assess risk. As the pace of financial innovation increased in the last 30 years, accounting and financial reporting requirements have also had to keep pace, with 72 percent of the current 163 standards having been issued since 1980—some of which were revisions and amendments to recently established standards, which evidences the challenge of establishing accounting and financial reporting requirements that respond to needs created by financial innovation.

As a result of the growth in complex financial instruments and a desire to improve the usefulness of financial information about them, U.S. standard setters and regulators currently are dealing with accounting and auditing challenges associated with recently developed standards related to valuing financial instruments and special-purpose entities. Over the last year, owners and issuers of financial instruments have expressed concerns about implementing the new fair value accounting standard, which requires that financial assets and liabilities be recorded at fair or market value. SEC and FASB have recently issued clarifications of measuring fair value when there is not an active market for the financial instrument.[70] In addition, market participants raised concerns about the availability of useful accounting and financial reporting information to assess the risks posed by special-purpose entities. Under current accounting rules, publicly traded companies that create qualifying special-purpose entities are allowed to move qualifying assets and liabilities associated with certain complex financial instruments off the issuing company's balance sheets, which results in virtually no accounting and financial reporting information being available about the entities' activities. Due to the accounting and financial reporting treatment for these special-purpose entities, as the subprime crisis worsened, banks initially refused to negotiate loans with homeowners because banks were concerned that the accounting and financial reporting requirements would have the banks put the assets and liabilities back onto their balance sheets. In response to questions regarding modification of loans in special-purpose entities, the SEC's Chief Accountant issued a letter that concluded his office would not object to loans being modified pursuant to specific screening criteria. In response to these concerns, FASB expedited its standards-setting process in order to reduce the amount of time before the issuance of a new accounting standard that would effectively eliminate qualified special-purpose entities.[71]

Standard setters and regulators also face new challenges in dealing with global convergence of accounting and auditing standards. The rapid integration of the world's capital markets has made establishing a single set of effective accounting and financial reporting standards increasingly relevant. FASB and SEC have acknowledged the need to address the convergence of U.S. and international accounting standards, and SEC has proposed having U.S. public companies use International Financial Reporting Standards by 2014. As the globalization of accounting standards moves forward, U.S. standard setters and regulators need to anticipate and manage the challenges posed by their development and implementation, such as how to apply certain standards in unique legal and regulatory environment frameworks in the United States as well as in certain unique industry niches. Ensuring that auditing standards applicable to U.S. public companies continue to provide the financial markets with the important and independent assurances associated with existing U.S. auditing standards will also prove challenging to the Public Company Accounting Oversight Board.

Globalization Will Further Challenge the Existing U.S. Regulatory System

Just as global accounting and auditing standards are converging, financial markets around the world are becoming increasingly interlinked and global in nature, requiring U.S. regulators to work with each other and other countries to effectively adapt. To effectively oversee large financial services firms that have operations in many countries, regulators from various countries must coordinate regulation and supervision of financial services across national borders and must communicate regularly. Although financial regulators have effectively coordinated in a number of ways to accommodate some changes, the current fragmented regulatory structure has complicated some of these efforts.

For example, the current U.S. regulatory system complicates the ability of financial regulators to convey a single U.S. position in international discussions, such as those related to the Basel Accords process for developing international capital standards. Each federal regulator involved in these efforts oversees a different set of institutions and represents an important regulatory perspective, which has made reaching consensus on some issues more difficult than others. Although U.S. regulators generally agree on the broad underlying principles at the core of Basel II, including increased risk sensitivity of capital requirements and capital neutrality, in a 2004 report we noted that although regulators communicated and coordinated, they sometimes had difficulty agreeing on certain aspects of the process.[72] As we reported, in November 2003, members of the House Financial Services Committee warned in a letter to the bank regulatory agencies that the discord surrounding Basel II had weakened the negotiating position of the United States and resulted in an agreement that was less than favorable to U.S. financial institutions.[73] International officials have also indicated that the lack of a single point of contact on, for example, insurance issues has complicated regulatory decision making. However, regulatory officials told us that the final outcome of the Basel II negotiations was better than it would have been with a single U.S. representative because of the agencies' varying perspectives and expertise. In particular, one regulator noted that, in light of the magnitude of recent losses at banks and the failure of banks and rating agencies to predict such losses, the additional safeguards built into how U.S. regulators adopted Basel II are an example of how more than one regulatory perspective can improve policymaking.

A Framework for Crafting and Assessing Alternatives for Reforming the U.S. Financial Regulatory System

The U.S. regulatory system is a fragmented and complex system of federal and state regulators—put into place over the past 150 years—that has not kept pace with the major developments that have occurred in financial markets and products in recent decades. In 2008, the United States finds itself in the midst of one of the worst financial crises ever, with instability threatening global financial markets and the broader economy. While much of the attention of policymakers understandably has been focused on taking short-term steps to address the immediate nature of the crisis, attention has also turned to the need to consider significant reforms to the financial regulatory system to keep pace with existing and anticipated challenges in financial regulation.

While the current U.S. system has many features that could be preserved, the significant limitations of the system, if not addressed, will likely fail to prevent future crises that could be as harmful as or worse than those that have occurred in the past. Making changes that better position regulators to oversee firms and products that pose risks to the financial system and consumers and to adapt to new products and participants as these arise would seem essential to ensuring that our financial services sector continues to serve our nation's needs as effectively as possible.

We have conducted extensive work in recent decades reviewing the impacts of market developments and overseeing the effectiveness of financial regulators' activities. In particular, we have helped Congress address financial crises dating back to the savings and loan and LTCM crises, and more recently over the past few years have issued several reports citing the need to modernize the U.S. financial regulatory structure. In this chapter, consistent with our past work, we are not proposing the form and structure of what a new financial regulatory system should look like. Instead, we are providing a framework, consisting of the following nine elements, that Congress and others can use to evaluate or craft proposals for financial regulatory reform. By applying the elements of this framework to proposals, the relative strengths and weaknesses of each one should be better revealed. Similarly, the framework we present could be used to craft a proposal or to identify aspects to be added to existing proposals to make them more effective and appropriate for addressing the limitations of the current system. The nine elements could be addressed in a variety of ways, but each is critically important in establishing the most effective and efficient financial regulatory system possible.

1. ***Clearly defined regulatory goals.* A regulatory system should have goals that are clearly articulated and relevant, so that regulators can effectively conduct activities to implement their missions.**

A critical first step to modernizing the regulatory system and enhancing its ability to meet the challenges of a dynamic financial services industry is to clearly define regulatory goals and objectives. In the background of this chapter, we identify four broad goals of financial regulation that regulators have generally sought to achieve. These include ensuring adequate consumer protections, ensuring the integrity and fairness of markets, monitoring the safety and soundness of institutions, and acting to ensure the stability of the overall financial system. However, these goals are not always explicitly set in the federal statutes and regulations that govern these regulators. Having specific goals clearly articulated in legislation could serve to better focus regulators on achieving their missions with greater certainty and purpose, and provide continuity over time.

Given some of the key changes in financial markets discussed earlier in this chapter—particularly the increased interconnectedness of institutions, the increased complexity of products, and the increasingly global nature of financial markets—Congress should consider the benefits that may result from re-examining the goals of financial regulation and making explicit a set of comprehensive and cohesive goals that reflect today's environment. For example, it may be beneficial to have a clearer focus on ensuring that products are not sold with unsuitable, unfair, deceptive, or abusive features; that systemic risks and the stability of the overall financial system are specifically addressed; or that U.S. firms are competitive in a global environment. This may be especially important given the history of financial regulation and the ad hoc approach through which the existing goals have been established, as discussed earlier.

We found varying views about the goals of regulation and how they should be prioritized. For example, representatives of some regulatory agencies and industry groups emphasized the importance of creating a competitive financial system, whereas members of one consumer advocacy group noted that reforms should focus on improving regulatory effectiveness rather than addressing concerns about market competitiveness. In addition, as the Federal Reserve notes, financial regulatory goals often will prove interdependent and at other times may conflict.

Revisiting the goals of financial regulation would also help ensure that all involved entities—legislators, regulators, institutions, and consumers—are able to work jointly to meet the intended goals of financial regulation. Such goals and objectives could help establish agency priorities and define responsibility and accountability for identifying risks, including those that cross markets and industries. Policymakers should also carefully define jurisdictional lines and weigh the advantages and disadvantages of having overlapping authorities. While ensuring that the primary goals of financial regulation—including system soundness, market integrity, and consumer protection—are better articulated for regulators, policymakers will also have to ensure that regulation is balanced with other national goals, including facilitating capital raising, innovation, and other benefits that foster long-term growth, stability, and welfare of the United States.

Once these goals are agreed upon, policymakers will need to determine the extent to which goals need to be clarified and specified through rules and requirements, or whether to avoid such specificity and provide regulators with greater flexibility in interpreting such goals. Some reform proposals suggest "principles-based regulation" in which regulators apply broad-based regulatory principles on a case-by-case basis. Such an approach offers the potential advantage of allowing regulators to better adapt to changing market developments. Proponents also note that such an approach would prevent institutions in a more rules-based system from complying with the exact letter of the law while still engaging in unsound or otherwise undesirable financial activities. However, such an approach has potential limitations. Opponents note that regulators may face challenges to implement such a subjective set of principles. A lack of clear rules about activities could lead to litigation if financial institutions and consumers alike disagree with how regulators interpreted goals. Opponents of principles-based regulation note that industry participants who support such an approach have also in many cases advocated for bright-line standards and increased clarity in regulation, which may be counter to a principles-based system. The most effective approach may involve both a set of broad underlying principles and some clear technical rules prohibiting specific activities that have been identified as problematic.

Key issues to be addressed:

- Clarify and update the goals of financial regulation and provide sufficient information on how potentially conflicting goals might be prioritized.
- Determine the appropriate balance of broad principles and specific rules that will result in the most effective and flexible implementation of regulatory goals.

2. ***Appropriately comprehensive.* A regulatory system should ensure that financial institutions and activities are regulated in a way that ensures regulatory goals are fully met. As such, activities that pose risks to consumer protection, financial stability, or other goals should be comprehensively regulated, while recognizing that not all activities will require the same level of regulation.**

A financial regulatory system should effectively meet the goals of financial regulation, as articulated as part of this process, in a way that is appropriately comprehensive. In doing so, policymakers may want to consider how to ensure that both the breadth and depth of regulation are appropriate and adequate. That is, policymakers and regulators should consider how to make determinations about which activities and products, both new and existing, require some aspect of regulatory involvement to meet regulatory goals, and then make determinations about how extensive such regulation should be. As we have noted, gaps in the current level of federal oversight of mortgage lenders, credit rating agencies, and certain complex financial products such as CDOs and credit default swaps likely have contributed to the current crisis. Congress and regulators may also want to revisit the extent of regulation for entities such as banks that have traditionally fallen within full federal oversight but for which existing regulatory efforts, such as oversight related to risk management and lending standards, have been proven in some cases inadequate by recent events. However, overly restrictive regulation can stifle the financial sectors' ability to innovate and stimulate capital formation and economic growth. Regulators have struggled to balance these competing objectives, and the current crisis appears to reveal that the proper balance was not in place in the regulatory system to date.

Key issues to be addressed:

- Identify risk-based criteria, such as a product's or institution's potential to harm consumers or create systemic problems, for determining the appropriate level of oversight for financial activities and institutions.
- Identify ways that regulation can provide protection but avoid hampering innovation, capital formation, and economic growth.

3. ***Systemwide focus.* A regulatory system should include a mechanism for identifying, monitoring, and managing risks to the financial system regardless of the source of the risk or the institutions in which it is created.**

A regulatory system should focus on risks to the financial system, not just institutions. As noted earlier, with multiple regulators primarily responsible for individual institutions or markets, none of the financial regulators is tasked with assessing the risks posed across the entire financial system by a few institutions or by the collective activities of the industry. As we noted earlier in the report, the collective activities of a number of entities—including mortgage brokers, real estate professionals, lenders, borrowers, securities underwriters, investors, rating agencies and others—likely all contributed to the recent market crisis, but no one regulator had the necessary scope of oversight to identify the risks to the broader financial system. Similarly, once firms began to fail and the full extent of the financial crisis began to become clear, no formal mechanism existed to monitor market trends and potentially stop or help mitigate the fallout from these events.

Having a single entity responsible for assessing threats to the overall financial system could prevent some of the crises that we have seen in the past. For example, in its *Blueprint for a Modernized Financial Regulatory Structure*, Treasury proposed expanding the responsibilities of the Federal Reserve to create a "market stability regulator" that would have broad authority to gather and disclose appropriate information, collaborate with other regulators on rulemaking, and take corrective action as necessary in the interest of overall financial market stability. Such a regulator could assess the systemic risks that arise at financial institutions, within specific financial sectors, across the nation, and globally. However, policymakers should consider that a potential disadvantage of providing the agency with such broad responsibility for overseeing nonbank entities could be that it may imply an official government support or endorsement, such as a government guarantee, of such activities, and thus encourage greater risk taking by these financial institutions and investors.

Regardless of whether a new regulator is created, all regulators under a new system should consider how their activities could better identify and address systemic risks posed by their institutions. As the Federal Reserve Chairman has noted, regulation and supervision of financial institutions is a critical tool for limiting systemic risk. This will require broadening the focus from individual safety and soundness of institutions to a systemwide oversight approach that includes potential systemic risks and weaknesses.

A systemwide focus should also increase attention on how the incentives and constraints created by regulations affects risk taking throughout the business cycle, and what actions regulators can take to anticipate and mitigate such risks. However, as the Federal Reserve Chairman has noted, the more comprehensive the approach, the more technically demanding and costly it would be for regulators and affected institutions.

Key issues to be addressed:

- Identify approaches to broaden the focus of individual regulators or establish new regulatory mechanisms for identifying and acting on systemic risks.
- Determine what additional authorities a regulator or regulators should have to monitor and act to reduce systemic risks.

4. ***Flexible and adaptable.*** **A regulatory system should be adaptable and forward-looking such that regulators can readily adapt to market innovations and changes and include a mechanism for evaluating potential new risks to the system.**

A regulatory system should be designed such that regulators can readily adapt to market innovations and changes and include a formal mechanism for evaluating the full potential range of risks of new products and services to the system, market participants, and customers. An effective system could include a mechanism for monitoring market developments— such as broad market changes that introduce systemic risk, or new products and services that may pose more confined risks to particular market segments—to determine the degree, if any, to which regulatory intervention might be required. The rise of a very large market for credit derivatives, while providing benefits to users, also created exposures that warranted actions by regulators to rescue large individual participants in this market. While efforts are under way to create risk-reducing clearing mechanisms for this market, a more adaptable and responsive regulatory system might have recognized this need earlier and addressed it sooner. Some industry representatives have suggested that principles-based regulation, as discussed above, would provide such a mechanism. Designing a system to be flexible and proactive also involves determining whether Congress, regulators, or both should make such determinations, and how such an approach should be clarified in laws or regulations.

Important questions also exist about the extent to which financial regulators should actively monitor and, where necessary, approve new financial products and services as they are developed to ensure the least harm from inappropriate products. Some individuals commenting on this framework, including industry representatives, noted that limiting government intervention in new financial activities until it has become clear that a particular activity or market poses a significant risk and therefore warrants intervention may be more appropriate. As with other key policy questions, this may be answered with a combination of both approaches, recognizing that a product approval approach may be appropriate for some innovations with greater potential risk, while other activities may warrant a more reactive approach.

Key issues to be addressed:

- Determine how to effectively monitor market developments to identify potential risks; the degree, if any, to which regulatory intervention might be required; and who should hold such a responsibility.
- Consider how to strike the right balance between overseeing new products as they come onto the market to take action as needed to protect consumers and investors, without unnecessarily hindering innovation.

5. ***Efficient and effective.* A regulatory system should provide efficient oversight of financial services by eliminating overlapping federal regulatory missions, where appropriate, and minimizing regulatory burden while effectively achieving the goals of regulation.**

A regulatory system should provide for the efficient and effective oversight of financial services. Accomplishing this in a regulatory system involves many considerations. First, an efficient regulatory system is designed to accomplish its regulatory goals using the least amount of public resources. In this sense, policymakers must consider the number, organization, and responsibilities of each agency, and eliminate undesirable overlap in agency activities and responsibilities. Determining what is undesirable overlap is a difficult decision in itself. Under the current U.S. system, financial institutions often have several options for how to operate their business and who will be their regulator. For example, a new or existing depository institution can choose among several charter options. Having multiple regulators performing similar functions does allow for these agencies to potentially develop alternative or innovative approaches to regulation separately, with the approach working best becoming known over time. Such proven approaches can then be adopted by the other agencies. On the other hand, this could lead to regulatory arbitrage, in which institutions take advantage of variations in how agencies implement regulatory responsibilities in order to be subject to less scrutiny. Both situations have occurred under our current structure.

With that said, recent events clearly have shown that the fragmented U.S. regulatory structure contributed to failures by the existing regulators to adequately protect consumers and ensure financial stability. As we noted earlier, efforts by regulators to respond to the increased risks associated with new mortgage products were sometimes slowed in part because of the need for five federal regulators to coordinate their response. The Chairman of the Federal Reserve has similarly noted that the different regulatory and supervisory regimes for lending institutions and mortgage brokers made monitoring such institutions difficult for both regulators and investors. Similarly, we noted earlier in the report that the current fragmented U.S. regulatory structure has complicated some efforts to coordinate internationally with other regulators.

One first step to addressing such problems is to seriously consider the need to consolidate depository institution oversight among fewer agencies. Since 1996, we have been recommending that the number of federal agencies with primary responsibilities for bank oversight be reduced. Such a move would result in a system that was more efficient and improve consistency in regulation, another important characteristic of an effective regulatory system. In addition, Congress could consider the advantages and disadvantages of providing a federal charter option for insurance and creating a federal insurance regulatory entity. We have not studied the issue of an optional federal charter for insurers, but have through the years noted difficulties with efforts to harmonize insurance regulation across states through the NAIC-based structure. The establishment of a federal insurance charter and regulator could help alleviate some of these challenges, but such an approach could also have unintended consequences for state regulatory bodies and for insurance firms as well.

Also, given the challenges associated with increasingly complex investment and retail products as discussed earlier, policymakers will need to consider how best to align agency responsibilities to better ensure that consumers and investors are provided with clear, concise, and effective disclosures for all products.

Organizing agencies around regulatory goals as opposed to the existing sector-based regulation may be one way to improve the effectiveness of the system, especially given some of the market developments discussed earlier. Whatever the approach, policymakers should seek to minimize conflict in regulatory goals across regulators, or provide for efficient mechanisms to coordinate in cases where goals inevitably overlap. For example, in some cases, the safety and soundness of an individual institution may have implications for systemic risk, or addressing an unfair or deceptive act or practice at a financial institution may have implications on the institution's safety and soundness by increasing reputational risk. If a regulatory system assigns these goals to different regulators, it will be important to establish mechanisms for them to coordinate.

Proposals to consolidate regulatory agencies for the purpose of promoting efficiency should also take into account any potential trade-offs related to effectiveness. For example, to the extent that policymakers see value in the ability of financial institutions to choose their regulator, consolidating certain agencies may reduce such benefits. Similarly, some individuals have commented that the current system of multiple regulators has led to the development of expertise among agency staff in particular areas of financial market activities that might be threatened if the system were to be consolidated. Finally, policymakers may want to ensure that any transition from the current financial system to a new structure should minimize as best as possible any disruption to the operation of financial markets or risks to the government, especially given the current challenges faced in today's markets and broader economy.

A financial system should also be efficient by minimizing the burden on regulated entities to the extent possible while still achieving regulatory goals. Under our current system, many financial institutions, and especially large institutions that offer services that cross sectors, are subject to supervision by multiple regulators. While steps toward consolidated supervision and designating primary supervisors have helped alleviate some of the burden, industry representatives note that many institutions face significant costs as a result of the existing financial regulatory system that could be lessened. Such costs, imposed in an effort to meet certain regulatory goals such as safety and soundness and consumer protection, can run counter to other goals of a financial system by stifling innovation and competitiveness. In addressing this concern, it is also important to consider the potential benefits that might result in some cases from having multiple regulators overseeing an institution. For example, representatives of state banking and other institution regulators, and consumer advocacy organizations, note that concurrent jurisdiction— between two federal regulators or a federal and state regulator—can provide needed checks and balances against individual financial regulators who have not always reacted appropriately and in a timely way to address problems at institutions. They also note that states may move more quickly and more flexibly to respond to activities causing harm to consumers. Some types of concurrent jurisdiction, such as enforcement authority, may be less burdensome to institutions than others, such as ongoing supervision and examination.

Key issues to be addressed:

- Consider the appropriate role of the states in a financial regulatory system and how federal and state roles can be better harmonized.
- Determine and evaluate the advantages and disadvantages of having multiple regulators, including nongovernmental entities such as SROs, share responsibilities for regulatory oversight.
- Identify ways that the U.S. regulatory system can be made more efficient, either through consolidating agencies with similar roles or through minimizing unnecessary regulatory burden.
- Consider carefully how any changes to the financial regulatory system may negatively impact financial market operations and the broader economy, and take steps to minimize such consequences.

6. ***Consistent consumer and investor protection.* A regulatory system should include consumer and investor protection as part of the regulatory mission to ensure that market participants receive consistent, useful information, as well as legal protections for similar financial products and services, including disclosures, sales practice standards, and suitability requirements.**

A regulatory system should be designed to provide high-quality, effective, and consistent protection for consumers and investors in similar situations. In doing so, it is important to recognize important distinctions between retail consumers and more sophisticated consumers such as institutional investors, where appropriate considering the context of the situation. Different disclosures and regulatory protections may be necessary for these different groups. Consumer protection should be viewed from the perspective of the consumer rather than through the various and sometimes divergent perspectives of the multitude of federal regulators that currently have responsibilities in this area.

As discussed earlier, many consumers that received loans in the last few years did not understand the risks associated with taking out their loans, especially in the event that housing prices would not continue to increase at the rate they had in recent years. In addition, increasing evidence exists that many Americans are lacking in financial literacy, and the expansion of new and more complex products will continue to create challenges in this area. Furthermore, as noted above, regulators with existing authority to better protect consumers did not always exercise that authority effectively. In considering a new regulatory system, policymakers should consider the significant lapses in our regulatory system's focus on consumer protection and ensure that such a focus is prioritized in any reform efforts. For example, policymakers should identify ways to improve upon the existing, largely fragmented, system of regulators that must coordinate to act in these areas. As noted above, this should include serious consideration of whether to consolidate regulatory responsibilities to streamline and improve the effectiveness of consumer protection efforts. Another way that some market observers have argued that consumer protections could be enhanced and harmonized across products is to extend suitability requirements—which require securities brokers making recommendations to customers to have reasonable grounds for believing that the recommendation is suitable for the customer—to mortgage and other products. Additional consideration could also be given to determining whether certain products are simply too complex to be well understood and make judgments about limiting or curtailing their use.

Key issues to be addressed:

- Consider how prominent the regulatory goal of consumer protection should be in the U.S. financial regulatory system.
- Determine what amount, if any, of consolidation of responsibility may be necessary to enhance and harmonize consumer protections, including suitability requirements and disclosures across the financial services industry.
- Consider what distinctions are necessary between retail and wholesale products, and how such distinctions should affect how products are regulated.
- Identify opportunities to protect and empower consumers through improving their financial literacy.

7. ***Regulators provided with independence, prominence, authority, and accountability.*** **A regulatory system should ensure that regulators have independence from inappropriate influence; have sufficient resources, clout, and authority to carry out and enforce statutory missions; and are clearly accountable for meeting regulatory goals.**

A regulatory system should ensure that any entity responsible for financial regulation is independent from inappropriate influence; has adequate prominence, authority, and resources to carry out and enforce its statutory mission; and is clearly accountable for meeting regulatory goals. With respect to independence, policymakers may want to consider advantages and disadvantages of different approaches to funding agencies, especially to the extent that agencies might face difficulty remaining independent if they are funded by the institutions they regulate. Under the current structure, for example, the Federal Reserve primarily is funded by income earned from U.S. government securities that it has acquired through open market operations and does not assess charges to the institutions it oversees. In contrast, OCC and OTS are funded primarily by assessments on the firms they supervise. Decision makers should consider whether some of these various funding mechanisms are more likely to ensure that a regulator will take action against its regulated institutions without regard to the potential impact on its own funding.

With respect to prominence, each regulator must receive appropriate attention and support from top government officials. Inadequate prominence in government may make it difficult for a regulator to raise safety and soundness or other concerns to Congress and the administration in a timely manner. Mere knowledge of a deteriorating situation would be insufficient if a regulator were unable to persuade Congress and the administration to take timely corrective action. This problem would be exacerbated if a regulated institution had more political clout and prominence than its regulator because the institution could potentially block action from being taken.

In considering authority, agencies must have the necessary enforcement and other tools to effectively implement their missions to achieve regulatory goals. For example, as noted earlier, in a 2007 report we expressed concerns over the appropriateness of having OTS oversee diverse global financial firms given the size of the agency relative to the institutions for which it was responsible.[74] It is important for a regulatory system to ensure that agencies are provided with adequate resources and expertise to conduct their work effectively. A regulatory system should also include adequate checks and balances to ensure the appropriate use of agency authorities. With respect to accountability, policymakers may also want to consider different governance structures at agencies—the current system includes a combination of agency heads and independent boards or commissions—and how to ensure that agencies are recognized for successes and held accountable for failures to act in accordance with regulatory goals.

Key issues to be addressed:

- Determine how to structure and fund agencies to ensure each has adequate independence, prominence, tools, authority and accountability.
- Consider how to provide an appropriate level of authority to an agency while ensuring that it appropriately implements its mission without abusing its authority.
- Ensure that the regulatory system includes effective mechanisms for holding regulators accountable.

8. ***Consistent financial oversight.* A regulatory system should ensure that similar institutions, products, risks, and services are subject to consistent regulation, oversight, and transparency, which should help minimize negative competitive outcomes while harmonizing oversight, both within the United States and internationally.**

A regulatory system should ensure that similar institutions, products, and services posing similar risks are subject to consistent regulation, oversight, and transparency. Identifying which institutions and which of their products and services pose similar risks is not easy and involves a number of important considerations. Two institutions that look very similar may in fact pose very different risks to the financial system, and therefore may call for significantly different regulatory treatment. However, activities that are done by different types of financial institutions that pose similar risks to their institutions or the financial system should be regulated similarly to prevent competitive disadvantages between institutions.

Streamlining the regulation of similar products across sectors could also help prepare the United States for challenges that may result from increased globalization and potential harmonization in regulatory standards. Such efforts are under way in other jurisdictions. For example, at a November 2008 summit in the United States, the Group of 20 countries pledged to strengthen their regulatory regimes and ensure that all financial markets, products, and participants are consistently regulated or subject to oversight, as appropriate to their circumstances. Similarly, a working group in the European Union is slated by the spring of 2009 to propose ways to strengthen European supervisory arrangements, including addressing how their supervisors should cooperate with other major jurisdictions to help safeguard financial stability globally. Promoting consistency in regulation of similar products should be done in a way that does not sacrifice the quality of regulatory oversight.

As we noted in a 2004 report, different regulatory treatment of bank and financial holding companies, consolidated supervised entities, and other holding companies may not provide a basis for consistent oversight of their consolidated risk management strategies, guarantee competitive neutrality, or contribute to better oversight of systemic risk. Recent events further underscore the limitations brought about when there is a lack of consistency in oversight of large financial institutions. As such, Congress and regulators will need to seriously consider how best to consolidate responsibilities for oversight of large financial conglomerates as part of any reform effort.

Key issues to be addressed:

- Identify institutions and products and services that pose similar risks.
- Determine the level of consolidation necessary to streamline financial regulation activities across the financial services industry.
- Consider the extent to which activities need to be coordinated internationally.

9. ***Minimal taxpayer exposure.* A regulatory system should have adequate safeguards that allow financial institution failures to occur while limiting taxpayers' exposure to financial risk.**

A regulatory system should have adequate safeguards that allow financial institution failures to occur while limiting taxpayers' exposure to financial risk. Policymakers should consider identifying the best safeguards and assignment of responsibilities for responding to situations where taxpayers face significant exposures, and should consider providing clear guidelines when regulatory intervention is appropriate. While an ideal system would allow firms to fail without negatively affecting other firms— and therefore avoid any moral hazard that may result—policymakers and regulators must consider the realities of today's financial system. In some cases, the immediate use of public funds to prevent the failure of a critically important financial institution may be a worthwhile use of such funds if it ultimately serves to prevent a systemic crisis that would result in much greater use of public funds in the long run. However, an effective regulatory system that incorporates the characteristics noted above, especially by ensuring a systemwide focus, should be better equipped to identify and mitigate problems before it become necessary to make decisions about whether to let a financial institution fail.

An effective financial regulatory system should also strive to minimize systemic risks resulting from interrelationships between firms and limitations in market infrastructures that prevent the orderly unwinding of firms that fail. Another important consideration in minimizing taxpayer exposure is to ensure that financial institutions provided with a government guarantee that could result in taxpayer exposure are also subject to an appropriate level of regulatory oversight to fulfill the responsibilities discussed above.

Key issues to be addressed:

- Identify safeguards that are most appropriate to prevent systemic crises while minimizing moral hazard.
- Consider how a financial system can most effectively minimize taxpayer exposure to losses related to financial instability.

Finally, although significant changes may be required to modernize the U.S. financial regulatory system, policymakers should consider carefully how best to implement the changes in such a way that the transition to a new structure does not hamper the functioning of the financial markets, individual financial institutions' ability to conduct their activities, and consumers' ability to access needed services. For example, if the changes require regulators or institutions to make systems changes, file registrations, or other activities that could require extensive time to complete, the changes could be implemented in phases with specific target dates around which the affected entities could formulate plans.

In addition, our past work has identified certain critical factors that should be addressed to ensure that any large-scale transitions among government agencies are implemented successfully.[75] Although all of these factors are likely important for a successful transformation for the financial regulatory system, Congress and existing agencies should pay particular attention to ensuring there are effective communication strategies so that all affected parties, including investors and consumers, clearly understand any changes being implemented. In addition, attention should be paid to developing a sound human capital strategy to ensure that any new or consolidated agencies are able to retain and attract additional quality staff during the transition period. Finally, policymakers should consider how best to retain and utilize the existing skills and knowledge base within agencies subject to changes as part of a transition.

COMMENTS FROM AGENCIES AND OTHER ORGANIZATIONS, AND OUR EVALUATION

We provided the opportunity to review and comment on a draft of this chapter to representatives of 29 agencies and other organizations, including federal and state financial regulatory agencies, consumer advocacy groups, and financial service industry trade associations. A complete list of organizations that reviewed the draft is included in appendix II. All reviewers provided valuable input that was used in finalizing this chapter. In general, reviewers commented that the report represented a high-quality and thorough review of issues related to regulatory reform. We made changes throughout the report to increase its precision and clarity and to provide additional detail. For example, the Federal Reserve provided comments indicating that our report should emphasize that the traditional goals of regulation that we described in the background section are incomplete unless their ultimate purpose is considered, which is to promote the long-term growth, stability, and welfare of the United States. As a result, we expanded the discussion of our framework element concerning the need to have clearly defined regulatory goals to emphasize that policymakers will need to ensure that such regulation is balanced with other national goals, including facilitating capital raising and fostering innovation.

In addition, we received formal written responses from the American Bankers Association, the American Council of Life Insurers, the Conference of State Bank Supervisors, Consumers Union, the Credit Union National Association, the Federal Deposit Insurance Corporation, the Mortgage Bankers Association, and the National Association of Federal Credit Unions, and a joint letter from the Center for Responsible Lending, the National Consumer Law Center, and U.S. PIRG; all formal written responses are included as appendixes to this chapter.

Among the letters we received, various commenters raised additional issues regarding consumer protection and risky products. For example, in a joint letter, the Center for Responsible Lending, the National Consumer Law Center, and the U.S. PIRG noted that the best way to avoid systemic risk is to address problems that exist at the level of individual consumer transactions, before they pose a threat to the system as a whole. They also noted that although most of the subprime lending was done by nonbank lenders, overly aggressive practices for other loan types and among other lenders also contributed to the current crisis. In addition, they noted that to effectively protect consumers, the regulatory system must prohibit unsustainable lending and that disclosures and financial literacy are not enough. The letter from FDIC agreed that effective reform of the U.S. financial regulatory system would help avoid a recurrence of the economic and financial problems we are now experiencing. It also noted that irresponsible lending practices were not consistent with sound banking practices. FDIC's letter also notes that the regulatory structure collectively permitted excessive levels of leverage in the nonbank financial system and that statutory mandates that address consumer protection and aggressive lending practices and leverage among firms would be equally important for improving regulation as would changing regulatory structure. In a letter from Consumers Union, that group urged that consumer protection be given equal priority as safety and soundness and that regulators act more promptly to address emerging risks rather than waiting until a problem has become national in scope. The letter indicates that Consumers Union supports an independent federal consumer protection agency for financial services and the ability of states to also develop and enforce consumer protections. We made changes in response to many of these comments. For example, we enhanced our discussion of weaknesses in regulators' efforts to oversee the sale of mortgage products that posed risks to consumers and the stability of the financial system, and we made changes to the framework to emphasize the importance of consumer protection.

Several of the letters addressed issues regarding potential consolidation of regulatory agencies and the role of federal and state regulation. The letter from the American Bankers Association said that the current system of bank regulation and oversight has many advantages and that any reform efforts should build on those advantages. The letter also noted that there are benefits to having multiple federal regulators, as well as a dual banking system. The letter from the Conference of State Bank Supervisors agreed with our report that the U.S. regulatory system is complex and clearly has gaps, but cautioned that consolidating regulation and making decisions that could indirectly result in greater industry consolidation could exacerbate problems. The letter also indicates concern that our report does not fully acknowledge the importance of creating an environment that promotes a diverse industry to serve the nation's diverse communities and prevents concentration of economic power in a handful of institutions. Our report does discuss the benefits of state regulation of financial institutions, but we did not address the various types of state institutions because we focused mainly on the federal role over our markets. In the past, our work has acknowledged the dual banking system has benefits and that concentration in markets can have disadvantages. The Conference of State Bank Supervisors letter also notes that state efforts to respond to consumer abuses were stymied by federal pre-emption and that a regulatory structure should preserve checks and balances, avoid concentrations of power, and be more locally responsive. In response to this letter, we also added information about the enactment of the Secure and Fair Enforcement for Mortgage Licensing Act, as part of the Housing and Economic Recovery Act, which requires enhanced licensing and registration of mortgage brokers.

The letter from the National Association of Federal Credit Unions urged that an independent regulator for credit unions be retained because of the distinctive characteristics of federal credit unions. A letter from the Credit Union National Association also strongly opposes combining the credit union regulator or its insurance function with another agency. The letter from the Mortgage Bankers Association urges that a federal standard for mortgage lending be developed to provide greater uniformity than the currently diffuse set of state laws. They also supported consideration of federal regulation of independent mortgage bankers and mortgage brokers as a way of improving uniformity and effectiveness of the regulation of these entities. A letter from the American Council of Life Insurers noted that the lack of a federal insurance regulatory office provides for uneven consumer protections and policy availability nationwide and hampers the country's ability to negotiate internationally on insurance industry issues, and urged that we include a discussion of the need to consider a greater federal role in the regulation of insurance. As a result, in the section where we discuss the need for efficient and effective regulation we noted that harmonizing insurance regulation across states has been difficult, and that Congress could consider the advantages and disadvantages of providing a federal charter option for insurance and creating a federal insurance regulatory entity.

Gene L. Dodaro
Acting Comptroller General of the United States

List of Congressional Addressees

The Honorable Christopher J. Dodd
Chairman
The Honorable Richard C. Shelby
Ranking Member
Committee on Banking, Housing, and Urban Affairs
United States Senate

The Honorable Joseph I. Lieberman
Chairman

The Honorable Susan M. Collins
Ranking Member
Committee on Homeland Security and Governmental Affairs
United States Senate

The Honorable Barney Frank
Chairman
The Honorable Spencer Bachus
Ranking Member
Committee on Financial Services
House of Representatives

The Honorable Edolphus Towns
Chairman
The Honorable Darrell E. Issa
Ranking Member
Committee on Oversight and Government Reform
House of Representatives

The Honorable Richard J. Durbin
The Honorable Tim Johnson
The Honorable Jack Reed
United States Senate

The Honorable Judy Biggert
The Honorable Paul E. Kanjorski
The Honorable Carolyn B. Maloney
The Honorable José E. Serrano
House of Representatives

APPENDIX I: SCOPE AND METHODOLOGY

Our report objectives were to (1) describe the origins of the current financial regulatory system, (2) describe various market developments and changes that have raised challenges for the current system, and (3) present an evaluation framework that can be used by Congress and others to craft or evaluate potential regulatory reform efforts going forward.

To address all of these objectives, we synthesized existing GAO work on challenges to the U.S. financial regulatory structure and on criteria for developing and strengthening effective regulatory structures. These reports are referenced in footnotes in this chapter and noted in the Related GAO Products appendix. In particular, we relied extensively on our recent body of work examining the financial regulatory structure, culminating in reports issued in 2004 and 2007.[76] We also reviewed existing studies, government documents, and other research for illustrations of how current and past financial market events have revealed limitations in our existing regulatory system and suggestions for regulatory reform.

In addition, to gather input on challenges with the existing system and important considerations in evaluating reforms, we interviewed several key individuals with broad and substantial knowledge about the U.S. financial regulatory system—including a former Chairman of the Board of Governors of the Federal Reserve System (Federal Reserve), a former high-level executive at a major investment bank that had also served in various regulatory agencies, and an international financial organization official that also served in various regulatory agencies. We selected these individuals from a group of notable officials, academics, legal scholars, and others we identified as part of this and other GAO work, including a 2007 expert panel on financial regulatory structure. We selected individuals to interview in an effort to gather government, industry, and academic perspectives, including on international issues. In some cases, due largely to the market turmoil at the time of our study, we were unable to or chose not to reach out to certain individuals, but took steps to ensure that we selected other individuals that would meet our criteria.

To develop the evaluation framework, we also convened a series of three forums in which we gathered comments on a preliminary draft of our framework from a wide range of representatives of federal and state financial regulatory agencies, financial industry associations and institutions, and consumer advocacy organizations. In particular, at a forum held on August 19, 2008, we gathered comments from representatives of financial industry associations and institutions, including the American Bankers Association, the American Council of Life Insurers, The Clearing House, Columbia Bank, the Independent Community Bankers of America, The Financial Services Roundtable, Fulton Financial Corporation, the Futures Industry Association, the Managed Funds Association, the Mortgage Bankers Association, the National Association of Federal Credit Unions, the Securities Industry and Financial Markets Association, and the U.S. Chamber of Commerce. We worked closely with representatives at the American Bankers Association—which hosted the forum at its Washington, D.C., headquarters—to identify a comprehensive and representative group of industry associations and institutions.

At a forum held on August 27, 2008, we gathered comments from representatives of consumer advocacy organizations, including the Center for Responsible Lending, the Consumer Federation of America, the Consumers Union, the National Consumer Law Center, and the U.S. PIRG. We invited a comprehensive list of consumer advocacy organization representatives—compiled based on extensive dealings with these groups from current and past work—to participate in this forum and hosted it at GAO headquarters in Washington, D.C.

At a forum held on August 28, 2008, we gathered comments from representatives of federal and state banking, securities, futures, insurance and housing regulatory oversight agencies, including the Commodity Futures Trading Commission, the Conference of State Bank Supervisors, the Department of the Treasury, the Federal Deposit Insurance Corporation, the Federal Housing Finance Agency, the Federal Reserve, the Financial Industry Regulatory Authority, the National Association of Insurance Commissioners, the National Credit Union Administration, the North American Securities Administrators Administration, the Office of the Comptroller of the Currency, the Office of Thrift Supervision, the Public Company Accounting Oversight Board, and the Securities and Exchange Commission. We worked closely with officials at the Federal Reserve—which hosted the forum at its Washington, D.C., headquarters— to identify a comprehensive and representative group of federal and state financial regulatory agencies.

We conducted this work from April 2008 to December 2008 in accordance with generally accepted government auditing standards. Those standards require that we plan and perform the audit to obtain sufficient, appropriate evidence to provide a reasonable basis for our findings and conclusions based on our audit objectives. We believe that the evidence obtained provides a reasonable basis for our findings and conclusions based on our audit objectives.

APPENDIX II: AGENCIES AND OTHER ORGANIZATONS THAT REVIEWD THE DRAFT REPORT

American Bankers Association
American Council of Life Insurers
Center for Responsible Lending
Commodity Futures Trading Commission
Conference of State Bank Supervisors
Consumer Federation of America
Consumers Union
Credit Union National Association
Department of the Treasury
Federal Deposit Insurance Corporation
Federal Housing Finance Agency
Federal Reserve
Financial Industry Regulatory Authority
Financial Services Roundtable
Futures Industry Association
Independent Community Bankers of America
International Swaps and Derivates Association
Mortgage Bankers Association
National Association of Federal Credit Unions
National Association of Insurance Commissioners
National Consumer Law Center
National Credit Union Administration
National Futures Association
Office of the Comptroller of the Currency
Office of Thrift Supervision
Public Company Accounting Oversight Board
Securities and Exchange Commission
Securities Industry and Financial Markets Association
U.S. PIRG

APPENDIX III: COMMENTS FROM THE AMERICAN BANKERS ASSOCIATION

AMERICAN BANKERS ASSOCIATION

1120 Connecticut Avenue, NW
Washington, DC 20036

1-800-BANKERS
www.aba.com

World-Class Solutions,
Leadership & Advocacy
Since 1875

Denyette DePierro
Senior Counsel
Office of Regulatory Policy
Phone: 202-663-5333
Fax: 202-828-5047
ddepierr@aba.com

December 19, 2008

Ms. Orice M. Williams
Director
Financial Markets and Community Investment
U.S. Government Accountability Office
441 G Street, N.W.
Washington, D.C. 20548

Dear Ms. Williams:

The American Bankers Association[1] (ABA) appreciates the opportunity to provide comments in connection with the Government Accountability Office's (GAO) draft report entitled, *A Framework for Crafting and Assessing Proposals to Modernize the Outdated U.S. Financial Regulatory System*, which we understand is to be published in January, 2009. The purpose of the report is to identify existing problems with the financial regulatory system and craft a framework to assist in the evaluation of reform proposals.

We believe that any review of the current regulatory system should begin with the recognition that banks have been and continue to be the primary institutions for saving, lending, and financing economic growth in our nation's communities. Banks are also the leading players in the payments system and the only institutions that can be found participating in every stage of the payments system. Held to high standards of financial strength and integrity of operations, banks are well-poised to be engines of economic recovery and continued economic growth and development thereafter.

Our customers include people and families from all walks of life and involve businesses of all sizes. The innovation and the diversity of the banking industry enable us to meet changing customer needs and interests. Through these efforts in recent decades more people have gained access to a wider array of banking products—and at lower costs—than ever before, and better than anywhere else in the world.

1 The American Bankers Association brings together banks of all sizes and charters into one association. ABA works to enhance the competitiveness of the nation's banking industry and strengthen America's economy and communities. Its members – the majority of which are banks with less than $125 million in assets – represent over 95 percent of the industry's $13.6 trillion in assets and employ over 2 million men and women.

We support a regulatory program that fosters a climate in which we can build on these accomplishments and continue our progress in providing more and better services to more people and businesses at lower costs. With that in mind, we offer the following observations about ways in which changes to the current system could achieve these objectives.

The central objective of regulatory reform efforts should be to enhance banks' ability to meet the needs of their customers. This objective has several facets. First, regulation needs to foster safe and sound operations. Second, it must provide appropriate consumer protections. Third, it needs to promote competition. And fourth, it must foster innovation and facilitate banks' ability to meet changing customer needs. These facets, while distinct, are wholly compatible. A financial institution will best be able to achieve its business objectives by responsibly managing its risks; by providing a full range of products and services to all customers who can responsibly manage *their* risks; and by competing against others based on price, product quality, reputation, and other customer interests, not by undermining standards of integrity. We believe it is incumbent upon policy makers to create the legal framework that supports these goals.

Any regulatory reform effort must focus on solving the problems that caused the current market turmoil. This necessarily entails identifying what those problems are so that responses can be tailored accordingly. A business model that combines activities that are financial in nature and thereby draws from a diversified revenue mix has shown to be a solution to, and not a part of, the current problems. Thus reform efforts should facilitate banks offering a broad range of financial products and services. Conversely, reform efforts should be careful not merely to impose new regulations on the banking sector, which did not cause the crisis and which continues to provide credit; rather it should remove unnecessary regulations that impede sound lending and efficient operations.

The current system of bank regulation and oversight has many advantages, and we believe any reform efforts should build on those advantages. As the recent rush by non-bank actors to obtain bank charters has demonstrated, bank regulation and supervision has proven to be the most durable method to minimize risks to safety and soundness. Moreover, it provides a useful check against any one regulator neglecting its duties, becoming too calcified for an ever-changing financial marketplace, growing overly bureaucratic and ineffective, or otherwise imposing regulatory conditions inconsistent with the ability of financial firms to serve their customers. Thus, the ABA supports the Office of the Comptroller of the Currency, Federal Deposit Insurance Corporation, Federal Reserve Board, and the Office of Thrift Supervision with regard to their diverse supervision and oversight responsibilities within the U.S. banking system.

Just as there is a benefit in having multiple federal regulators, so too is there a benefit in having a dual banking system. States have for years operated as incubators for new products and services, such as NOW accounts and adjustable rate mortgages. The dual banking system has proven vital to the continued evolution of the U.S. banking. Close coordination between federal bank regulators and state banking commissioners within the Federal Financial Institutions Examination Council (FFIEC) as well as during joint bank examinations is a dynamic element of the dual banking system, resulting in a system of complementary supervision.

Recent economic turmoil has drawn attention to the need for a regulator with explicit jurisdiction to manage systemic risk. The primary responsibility of systemic risk regulation should be protecting the economy from major shocks and working with bank supervisors to avoid pro-cyclical directives within the supervisory process. The systemic risk regulator would gather information, monitor exposures throughout the system and take action in concert with domestic and international supervisors to minimize risks to the economy. For maximum effectiveness and ease of implementation, systemic risk regulation should rely on existing regulatory structures and restrict its oversight to a limited number of large market participants, both bank and non-bank.

There clearly is a need for better supervision and regulation of many non-bank actors, such as mortgage banks and brokers that are not affiliated with an insured depository institution. Consumer confidence in the financial sector as a whole suffers when non-bank actors offer bank-like services while operating under substandard or non-existent guidelines for safety and soundness. Lesser-regulated companies and individuals participating in bank-like activities or offering bank-like products and services should be subject to bank-like regulation and capital requirements. Regulatory reform should tackle these issues and bring appropriate oversight to inadequately or ineffectively regulated financial products and services.

This should be done within the context of agencies that have the authority and responsibility to supervise all aspects of an institution's activities. Safety and soundness issues and consumer protection are closely linked for banks and should be supervised as such. Treating consumers unfairly is inconsistent with safe and sound operations; so, too, is attempting to insulate consumers from any risk. Well-run institutions keep both facets in mind, and their regulators should as well. This argues in favor of continuing to place responsibility for both consumer protection and safety and soundness with the banking agencies.

It also should be done in a manner that preserves the independence of the Federal Reserve Board (Board) and keeps the Board's primary focus on the conduct of monetary policy. Any expansion of the Board's authority to serve as the systemic risk regulator should be made only if such authority would not create conflicts of interest for the Board or otherwise compromise its ability to carry out its responsibilities for monetary policy.

Any regulatory restructuring effort must recognize the benefits of charter choice. A robust banking sector requires participants of all sizes and business models, including community banks, development banks, and niche-focused financial institutions as well as regional, national, and international banks. Federal and state bank charter alternatives, a broad range of business models, as well as choice of ownership structure (encompassing S corporations, limited liability corporations, mutual ownership, and other forms of publicly-traded and privately-held banks) promotes responsiveness to changing customer needs, consumer preferences, and economic conditions. Only a diverse, well-regulated banking system can bring sustainable increases in homeownership and community development that are essential to economic recovery.

This diversity is not well-served by a system that treats any financial institution as if it were too big or too complex to fail. Such a policy can have serious competitive consequences for the banking industry as a whole. Clear actions strengthening the competitive position of all banks are needed to address and ameliorate the negative effect on the majority of financial institutions when a select few are designated as too big to fail. Moreover, financial regulators should develop a program to identify, monitor, and respond effectively to market developments arising to the perception of an institution as too big or too complex to fail—particularly in times of financial stress. The ad hoc approach used in the resolution of Lehman Brothers and Bear Sterns is inadequate. Specific authorities and programs must be developed to manage the orderly transition or resolution of any systemically significant financial institution, bank or non-bank.

Any reform effort also must address issues in our accounting rules that create a pro-cyclical downward drag on the financial sector and the economy as a whole. Accounting should be a reflection of economic reality, not a driver. Reforms to accounting standards should make the standard setting process accountable to the market and implement standards that consider the real-world effects of the rules. Rules governing loan-loss reserves and fair value accounting should minimize pro-cyclical effects that reinforce economic highs and lows. A reformed accounting system would recognize that functioning accounting rules are essential to minimizing systemic risk and fostering economic growth.

Thank you for the opportunity to comment on this proposal. Should you have any questions, please contact the undersigned at 202-663-5333 or ddepierr@aba.com.

Sincerely,

Denyette DePierro

Appendix IV: Comments from the American Council of Life Insurers

ACLI
Financial Security. For Life.

Julie A. Spiezio
Senior Vice President, Insurance Regulation & Deputy General Counsel

December 15, 2008

Ms. Orice M. Williams
Director, Financial Markets and Community Investment
U.S. Government Accountability Office
441 G Street, N.W.
Washington, D.C. 20548
williamso@gao.gov

RE: Draft Report on Reforming the Financial Regulatory System

Dear Ms. Williams:

These comments are submitted on behalf of the American Council of Life Insurers (ACLI). The ACLI is a national trade association with 353 member companies that account for 93 percent of the industry's total assets, 93 percent of U.S life insurance premiums and 95 percent of U.S. annuity considerations. We appreciate being given an opportunity to comment on the draft report.

At GAO's invitation, ACLI staff undertook a brief review of the draft report at GAO headquarters early last week. Speaking from an insurance industry perspective, we were surprised that the draft report did not include discussion of the need for insurance regulatory reform as part of the broader financial services industry reform effort. We believe this is an important oversight and one that should be addressed before the final report is issued by the GAO.

Currently there is no insurance expertise in the federal government. Prior to the crisis that has beset the financial service industry since September of this year, this fact was proving to be a costly problem for American consumers and insurers alike. A regulatory system that provides for uneven consumer protections and policy availability nationwide is not compatible with the economic model of the 21st century. In addition, the lack of a federal insurance regulatory office prevents the United States from adequately addressing its citizens' needs in international trade negotiations and treaty developments involving insurance industry issues. These issues alone warrant discussion of the need for a federal role in insurance regulation via the availability of an optional federal insurance charter (OFC).

The economic crisis has only served to underscore this need. The crisis has highlighted for policymakers and the general public alike that insurers play a systemic role in our economy, both nationally and internationally. And today, after all that has taken place over the past few months, both the executive and legislative branches of the federal government remain handicapped in their ability to completely understand and respond to the underlying insurance issues that are part of the financial crisis because they lack any insurance industry regulatory expertise.

These facts make the lack of reference to the issue of insurance regulatory reform in the draft GAO report just that much more puzzling. The report directly addresses the need for the federal government

American Council of Life Insurers
101 Constitution Avenue, NW, Washington, DC 20001-2133
(202) 624-2194 t (202) 572-4843 f juliespiezio@acli.com
www.acli.com

to assume some regulatory responsibility over other areas of the financial services industry where it currently lacks such authority (e.g., hedge funds), but remains conspicuously silent on the insurance regulatory reform/OFC issue. We feel this is not simply an oversight, but is a lost opportunity to help Congress in its effort to effectively reform and modernize the whole of financial services industry regulation moving forward.

For all of these reasons, we respectfully request that prior to the final publication of this GAO report be revised to include discussion of the need for insurance regulatory reform. It is our opinion that releasing the report without such a revision will render the report incomplete and therefore of less value to both the Congress and the public at large then it otherwise might be.

Thank you again for this opportunity to comment on the draft report. Please feel free to contact me directly if you have any questions or would like to discuss this issue further.

Very truly yours,

Julie A. Splezio

Cc: Randy Fasnacht
Cody Goebel

Appendix V: Comments from the Conference of State Bank Supervisors

December 17, 2008

Orice M. Williams
Director
Financial Markets and Community Investment
U.S. Government Accountability Office
441 G Street, NW
Washington, DC 20548

Dear Ms. Williams:

Thank you for the opportunity to submit a second written comment in response to the GAO's upcoming report on the financial regulatory framework of the United States.

The Conference of State Bank Supervisors (CSBS) recognizes the current regulatory structure at both the state and federal level is sometimes complex for the industry, regulators, consumers, and policymakers to navigate. As financial institutions and service providers increase in size, complexity, and operations, our regulatory system must reflect this evolution. The current economic stresses have also shown that our financial regulatory system must better address the interconnected risks of the capital markets and our banking system.

CSBS is committed to working with the GAO, our federal counterparts, Congress, industry associations, and consumer advocates to further the development of a fair and efficient regulatory system that provides sufficient consumer protection and serves the interests of financial institutions and financial service providers, while ultimately strengthening the U.S. economy as a whole.

We believe that changes are needed in both regulation and the way our regulatory structure functions to better respond to consumer needs and address systemic risks and market integrity. We are very concerned, however, that federal policy that addresses nationwide and global regulatory business models continues to threaten—or perhaps eliminate—the greatest strengths of our system. Specifically, we see policies that promote the needs of the very largest financial institutions at the expense of consumers, important federal checks and balances and diversity of banking and other financial institutions that are critical to our state economies.

The current financial regulatory structure allows for a diverse universe of financial institutions of varying sizes. While the financial industry continues to consolidate at a rapid pace, there are still well over 8,000 financial institutions operating within the United

CONFERENCE OF STATE BANK SUPERVISORS
1155 Connecticut Ave., NW, 5th Floor • Washington DC 20036-4306 • (202) 296-2840 • Fax: (202) 296-1928

States, some of which are as small as $1 million in assets. Obviously, our nation's largest money center banks play a critical role in the economy. However, even the smallest bank in the country is absolutely critical to the economic health of the community in which it operates.

The complexity of the system is presented as a major source of the current financial crisis. While there are clearly gaps in our regulatory system and the system is undeniably complex, CSBS has observed that the greater failing of the system has been one of insufficient political and regulatory will, primarily at the federal level. We believe that decisions to consolidate regulation do not fix, but rather exacerbate this problem. Moreover, CSBS is deeply concerned that the GAO study does not fully appreciate the importance of creating an environment that promotes a diverse industry which serves our nation's diverse communities and avoids a concentration of economic and political power in a handful of institutions.

Specifically, we are offering the following comments to the elements of a successful supervisory framework.

Clearly Defined Regulatory Goals
Generally, we agree with the GAO's goals of a regulatory system that ensures adequate consumer protections, ensures the integrity and fairness of markets, monitors the safety and soundness of institutions, and acts to ensure the stability of the overall financial system. We disagree, however, with the GAO's claim that the safety and soundness goal is necessarily in direct conflict with the goal of consumer protection. It has been the experience of state regulators that the very opposite can be true. Indeed, consumer protection should be recognized as integral to safety and soundness of financial institutions and service providers. The health of a financial institution ultimately is connected to the health of its customers. However, we have observed that federal regulators, without the checks and balances of more locally responsive state regulators or state law enforcement do not always give fair weight to consumer issues or have the perspective to understand consumer issues. We consider this a significant weakness of the current system. Federal preemption of state law and state law enforcement by the Office of the Comptroller of the Currency and the Office of Thrift Supervision has resulted in less responsive consumer protections and institutions that are much less responsive to needs of consumers in our states.

Appropriately Comprehensive
CSBS disagrees that federal regulators were unable to identify the risks to the financial system because they did not have the necessary scope of oversight. As previously noted, we believe it was a failure of regulatory will and a philosophy of self-regulating markets that allowed for risks to develop. CSBS strongly believes a "comprehensive" system of regulation should not be construed as a consolidated regime under one single regulator. Instead, "comprehensive" should describe a regulatory system that is able to adequately supervise a broad, diverse, and dynamic financial industry. We believe that the checks and balances of the dual system of federal and state supervision are more likely to result in

comprehensive and meaningful coverage of the industry. From a safety and soundness perspective and from a consumer protection standpoint, the public is better served by a coordinated regulatory network that benefits from both the federal and state perspectives. We believe the Federal Financial Institutions Examination Council (FFIEC) could be much better utilized to accomplish this approach.

Systemwide Focus

The GAO report states "a regulatory system should include a mechanism for identifying, monitoring, and managing risks to the financial system regardless of the source of the risk or the institutions in which it was created." CSBS agrees with this assessment. Our current crisis has shown us that our regulatory structure was incapable of effectively managing and regulating the nation's largest institutions. CSBS believes the solution, however, is not to expand the federal government bureaucracy by creating a new super regulator. Instead, we should enhance coordination and cooperation among the federal government and the states. We believe regulators must pool resources and expertise to better manage systemic risk. The FFIEC provides a vehicle for working towards this goal of seamless federal and state cooperative supervision.

In addition, CSBS provides significant coordination among the states as well as with federal regulators. This coordinating role reached new levels when Congress adopted the Riegle-Neil Act to allow for interstate banking and branching. The states, through CSBS, quickly followed suit by developing the Nationwide Cooperative Agreement and the State-Federal Supervisory Agreement for the supervision of multi-state banks. Most recently, the states launched the Nationwide Mortgage Licensing System (NMLS) and a nationwide protocol for mortgage supervision. Further, the NMLS is the foundation for the recently enacted Secure and Fair Enforcement for Mortgage Licensing Act of 2008, or the S.A.F.E. Act. The S.A.F.E. Act establishes minimum mortgage licensing standards and a coordinated network of state and federal mortgage supervision.

Flexible and Adaptable

CSBS agrees that a regulatory system should be adaptable and forward-looking so that regulators can readily adapt to market innovations and chances to include a mechanism for evaluating potential new risks to the system. In fact, this is one of the greatest strengths of the state system. The traditional dynamic of the dual-banking system of regulation has been that the states experiment with new products, services, and practices that, upon successful implementation, Congress later enacts on a nationwide basis. In addition, state bank examiners are often the first to identify and address economic problems. Often, states are the first responders to almost any problem in the financial system. The states can—and do—respond to these problems much more quickly than the federal government as evidenced by escalating state responses to the excesses and abuses of mortgage lending over the past decade. Unfortunately, the federal response was to thwart rather than encourage these policy responses.

Efficient and Effective

In the report, GAO asserts that a system should provide for efficient and effective oversight by eliminating overlapping federal regulatory missions and minimizing regulatory burden. CSBS believes efficiency must not be achieved at the cost of protecting consumers, providing for a competitive industry that serves all communities or maintaining the safety and soundness of financial institutions. We recognize that our regulatory structure is complex and may not be as efficient as some in the industry would prefer. There is undoubtedly a need for improved coordination and cooperation among functional regulators. However, this efficiency must not be met through the haphazard consolidation or destruction of supervisory agencies and authorities. CSBS strongly believes that it is more important to preserve a regulatory framework with checks and balances among and between regulators. This overlap does not need to be a negative characteristic of our system. Instead, it has most often offered additional protection for our consumers and institutions. We believe that the weakening of these overlays in recent years weakened our system and contributed to the current crisis.

In addition, we should consider how "efficient" is defined. Efficient does not inherently mean effective. Our ideal regulatory structure should balance what is efficient for large and small institutions as well as what is efficient for consumers and our economy. While a centralized and consolidated regulatory system may look efficient on paper or benefit our largest institutions, the outcomes may be inflexible and be geared solely at the largest banks at the expense of the small community institutions, the consumer or our diverse economy.

Consistent Consumer and Investor Protection

The states have long been regarded as leaders in the consumer protection arena. This is an area where the model of states acting as laboratories of innovation is clearly working. State authorities often discover troubling practices, trends, or warning signs before the federal agencies can identify these emerging concerns. State authorities and legislature then are able to respond quickly to protect consumers. Ultimately, Congress and federal regulators can then rely on state experience to develop uniform and nationwide standards or best practices. Ultimately, we believe the federal government is simply not able to respond quickly enough to emerging threats and consumer protection issues. State authorities have also been frustrated by federal preemption of state consumer protection laws. If Congress were to act to repeal or more clearly limit these preemptions, states would be able to more effectively and consistently enforce consumer protection laws.

CSBS also agrees that there were significant loopholes and unequal regulation and examination of the mortgage industry. In fact, the states led the way to address these regulatory gaps. However, in describing where subprime lending occurred, we believe the report should acknowledge the fact that subprime lending took place in nearly equal parts between nonbank lenders and institutions subject to federal bank regulation. Federal regulation of operating subsidiaries has been inconsistent at best and nonexistent at worst. As acknowledged in the report, affiliate regulation for consumer compliance simply did not exist at the federal level until a recent pilot project led by the Federal Reserve was initiated.

The report also fails to acknowledge the very significant reforms of mortgage regulation adopted by Congress under the S.A.F.E. Act or the major efforts the states have engaged in to regulate the nonbank mortgage lenders and originators.

Regulators Provided with Independence, Prominence, Authority, and Accountability
The dual-banking system helps preserve both regulator independence and accountability. The state system of chartering, with an independent primary federal regulator probably serves as the best model for this goal.

Consistent Financial Oversight
Consistency in regulation is important, but our financial system must also be flexible enough to allow our diverse institutions all to flourish. The diversity of our nation's banking system has created the most dynamic and powerful economy in the world, regardless of the current problems we are experiencing. The strength at the core of our banking system is that it is comprised of thousands of financial intuitions of vastly different sizes. Even as our largest banks are struggling to survive, the vast majority of community banks remains strong and continues to provide financial services to their local citizens. It is vital that a one-size-fits-all regulatory system does not adversely affect the industry by putting smaller banks at a competitive disadvantage with larger, more complex institutions.

It is our belief that the report should acknowledge the role of federal preemption of state consumer protections and the lack of responsiveness of federal law and regulation to mortgage lending and consumer protection issues. For example, the states began responding in 1999 to circumventions of HOEPA and consumer abuses related to subprime lending. Nine years later and two years into a nationwide subprime crisis and Congress has not yet been able to adopt a predatory lending law. We believe that some industry advocates have pushed for preemption to prevent the states from being able to develop legislative and regulatory models for consumer protection and because they have been successful in thwarting legislation and significant regulation at the federal level.

Minimal Taxpayer Exposure
CSBS strongly agrees that a regulatory system should have adequate safeguards that allow financial institution failures to occur while limiting taxpayers' exposure to financial risk. Part of this process must be to prevent institutions from becoming "too big to fail," "too systemic to fail," or simply too big to regulate. Specifically, the federal government must have regulatory tools in place to manage the orderly failure of the largest institutions rather than continuing to prop up failed systemic institutions.

CSBS Principles of Regulatory Reform
While numerous proposals will be advanced to overhaul the financial regulatory system, CSBS believes the structure of the regulatory system should:

1. Usher in a new era of cooperative federalism, recognizing the rights of states to protect consumers and reaffirming the state role in chartering and supervising financial institutions.
2. Foster supervision that is tailored to the size, scope, and complexity of the institution and the risk they pose to the financial system.
3. Assure the promulgation and enforcement of consumer protection standards that are applicable to both state and nationally chartered financial institutions and are enforceable by locally-responsive state officials against all such institutions.
4. Encourage a diverse universe of financial institutions as a method of reducing risk to the system, encouraging competition, furthering innovation, insuring access to financial markets, and promoting efficient allocation of credit.
5. Support community and regional banks, which provide relationship lending and fuel local economic development.
6. Require financial institutions that are recipients of governmental protection or pose systemic risk to be subject to safety and soundness and consumer protection oversight.

The states, through CSBS and the State Liaison Committee's involvement on the FFIEC, will be part of any solution to regulatory restructuring or our current economic condition. We want to ensure consumers are protected, and preserve the viability of both the federal and state charter to ensure the success of our dual-banking system and our economy as a whole.

CSBS believes there is significant work to be done on this issue, and we commend the GAO for undertaking this report.

Best regards,

John W. Ryan
Executive Vice President

APPENDIX VI: COMMENTS FROM CONSUMERS UNION

Consumers Union

Via Electronic Mail

December 16, 2008

Ms. Orice M. Williams
Director, Financial Markets and Community Investment
U.S. Government Accountability Office
441 G Street, N.W.
Washington, DC 20548

Re: GAO Report on Reforming the Financial Regulatory System

Dear Ms. Williams,

Consumers Union, the nonprofit publisher of *Consumer Reports*, is deeply interested in creating a more effective structure for the regulation of financial institutions and other participants in the financial markets. Financial regulation must be designed to protect individuals as consumers of credit and deposit services, as investors, and as taxpayers.

The spark for the financial crisis was unsuitable, poorly underwritten loans being sold to individual homeowners. The risk was amplified by widespread sale of financial instruments based on those mortgages. The resulting crisis of confidence has led to reduced credibility for the U.S. financial system, gridlocked credit markets, loss of equity for homeowners who accepted subprime mortgages and for their neighbors who did not, empty houses and reduced property tax revenue.

Any future financial regulatory structure must include active federal and state oversight, a priority on consumer protection, steps to make the pricing and features of financial products less complex, and more accountability by financial entities at each step of a financial transaction.

1. **Regulators must be required to proactively monitor new products and practices to address dangers before they spread.** Financial system regulators must identify, evaluate, and mitigate emerging risks both to the financial system and to individuals. Regulators must abandon the old "wait and see" regulatory approach, where a problem has to grow to be national in scope, and perhaps be in the public eye, before it is addressed. Financial regulators must have independence from the entities they oversee and an express charge to regulate for the prevention of harm both to individuals and to the financial system.

2. **Financial system regulators should give the same priority to consumer protection as to safety and soundness.** The mortgage crisis and its aftermath dramatically illustrate that the consumer protection and safety and soundness are inextricably linked. Regulators must increase the priority placed on consumer protection.

West Coast Office
1535 Mission Street • San Francisco, CA 94104
tel: 415.431.6747 • fax: 415.431.0906 • www.consumersunion.org

3. Practices and features that make financial products sold to individuals too complex to understand must be stopped. The report speaks in several places about the need for financial literacy or improved disclosure. However, financial products which are too complex for the intended consumer carry special risks that no amount of additional disclosure or information will fix. In subprime mortgages, for example, many homeowners were induced to refinance an existing loan for one that would offer a reduced payment for just the first two years. Others were assured that they could refinance later, yet the loan documents contained an expensive prepayment penalty. Many of the tens of thousands of individuals who filed comments in the Federal Reserve Board's Regulation AA docket on unfair or deceptive credit card practices reported that they learned about harmful card issuer practices apparently permitted by the cardholder agreement only when the practice was first invoked against them. Regulatory reform will be incomplete unless regulators identify and stop practices that make credit and deposit products difficult for individuals to understand and evaluate.

4. Federal and state regulatory diversity is essential to robust oversight. We agree with report that it is important to eliminate the bottlenecks that can be caused by the coordination process between multiple federal regulators. However, no single federal agency leader can foresee all of the consequences of new practices and products. For this reason, Consumers Union supports both an independent federal consumer protection agency for financial services products (with concurrent jurisdiction with existing banking agencies), and the power of states to develop and enforce consumer protections. The swift and troubling developments in the financial meltdown show that we cannot rely on a single federal agency leader to anticipate all of the risks in new practices and products, nor to have the inclination or the resources to pursue all of the areas where law enforcement is needed.

5. Accountability must be built into the financial system. During the build-up to the crisis, loan originators and securitization packagers got fees even if loans couldn't later be repaid. Regulatory restructuring should include changing the incentives in the private market by requiring that everyone who gets a fee in connection with a credit product also keeps some of the risk of future nonpayment and the risk of problems with the loan. In addition, everyone who offers financial products to consumers should be subject to suitability requirements and fiduciary duties.

We appreciate the work of the GAO in this important issue area. Creating a strong, trusted regulatory structure for financial products and the financial markets is essential to rebuilding the public confidence in the U.S. financial markets.

Very truly yours,

Gail Hillebrand
Financial Services Campaign Manager
Consumers Union of U.S., Inc.

APPENDIX VII: COMMENTS FROM THE CREDIT UNION NATIONAL ASSOCIATION

CUNA
Credit Union National Association
601 Pennsylvania Ave., NW | South Building, Suite 600 | Washington, DC 20004-2601 | PHONE: 202-638-5777 | FAX: 202-638-7734
cuna.org

December 18, 2008

Mr. Cody Goebel
Assistant Director
Financial Markets and Community Investment U.S. Government Accountability Office
441 G Street, NW, Room 2440B
Washington, DC 20548

Dear Mr. Goebel:

On behalf of the Credit Union National Association, thank you for the opportunity Bill Hampel, Ryan Donovan, and I had December 12, 2008 to review the Government Accountability Office's draft report on restructuring the financial regulatory system. CUNA is the largest advocacy organization representing the nation's 8,200 state and federal credit unions, which serve approximately 91 million members.

The report's treatment of credit unions is understandably abbreviated, given the fact that credit unions were not the cause of the financial market meltdown – although a limited number have experienced serious collateral effects. In line with GAO's approach, our letter focuses only on the independence of the National Credit Union Administration Board.

Unlike the Treasury's "Blueprint for Financial Modernization," which reflects a complete disregard for and lack of understanding of credit unions, the GAO draft stops short of offering specific recommendations. Even so, the report indicates there is merit to consideration of regulatory consolidation for certain purposes, such as consumer protection, and to address threats to the overall stability of the financial system. While we recognize the factors that support such consideration and appreciate that with four federal bank regulators, some consolidation there may be appropriate, we would strongly oppose any efforts to combine NCUA or its insurance function with another agency, as addressed below.

The draft report sets out several defined goals for an appropriate regulatory system, which include: a comprehensive approach to regulation that is system wide, flexible, efficient, and independent while providing consistent consumer protection and financial oversight.

CUNA likewise supports these objectives, which we believe are wholly consistent with the continuation of a separate regulator for credit unions. Earlier this month, CUNA's Governmental Affairs Committee reaffirmed strong support for a distinct

CREDIT UNIONS

Mary Dunn
December 18, 2008
Page 2 of 2

federal regulator as long as it provides rigorous, effective supervision that enhances their financial strength and is well-tailored to the level of risk credit unions demonstrate. At the same time, credit unions need and deserve a regulator that will facilitate, not stymie, their capabilities to provide innovative yet safe services to their consumer-members at favorable rates. While urging NCUA's independence, credit unions also appreciate the need for the agencies to address certain issues collectively, and to that end CUNA has recommended NCUA be included in the Presidential Working Group, which is currently comprised of the banking regulators but not NCUA.

Another goal the GAO draft includes is to minimize taxpayers' exposure in the event problems arise. To that end, the credit union regulatory structure combines the enforcement of demanding safety and soundness standards under NCUA's prompt corrective action provisions with an approach that seeks to contain credit union problems within the system. Virtually all of the funds to operate NCUA and the NCUSIF are provided by the credit union system, without reliance on taxpayer dollars, and since its inception in 1978, the NCUSIF has achieved a commendable record in managing problem cases and avoiding taxpayer losses. Another example of credit unions' self-sustaining efforts is their advocacy for the use of NCUSIF funds to purchase troubled assets from the limited number of natural person credit unions that might need such assistance first, before seeking back-up assistance from the Treasury's Troubled Asset Relief Program.

For many credit unions, maintaining a separate regulator is critical to their preservation as institutions with fundamentally different motivations than other financial intermediaries have. Credit unions are operated by volunteer boards who do not receive economic inducements to serve but rather serve to meet the financial needs of their member-owners. Banks are motivated by the need to reward their stockholders first, and then their customers. Because of these core differences, only a separate, effective regulator will provide the singular focus necessary to further credit unions' distinctiveness, thereby ensuring consumers will continue to have choices in the financial marketplace.

Again, thank you for the opportunity to provide these comments following the review of your draft. Please do not hesitate to contact any one of us if you have questions about credit unions or this letter. All the best for happy holidays.

Sincerely,

Mary Mitchell Dunn

Mary Mitchell Dunn
CUNA Deputy General Counsel and
Senior Vice President

APPENDIX VIII: COMMENTS FROM THE FEDERAL DEPOSIT INSURANCE CORPORATION

FDIC

Federal Deposit Insurance Corporation
550 17th Street NW, Washington, D.C. 20429-9990 Division of Supervision and Consumer Protection

December 10, 2008

Ms. Orice M. Williams
Director, Financial Markets and Community Investment
U.S. Government Accountability Office
441 G Street, N.W.
Washington, D.C. 20548

Dear Ms. Williams:

The FDIC appreciates the opportunity to provide comments on the GAO's report titled Financial Regulation: A Framework for Crafting and Assessing Proposals to Modernize the Outdated U.S. Financial Regulatory System. We understand that this report is self-initiated, and is intended to provide a set of principles by which policymakers can evaluate various proposals to restructure the U.S. financial regulatory system. We commend the GAO for undertaking this important project.

As an overarching premise, the report states that the U.S. financial regulatory structure is in need of modernization. The FDIC agrees that effective reform of the U.S. financial regulatory system would help avoid a recurrence of the economic and financial problems we are now experiencing.

As we consider recent experience, two issues related to U.S. financial regulatory performance stand out to us as being of particular concern. First, our regulatory structure collectively did not address a systematic breakdown in lending standards in wide segments of the U.S. mortgage market. An important lesson that should be incorporated in any regulatory reform proposal is that irresponsible or abusive lending practices are consistent neither with safe-and-sound banking nor with sustainable economic growth.

Second, the regulatory structure collectively permitted excessive leverage in the non-bank financial system. Facing no explicit leverage constraints, and lulled by quantitative models and agency ratings into believing risks were minimal, a variety of large investment banks, financial guarantee insurers and hedge funds operated with a degree of leverage that significantly diminished their ability to withstand financial stress. An important lesson from recent years is that unconstrained leverage places not only individual firms at risk, but greatly increases the severity of financial market downturns and imposes significant costs on taxpayers.

These two issues were not addressed as effectively as they should have been, in part because of regulatory gaps, and in part because of regulatory choices about how to exercise existing authority. Thus, while the role of regulatory structure is an important part of improving regulatory performance, statutory mandates for the regulators are of equal importance. Existing prompt corrective action law is a good example of a successful mandate. Any regulatory reform proposal should include consideration of appropriate mandates in the area of consumer protection. For example, some lending practices can be so egregious as to warrant their outright prohibition, as opposed to placing sole reliance on promoting financial literacy or improving disclosures. Regulatory reform proposals should also consider statutory mandates for leverage constraints for non-bank financial firms, and well-defined mechanisms to protect taxpayers from the cost of financial bailouts.

We believe the experience of recent years strongly supports the importance of an independent FDIC with the resources and authority to safeguard the government's financial stake in federal deposit insurance and promote public confidence in the banking system. The FDIC's independent perspective has been evidenced in recent years by its actions addressing both individual troubled financial institutions and systemic risk, strengthening our deposit insurance system, ensuring capital safeguards in the implementation of Basel II's advanced approaches, and promoting confidence in the banking system by promoting financial literacy, educating consumers about deposit insurance and taking actions to protect consumers.

Thank you once again for the opportunity to comment on this report. As always, we have appreciated the professionalism with which the GAO's review team conducted this assignment.

Sincerely,

Sandra L. Thompson
Director

APPENDIX IX: COMMENTS FROM THE MORTGAGE BANKERS ASSOCIATION

MORTGAGE BANKERS ASSOCIATION®
Investing in communities

December 18, 2008

Ms. Orice M. Williams
Director, Financial Markets and Community Investment
U.S. Government Accountability Office
441 G Street, N.W.
Washington, D.C. 20548

Dear Ms. Williams:

The Mortgage Bankers Association greatly appreciates the opportunity to comment on the forthcoming report of the United States Government Accountability Office entitled "Financial Regulation: A Framework for Crafting and Assessing Proposals to Modernize the Outdated U.S. Regulatory System." MBA strongly supports the improvement of the regulatory requirements and the regulatory structure for mortgage lending and commends GAO's efforts in this vital area.

MBA's main comments are that the report should recognize that: (1) responsibility for the current financial crisis is diffuse; (2) solutions recommended for the lending sphere should include consideration of a uniform mortgage lending standard that is preemptive of state lending standards; and (3) federal regulation of at least independent mortgage bankers deserves discussion.

In MBA's view, the factors contributing to the current crisis are manifold. They include, but are not limited to, traditional factors such as unemployment and family difficulties, high real estate prices and overbuilding, extraordinary appetites for returns, lowering of lending standards to satisfy investor and borrower needs, the growth of unregulated and lightly regulated entities and, to some degree, borrower misjudgment and even fraud.

In MBA's view no single actor or actors can fairly be assigned sole or even predominant blame for where we are today. On the other hand, MBA strongly believes that all of these factors contributing to the crisis deserve review as we fashion regulatory solutions. Specifically, respecting mortgage lending, MBA believes that the crisis presents an unparalleled opportunity to reevaluate the current regulatory requirements and structure for mortgage lending to protect the nation going forward.

MBA has long supported establishment of a uniform national mortgage lending standard that establishes strong federal protections, preempts the web of state laws and updates and expands federal requirements. Currently, lending is governed, and consumers are protected by, a patchwork of more than 30 different state laws which are piled on top of federal requirements. Some state laws are overly intrusive and some are weak. The federal requirements in some cases are duplicative and in some areas are out-of-date. In some states, there are no lending laws and borrowers have little protection beyond federal requirements.

December 18, 2008
GAO Comment Letter
Page 2

MBA believes legislators should look at the most effective state and federal approaches and work with stakeholders to fashion a new uniform standard which is appropriately up-to-date, robust, applies to every lender, and protects every borrower. It should be enacted by the Congress and preempt state laws. A uniform standard would help restore investor confidence and be the most effective and least costly means of protecting consumers against lending abuses nationwide. Having one standard would avoid undue compliance costs, facilitate competition and ultimately decrease consumer costs.

MBA recognizes that one of the key objections to a preemptive national standard is that it would not be flexible and adaptable and preclude state responses to future abuse. MBA believes this problem is surmountable and could be resolved by injecting dynamism into the law. One approach would be to supplement the law as needed going forward with new prohibitions and requirements formulated by federal and state officials in consultation.

Currently, some mortgage lenders are regulated as federal depository institutions, some as state depositories and some as state-regulated non-depositories. MBA believes that along with establishment of a uniform standard, a new federal regulator for independent mortgage bankers and mortgage brokers should be considered and MBA is interested in exploring that possibility.

A new regulator should have sufficient authorities to assure prudent operations to address financing needs of consumers. If such an approach is adopted, states also could maintain a partnership with the federal regulator in examination, enforcement and licensing. MBA believes the combined efforts of state and federal officials in regulatory reviews and enforcement under a uniform standard would greatly increase regulatory effectiveness and focus.

Notably, any new regulatory scheme should address the differing regulatory concerns presented by mortgage bankers and by mortgage brokers, considering their differing functions and the differing policy concerns which the respective industries present. MBA has written extensively on this subject and commends to GAO's attention the attached report entitled *Mortgage Bankers and Mortgage Brokers: Distinct Businesses Warranting Distinct Regulation* (2008).

Again, MBA strongly believes today's financial difficulties present an unparalleled opportunity to establish better regulation in the years to come. Today's financial crisis reminds us daily that financial markets are national and international in scope. As the crisis worsened, the world looked to national and international governments for solutions. MBA believes it would be unwise not to use this moment to establish a national standard and cease dispersing regulatory responsibility, to help prevent crises ahead.

Thank you again for the opportunity to comment.

Sincerely,

John A. Courson

John A. Courson
Chief Operating Officer
Mortgage Bankers Association

APPENDIX X: COMMENTS FROM THE NATIONAL ASSOCIATION OF FEDERAL CREDIT UNIONS

National Association of Federal Credit Unions
3138 10th Street North • Arlington, VA 22201-2149
(703) 522-4770 • (800) 336-4644 • Fax (703) 524-1082
NAFCU www.nafcu.org • nafcu@nafcu.org

December 15, 2008

Orice M. Williams
Director
Financial Markets and Community Investment
U.S. Government Accountability Office
441 G Street, NW
Washington, D.C. 20548

RE: Report of the U.S. Government Accountability Office on the Financial Markets and Financial Regulatory Structure

Dear Ms. Williams:

On behalf of the National Association of Federal Credit Unions (NAFCU), the only trade association that exclusively represents the interests of our nation's federal credit unions (FCUs), I am providing the following comments regarding the upcoming report by the U.S. Government Accountability Office (GAO) regarding the state of the financial industry and the regulatory structure.

NAFCU would first like to express our appreciation for the opportunity to meet with GAO staff and to review the draft GAO Report. As a trade association that represents federal credit unions, which are uniquely structured to provide provident thrift at lower cost to persons whom they are chartered to serve, we believe we provide unique and specific insight regarding the crisis in the financial sector and the regulatory structure under which financial institutions operate. We applaud the GAO for preparing a well written draft Report. We would like, however, to use this opportunity to provide the following specific comments and suggestions.

References to Credit Unions

The draft Report references comprehensive regulations to which "some institutions, such as banks ..." are subject. To ensure that readers of the Report do not misunderstand, we request the Report adds "credit unions." We specifically ask that the phrase "credit unions" is added in the following places of the draft report: (1) page 5 after "For example, some institutions, such as banks"; (2) page 8, line 1 after the word "banks"; and (3) on page 23, in the first full paragraph, add "credit unions" after "banks" and before "broker-dealers."

Ms. Orice M. Williams
December 15, 2008
Page 2 of 2

Also, we ask that the phrase "non-credit union" is added after "non-bank" on page 17, Figure 2. Similarly, "non-credit unions" should follow "non-banks" on page 23 in the subheading that presently reads "Activities of NonBank Mortgage Lenders Played A Significant Role." As you are aware, the non-banks referenced in the figure are also non-credit unions. As such, we believe the figure would be clearer if it more clearly explains that the non-banks are also not credit unions.

Framework for Regulatory Restructuring

A key aspect of the draft report is the provision of nine elements as a framework to restructure the financial regulatory system. While we believe the framework contains sound ideas, we strongly recommend that you fully incorporate the need to ensure that smaller institutions, particularly credit unions, are not inadvertently overlooked in any restructuring that Congress may institute.

We are particularly concerned about Element Two and Element Eight. Element Two recommends a single "market stability regulator." Element Eight recommends consistent financial oversight. As we have previously expressed to GAO staff, we believe an independent regulator should continue to oversee and examine federal credit unions. The distinctive characteristics of federal credit unions, including their cooperative structure and mission to provide provident service at lower cost to those they are chartered to serve, necessitates that they are regulated by an independent entity. Accordingly, we request that these two elements are revised to reflect the need of an independent regulator for federal credit unions.

NAFCU appreciates this opportunity to share its comments on this interim rule. Should you have any questions or require additional information please call me at (703) 522-4770 or (800) 336-4644 ext. 268.

Sincerely,

Tessema Tefferi
Associate Director of Regulatory Affairs

Appendix XI: Comments from the Center for Responsible Lending, the National Consumer Law Center, and the U.S. PIRG

December 16, 2008

VIA EMAIL AND U.S. MAIL

Ms. Orice M. Williams (williamso@gao.gov)
Director, Financial Markets and Community Investment
U.S. Government Accountability Office
441 G Street, N.W.
Washington, D.C. 20548

with copies via email to:
Mr. Cody Goebel, Assistant Director (goebelc@gao.gov)
Mr. Randall Fasnacht (fasnachtr@gao.gov)

Re: Comments on Draft Report, GAO-09-216

Dear Ms. Williams:

We appreciate the opportunity to review the draft report at your offices on December 4, and to offer comments. These are offered jointly by CRL, the National Consumer Law Center and USPIRG.

The report is a thoughtful and thorough review of the structural issues regarding regulatory reform.. We especially appreciate that your report notes the problem of charter competition and the distorting impact of the funding structure for the banking regulators.

We would like to preface our comments by stating the obvious – that this review does not occur in a vacuum, but rather in the context of a major crisis which exposed fundamental weaknesses on many fronts. The structural problems in the federal regulator system are but one. Some of these comments derive not from the specific content of the report, but the messages conveyed by some of the references to other aspects of the crisis, such as the nature of the market and consumer behavior. Another especially important comment derives as much from what is left unsaid. Perhaps it seems as though it should go without saying, but given much of the debate that this crisis has engendered, we fear that without at least an acknowledgement of what is not addressed by your report, necessary reminders of other integral parts of regulatory reform may be lost.

While the structure of regulation can create its own problems, such as the potential for charter competition and regulatory capture that you note, regulators also need tools (in the form of laws to enforce, or directives to promulgate rules in furtherance of such laws), adequate resources and, above all, the will to regulate. No amount of structural reform will succeed if regulators have no charge to fulfill in their job, nor the will to do so. We have had three decades of a deregulatory agenda, and without a change in that overarching view, structural changes will be insufficient. We recognize that the prevailing philosophy of regulation was not the focus of this report. However, we believe that any discussion of regulatory structural reform must be accompanied by an explicit caveat that it addresses only one aspect of the overall regulatory issues that contributed to this crisis, and that changing the structure, alone, will be insufficient if these other necessary conditions for effective oversight are not reformed, as well.

Beyond that overarching context for regulatory reform, we offer the following comments.

1. The best way to avoid systemic risk is to address problems that exist at the level of individual consumer transactions, before they pose a threat to the system as a whole.

The report appropriately addresses the need to effectively monitor and regulate problems that threaten the financial system as a whole. However, the most effective way to address systemic risk is to identify market failures that threaten abuse of individual consumers, and to address these failures before they threaten the system as a whole. The crisis today would not have reached its current state had problems been addressed and prevented before they evolved into the foreclosure epidemic now underway.

The report correctly notes that most *subprime* lending was done by nonbank lenders who were not subject to oversight by the federal banking agencies.[1] However, the market failures that contributed to the current crisis are not limited to the subprime market. The failure of the Alt-A market, including poorly underwritten non-traditional loans, are also significant contributors, as is becoming increasingly apparent. The failures of IndyMac and Washington Mutual, among others, are largely the function of overly aggressive lending of risky products that were unsuitable for far too many borrowers, and these did occur under the watch of the federal banking agencies. Though the federal banking agencies issued some guidelines for nontraditional lending, it was too little and too late. Further, to judge from the performance of the late vintages of these loans, even then, they were insufficiently enforced.

But in any case, neither bank nor nonbank lenders were subject to adequate consumer protection laws. Both banks and non-bank lenders pressed legislators and regulators not to enact such protections. Furthermore, banks subject to federal regulation also contributed to the problem by being part of the secondary market's demand for the risky products that permeated the subprime and Alt-A markets.[2] The report should make clear that to adequately protect consumers, and avoid systemic risk in the future, whatever regulatory structure emerges will need to be more robust and effective in protecting consumers than the current system has been to date.

---

[1] Further, the threat of federal preemption and its absence of suitable consumer protection gave the nonbank lenders the argument that they just wanted a "level playing field," --on a field largely without rules. To that extent, the regulatory structure played into the separate thread of whether there were adequate tools for regulators. The preemption agenda was part of the momentum to the lowest common denominator for the substance of regulation.

[2] Recent studies have found that the securitization process in fact contributed to the aggressive lending and poor underwriting. *See, e.g.* Benjamin J. Keys, Tanmoy Mikherjee, Amit Seru, Vikrant Vig, *Securitization and Screening: Evidence From Subprime Mortgage Backed Securities*, pp. 26-27 (January 2008), available at http://www2.law.columbia.edu/contracteconomics/conferences/laweconomics S08/Vig%20paper.pdf

2. To effectively protect consumers the regulatory system must prohibit unsustainable lending; disclosures and "financial literacy" are not enough.

The fundamental problem at the heart of today's crisis is that loan originators pushed borrowers into loan products that were inherently risky and unsustainable by design, and they did so notwithstanding the availability of the more suitable and affordable loans for which they qualified.[3] The most common product in the subprime market in recent years was not merely an adjustable rate mortgage, but rather an adjustable rate mortgage with built-in payment shock that lenders anticipated most borrowers could not afford, but that they could avoid only by refinancing before the payment shock took effect, typically paying typically 3% to 4% of the loan balance as a "prepayment penalty" in order to refinance.

According to a Wall Street Journal study, 55% of the borrowers who received such loans in 2005, and 60% of those who received them in 2006, had credit scores high enough to have qualified for lower cost prime loans.[4] And even those borrowers who did not qualify for prime could have had 30-year fixed rate loans for approximately 65 basis points above the introductory rate on the loans they received.[5] The report suggests incorrectly (pp. 43-44) that subprime loans "help[] borrowers afford houses" they could not otherwise afford, when in fact, most subprime loans refinanced existing loans, rather than purchased new homes.[6] But in either case, had borrowers been offered the more suitable loans for which many qualified, many more borrowers could have sustained homeownership.[7]

The experience with the recent vintages of Alt-A loans are similarly instructive: Chris Ferrell, an economics editor with the NPR program Marketplace referred to the Payment Option ARM product (many of which are Alt-A) as "the most complicated mortgage product ever marketed to consumers." The greater the complexity, the less suitable that disclosure is as a "market perfecting" tool. Further, the huge jump in payment option ARMS, (from $145 billion to $255 billion from 2004-2007), was primarily possible only by the increasingly poor underwriting. Countrywide, one of the major issuers of these

---

[3] For more detail on causes of the crisis, *see* Testimony of Eric Stein, Center for Responsible Lending, Before the U.S. Senate Committee on Banking, Housing and Urban Affairs (October 16, 2008), http://banking.senate.gov/public/_files/RevisedSenateTestimony101608HearingSteinFinalFinal.pdf.

[4] Rick Brooks and Ruth Simon, *Subprime Debacle Traps Even Very Credit-Worthy As Housing Boomed, Industry Pushed Loans To a Broader Market*, Wall Street Journal at A1 (Dec. 3, 2007).

[5] Letter from Coalition for Fair & Affordable Lending to Ben S. Bernanke, Sheila C. Bair, John C. Dugan, John M. Reich, JoAnn Johnson, and Neil Milner (Jan. 25, 2007) at 3.

[6] *See, e.g.* Subprime Lending: *A Net Drain on Homeownership*, CRL Issue Paper, No. 14 (March 27, 2007).

[7] *See, e.g.* Lei Ding, Roberto G. Quercia, Wei Li, and Janneke Ratcliffe, *Risky Borrowers or Risky Mortgages: Disaggregating Effects Using Propensity Score Models*, Center for Community Capital, Univ. of North Carolina & Center for Responsible Lending (Working Paper, Sept. 13, 2008).

loans (that issued them under both its national bank and federal thrift charters, as well as some of its non-depository entities) admitted that an estimated 80% of its recent PCARMs would not meet the late 2006 federal guidelines.[8]

The Federal Reserve has noted that, given the misaligned incentives of originators and the complexity of products and loan features, even with increased information or knowledge, borrowers could not have defended against poorly underwritten, risky products and deceptive practices. The main problem with these loans was not the inadequacy of the disclosures or the financial literacy of the borrowers. Rather, the fundamental problem was that -- as the federal banking regulators belatedly recognized with respect to non-traditional loans in late 2006 and subprime lending in 2007 -- lenders should not have made loans that they knew borrowers would be unable to sustain without refinancing.

3. To effectively protect consumers, the regulatory system must monitor and address market incentives that encourage loan originators to push risky or unsuitable loan products.

The report correctly notes that market incentives encouraged loan originators to extend excessive credit (p. 22). It should also note that these same incentives encouraged them to push riskier productions and features than the borrowers qualified for.[9] The report should note the need for regulatory oversight of market failures that reward market participants for irresponsible behavior.

We understand that philosophies of consumer protection and the adequacy of consumer protection laws is not your intended focus. However, there were occasional statements in the report which, intended or not, seemed to convey a message that improved disclosure or literacy would be adequate. Yet more people -- including some of the regulators themselves -- are recognizing that in an era of highly complex products and unseen perverse incentives, disclosure is an insufficient tool, and literacy is an elusive goal.

We would be happy to provide further information.

---

[8] Countrywide, *3Q 07 Earnings Supplemental Presentation* (October 26, 2007). To again emphasize that the federal banking regulators contributed to the problem, some $161 billion of those payment option ARMs were issued when Countrywide was under the OCC's watch.

[9] After filing for bankruptcy, the CEO of one mortgage lender explained it this way to the New York Times, "The market is paying me to do a no-income-verification loan more than it is paying me to do the full documentation loans," he said. "What would you do?" Vikas Bajaj and Christine Haughney, *Tremors at the Door: More People with Weak Credit Are Defaulting on Mortgages*, New York Times (January 26, 2007).

Sincerely,

Center for Responsible Lending

National Consumer Law Center

US PIRG

Contacts:

Ellen Harnick

Center for Responsible Lending

Ellen.Harnick@ResponsibleLending.org

919-313-8553

Kathleen Keest

Center For Responsible Lending

Kathleen.Keest@ResponsibleLending.org

919-313-8548

End Notes

[1] For more information about these activities, see GAO, *Troubled Asset Relief Program: Additional Actions Needed to Better Ensure Integrity, Accountability, and Transparency,* GAO-09-161 (Washington, D.C.: Dec. 2, 2008).

[2] Throughout this chapter, we use the term "financial regulatory system" to refer broadly to both the financial regulatory structure—that is, the number and organization of financial regulatory agencies—as well as other aspects of financial regulation, including agency responsibilities, and mechanisms and authorities available to agencies for fulfilling such responsibilities.

[3] See Department of the Treasury, *Blueprint for a Modernized Financial Regulatory Structure* (Washington, D.C., March 2008); Financial Services Roundtable, *The Blueprint for U.S. Financial Services Competitiveness* (Washington, D.C., Nov. 7, 2007); Timothy F. Geithner, President and Chief Executive Officer, Federal Reserve Bank of New York, "Reducing Systemic Risk in a Dynamic Financial System" (speech, New York, June 9, 2008); and Ben S. Bernanke, Chairman, Federal Reserve, "Reducing Systemic Risk" (speech, Jackson Hole, Wyo., Aug. 22, 2008).

[4] Pub. L. No. 110-343, § 105(c).

[5] For example, see GAO, *Financial Regulation: Industry Trends Continue to Challenge the Federal Regulatory Structure,* GAO-08-32 (Washington, D.C.: Oct. 12, 2007); and *Financial Regulation: Industry Changes Prompt Need to Reconsider U.S. Regulatory Structure,* GAO-05-61 (Washington, D.C.: Oct. 6, 2004). See Related GAO Products appendix for additional reports.

[6] Staff at the Federal Reserve Banks act as supervisors in conjunction with the Board.

[7] Thrifts, also known as savings and loans, are financial institutions that accept deposits and make loans, particularly for home mortgages. Until 1989, thrift deposits were federally insured by the Federal Savings and Loan Insurance Corporation (FSLIC), which was created by the National Housing Act of 1934. After experiencing solvency problems in connection with the savings and loan crisis of the 1980s, FSLIC was abolished and its insurance function was transferred to FDIC.

[8] The Securities Act of 1933 (1933 Act), 48 Stat. 74. et. seq., assigned federal supervision of securities to the Federal Trade Commission (FTC) by, among other things, requiring that securities offerings subject to the act's registration requirements be registered with the FTC. See 1933 Act, §§ 2, 5, 6 (May 27, 1933). In the 1934 act, Congress replaced the FTC's role by transferring its powers, duties, and functions under the 1933 act to SEC. See Securities Exchange Act of 1934, 48 Stat. 881, §§ 3(a), 210 (June 6, 1934).

[9] The National Securities Markets Improvement Act, Pub. L. No. 104-290 (Oct. 11, 1996), preempted state securities registration requirements for all but a subset of small securities products and limited state supervision of broker-dealers, but left intact the right of states to investigate securities fraud.

[10] Credit unions are member-owned financial institutions that generally offer their members services similar to those provided by banks.

[11] Home Owners' Loan Act of 1933, 48 Stat. 128 (June 13, 1933). The administration of the Federal Credit Union Act was originally vested in the Farm Credit Administration (Act of June 26, 1934, 48 Stat. 1216.) Executive Order No. 9148, dated April 27, 1942 (7 F.R. 3145), transferred the functions, powers and duties of the Farm Credit Administration to FDIC. Effective July 29, 1948, the powers, duties and functions transferred to FDIC were transferred to the Federal Security Agency. (Act of June 29, 1948, 62 Stat. 1091.) Reorganization Plan No. 1 of 1953, effective April 11, 1953, abolished the Federal Security Agency and transferred the Bureau of Federal Credit Unions, together with other agencies of the Federal Security Agency, to the Department of Health, Education, and Welfare. (67 Stat. 631, 18 F.R. 2053.).

[12] Public Law 91–206 (Mar. 10, 1970, 84 Stat. 49) created the National Credit Union Administration as an independent agency and transferred all of the functions of the Bureau of Federal Credit Unions to the new administration.

[13] Federally insured state credit unions also are subject to supervision by NCUA.

[14] Pub. L. No. 101-73 § 301 (Aug. 9, 1989).

[15] The five federal depository institution regulators discussed earlier coordinate formally through the Federal Financial Institutions Examination Council, an interagency body that was established in 1979 and is empowered to (1) prescribe uniform principles, standards, and report forms for the federal examination of financial institutions; and (2) make recommendations to promote uniformity in the supervision of financial institutions.

[16] The Grain Futures Act (ch. 369, 42 Stat. 998, Sept. 21, 1922). In 1936 the act was renamed the "Commodity Exchange Act (CEA)," which, among other things, created the Commodity Exchange Commission (CEC), a predecessor agency to the Commodity Futures Trading Commission. 49 Stat. 1491 (June 15, 1936).

[17] Commodity Futures Trading Commission Act, Pub. L. No. 93-463 (Oct. 23, 1974).

[18] A derivative is a financial instrument representing a right or obligation based on the value at a particular time of an underlying asset, reference rate, or index, such as a stock, bond, agricultural or other physical commodity, interest rate, currency exchange rate, or stock index. Derivatives contracts are used by firms around the world to manage market risk— the exposure to the possibility of financial loss caused by adverse changes in the values of assets or liabilities—by transferring it from entities less willing or able to manage it to those more willing and able to do so. Common types of derivatives include futures, options, forwards, and swaps and can be traded through an exchange, known as exchange-traded, or privately, known as over-the counter.

[19] Up until 1944, insurance was not considered interstate commerce and, therefore, was not subject to federal regulation. In *United States v. South-Eastern Underwriters Ass'n, 322 U.S. 533* (1944) the Supreme Court held that Congress could regulate insurance transactions that truly are interstate. Congress subsequently enacted the McCarranFerguson Act (Mar. 9, 1945), ch. 20, 59 Stat. 33, which provides that state laws apply to insurance unless they are specifically pre-empted by Congress. See 15 U.S.C. § 1011.

[20] NAIC is made up of the heads of the insurance departments of 50 states, the District of Columbia, and U.S. territories to provide a forum for the development of uniform policy when uniformity is appropriate.

[21] Housing and Economic Recovery Act of 2008, Pub. L. No. 110-289, title I, subtitle A (July 30, 2008).

[22] The 12 Federal Home Loan Banks form a system of regional cooperatives, each with its own president and board of directors, located in different regions of the country. Their statutory mission is to provide cost-effective funding to members for use in housing, community, and economic development; to provide regional affordable housing programs, which create housing opportunities for low- and moderate-income families; to support housing finance through advances and mortgage programs; and to serve as a reliable source of liquidity for its membership.

[23] OFHEO was created in title XIII of the Housing and Community Development Act (1992), Pub. L. No. 102-550 (Oct. 28, 1992). In 1932, the Federal Home Loan Bank Act created the Federal Home Loan Bank System to provide liquidity to thrifts to make home mortgages. Oversight of these responsibilities was later transferred to the Federal Housing Finance Board.

[24] Gramm-Leach-Bliley Act, Pub. L. No. 106-102 (Nov. 12, 1999). Although originally precluded from conducting significant securities underwriting activities, bank holding companies were permitted to conduct more of such activities over the years. For example, in 1987, the Federal Reserve allowed the subsidiaries of bank holding companies to engage in securities underwriting activities up to 5 percent of their revenue. Over time, the

Federal Reserve also expanded the types of securities that banks could conduct business in and raised the revenue limit to 10 percent in 1989 and to 25 percent in 1996.

[25] Pub. L. No. 107-204 (July 30, 2002).

[26] We include discussion of audit and accounting standards in this chapter because any new effort to examine the structure of financial regulation in the United States could include consideration of the process for creating and adopting these standards. However, determining whether the oversight of this process should be changed was not part of the scope of this chapter.

[27] Gianni De Nicoló, Philip Bartholomew, Jahanara Zaman, and Mary Zephirin, "Bank Consolidation, Internationalization, and Conglomeration: Trends and Implications for Financial Risk" (IMF Working Paper 03/158, Washington, D.C., July 2003).

[28] Group of Thirty, *The Structure of Financial Supervision: Approaches and Challenges in a Global Marketplace* (Washington, D.C., 2008). The Group of Thirty, established in 1978, is a private, nonprofit, international body—composed of very senior representatives of the private and public sectors and academia—that consults and publishes papers on international economic and monetary affairs.

[29] GAO, *Financial Market Regulation: Agencies Engaged in Consolidated Supervision Can Strengthen Performance Measurement and Collaboration,* GAO-07-154 (Washington, D.C.: Mar. 15, 2007).

[30] Under the CSE program, which SEC initiated pursuant to its capitalization requirements for broker-dealers, SEC instituted a system for supervising large broker-dealers at the holding company level. See 69 *Fed. Reg.* 34428 (June 21, 2004). Previously, SEC had focused its broker-dealer net capital regulations only upon the firms themselves, not their holding companies or other subsidiaries.

[31] 69 *Fed. Reg.* 34428 at n. 9.

[32] SEC Press Release (2008-230), *Chairman Cox Announces End of Consolidated Supervised Entities Program* (Sept. 26, 2008).

[33] Senate Committee on Banking, Housing, and Urban Affairs, *Condition of the Banking System,* 110th Cong., 2nd sess., June 5, 2008 (testimony of Federal Reserve Vice Chairman Donald L. Kohn).

[34] GAO-07-154.

[35] AIG is subject to OTS supervision as a savings and loan holding company because of its control of a thrift. See, e.g., 12 U.S.C. § 1467a(a)(1)(D), (H).

[36] The President's Working Group on Financial Markets consists of the Secretary of the Treasury, and the Chairmen of the Federal Reserve, SEC, and CFTC.

[37] We have noted limitations on effectively planning strategies that cut across regulatory agencies. See GAO-05-61.

[38] For the purposes of this chapter, nonbank lenders are those that are not banks, thrifts, or credit unions. Such entities include independent mortgage lenders, subsidiaries of national banks, subsidiaries of thrifts, and nonbank mortgage lending subsidiaries of holding companies. Although we include operating subsidiaries of national banks in the category of nonbanks, they are subject to the same federal requirements and OCC supervision and examination as their parent bank, according to an OCC official.

[39] Of the 21 nonbank lenders, 7 were subsidiaries of national banks, thrifts, or holding companies.

[40] GAO, *Consumer Protection: Federal and State Agencies Face Challenges in Combating Predatory Lending,* GAO-04-280 (Washington, D.C.: Jan. 30, 2004); *Alternative Mortgage Products: Impact on Defaults Remains Unclear, but Disclosure of Risks to Borrowers Could Be Improved,* GAO-06-1021 (Washington, D.C.: Sept. 19, 2006); and *Information on Recent Default and Foreclosure Trends for Home Mortgages and Associated Economic and Market Developments,* GAO-08-78R (Washington, D.C.: Oct. 16, 2007).

[41] GAO-08-78R.

[42] "Secure and Fair Enforcement for Mortgage Licensing Act of 2008" or "S.A.F.E. Mortgage Licensing Act of 2008", Pub. L. No. 110-289, title V.

[43] Although there is no statutory definition of hedge funds, the term is commonly used to describe pooled investment vehicles directed by professional managers that often engage in active trading of various types of assets such as securities and derivatives.

[44] See GAO, *Hedge Funds: Regulators and Market Participants Are Taking Steps to Strengthen Market Discipline, but Continued Attention Is Needed,* GAO-08-200 (Washington, D.C.: Jan. 24, 2008), 9.

[45] Under the Securities Act of 1933, a public offering or sale of securities must be registered with SEC, unless otherwise exempted. In order to exempt an offering or sale of hedge fund shares (ownership interests) to investors from registration under the Securities Act of 1933, most hedge funds restrict their sales to accredited investors in compliance with the safe harbor requirements of Rule 506 of Regulation D. See 15 U.S.C. § 77d and § 77e; 17 C.F.R. § 230.506 (2007). Such investors must meet certain wealth and income thresholds. In addition, hedge funds typically limit the number of investors to fewer than 500, so as not to fall within the purview of Section 12(g) of the Securities Exchange Act of 1934, which requires the registration of any class of equity securities (other than exempted securities) held of record by 500 or more persons. 15 U.S.C. § 78l(g).

[46] The registration and regulatory requirements applicable to Commodity Pool Operators and Commodity Trading Advisors are subject to various exceptions and exemptions contained in CFTC regulations. See, e.g., 17 C.F.R. Secs. 4.5 (exclusion from definition of CPO for pools subject to other types of regulation such as supervision as an insured depository institution, registration under the Investment Company Act of 1940, or state

regulation as an insurance company), 4.7 (exemptions from disclosure requirements for CPOs and CTAs offering or selling interests to qualified eligible persons or directing or guiding their accounts), 4.12(b) (disclosure exemption for CPOs operating pools offered and sold pursuant to the 1933 Securities Act or an exemption from the Act), 4.13 (exemption from CPO registration), 4.14 (exemption from CTA registration).

47 69 *Fed. Reg.* 72054 (Dec. 10, 2004).

48 See *Goldstein v. Securities and Exchange Commission*, 451 F.3d 873 (D.C. Cir. 2006). In Goldstein, the petitioner challenged an SEC regulation under the Investment Adviser's Act that defined "client" to include hedge fund investors and, therefore, prevented hedge fund advisers from qualifying for an exemption from registration for investment advisers with fewer than 15 clients. See Goldstein, 451 F.3d at 874-76. The Court of Appeals vacated the SEC's regulation. While hedge fund advisers may be exempt from registration, the antifraud provisions of the Advisers Act apply to all investment advisers, whether or not they are required to register under the Advisers Act. See Goldstein, 451 F.3d at 876. In August 2007, SEC adopted a final rule under the Investment Advisers Act (rule 206(4)–8 which prohibits advisers from (1) making false or misleading statements to investors or prospective investors in hedge funds and other pooled investment vehicles they advise, or (2) otherwise defrauding these investors. 72 Fed. Reg. 44756 (Aug. 9, 2007)).

49 A counterparty is the opposite party in a bilateral agreement, contract, or transaction.

50 GAO, *Long-Term Capital Management: Regulators Need to Focus Greater Attention on Systemic Risk*, GAO/GGD-00-3 (Washington, D.C.: Oct. 29, 1999).

51 See GAO-08-200. Counterparty credit risk is the risk that a loss will be incurred if a counterparty to a transaction does not fulfill its financial obligations in a timely manner.

52 SEC, *Summary Report of Issues Identified in the Commission Staff's Examinations of Select Credit Rating Agencies* (Washington, D.C., July 8, 2008).

53 Previously, SEC regulations referred to credit ratings by "nationally recognized statistical rating organizations," or NRSROs, but this designation was not established or defined in statute. SEC staff identified credit rating agencies as NRSROs through a no-action letter process in which they determine whether a rating agency had achieved broad market acceptance for its ratings.

54 Credit Rating Agency Reform Act of 2006, Pub. L. No. 109-291 (Sept. 29, 2006). Under the act, a credit rating agency seeking to be treated as an NRSRO must apply for, and be granted, registration with SEC, make public in its application certain information to help persons assess its credibility, and implement procedures to manage the handling of material nonpublic information and conflicts of interest. In addition, the act provides the SEC with rulemaking authority to prescribe: the form of the application (including requiring the furnishing of additional information); the records an NRSRO must make and retain; the financial reports an NRSRO must furnish to SEC on a periodic basis; the specific procedures an NRSRO must implement to manage the handling of material nonpublic information; the conflicts of interest an NRSRO must manage or avoid altogether; and the practices that an NRSRO must not engage in if SEC determines they are unfair, coercive, or abusive. The act expressly prohibits SEC from regulating the rating agencies' methodologies or the substance of their ratings. Pub. L. No. 109-291 § 4(a). SEC adopted rules implementing the act in June 2007. 72 *Fed. Reg.* 33564 (June 18, 2007).

55 CDO cash flows also can be affected by other contract terms, such as detailed provisions that divert payments from the junior classes to the more senior classes when certain conditions are met, such as if the portfolio value or interest proceeds fall below a certain level.

56 For more information, see The Joint Forum, Bank for International Settlements, *Credit Risk Transfer: Developments from 2005 to 2007* (Basel, Switzerland, April 2008).

57 See the Senior Supervisors Group, *Observations on Risk Management Practices during the Recent Market Turbulence* (New York, Mar. 6, 2008).

58 See the Financial Stability Forum, *Report of the Financial Stability Forum on Enhancing Market and Institutional Resilience* (Basel, Switzerland, Apr. 7, 2008). The Financial Stability Forum promotes international financial stability through information exchange and international cooperation in financial supervision and surveillance. It is composed of senior representatives of national financial authorities and various international financial organizations and the European Central Bank.

59 The notional amount is the amount upon which payments between parties to certain types of derivatives contracts are based. When this amount is not exchanged, it is not a measure of the amount at risk in a transaction. According to the Bank for International Settlements, the amount at risk, as measured by the gross market value of OTC derivatives outstanding, was $15 trillion, as of December 2007, or about 2 percent of the notional/contract amount. (The gross market value is the cost that would be incurred if the outstanding contracts were replaced at prevailing market prices.)

60 GAO, *Financial Derivatives: Actions Needed to Protect the Financial System*, GAO/GGD-94-133 (Washington, D.C.: May 18, 1994).

61 Subsequently, the Federal Reserve agreed to loan AIG up to an additional $38 billion. In November 2008, the Federal Reserve and U.S. Treasury restructured these lending arrangements with a new financial support package totaling over $150 billion.

62 See GAO-06-1021.

[63] Federal Trade Commission, *Improving Consumer Mortgage Disclosures: An Empirical Assessment of Current and Prototype Disclosure Forms: A Bureau of Economics Staff Report.* (Washington D.C.: June 2007).

[64] House of Representatives Committee on Financial Services, Subcommittee on Financial Institutions and Consumer Credit, *Subprime Mortgages,* 110th Cong. 2nd sess., Mar. 27, 2007 (testimony of Sandra F. Braunstein, Director, Division of Consumer and Community Affairs, Federal Reserve).

[65] 71 *Fed. Reg.* 58609 (Oct. 4, 2006) "Interagency Guidance on Nontraditional Mortgage Product Risks"; 72 *Fed. Reg.* 37569 (Jul. 10, 2007) "Statement on Subprime Mortgage Lending".

[66] See GAO, *Credit Cards: Increased Complexity in Rates and Fees Heightens Need for More Effective Disclosures to Consumers,* GAO-06-929 (Washington, D.C.: Sept. 12, 2006).

[67] See GAO-04-280.

[68] See GAO, *Financial Literacy and Education Commission: Further Progress Needed to Ensure an Effective National Strategy,* GAO-07-100 (Washington, D.C.: Dec. 4, 2006).

[69] FASB issues generally accepted accounting principles for financial statements prepared by nongovernmental entities in the United States. SEC issues financial reporting and disclosure requirements for U.S. publicly traded companies and recognizes the standards issued by FASB as "generally accepted" within the United States. SEC oversees FASB's standard-setting activities.

[70] FASB Staff Position No. FAS 157-3, *Determining the Fair Value of a Financial Asset When the Market for That Asset Is Not Active* (Oct. 10, 2008); and *SEC Press Release No. 2008-234, SEC Office of the Chief Accountant and FASB Staff Clarifications on Fair Value Accounting* (Sept. 30, 2008).

[71] On September 15, 2008, FASB issued an exposure draft, *Disclosures about Transfers of Financial Assets and Interests in Variable Interest Entities,* for a 30-day comment period that closed on October 15, 2008. On December 11, 2008, FASB issued FASB Staff Position (FSP) FAS 140-4 and FIN 46(R)-8, Disclosures by Public Entities (Enterprises) about Transfers of Financial Assets and Interests in Variable Interest Entities. This document requires additional disclosures about transfers of financial assets and variable interests in qualifying special purpose entities. It also requires public enterprises to provide additional disclosures about their involvement with variable interest entities.

[72] GAO-05-61.

[73] Letter from Representative Michael Oxley et al. to Chairman Alan Greenspan et al., Nov. 3, 2003.

[74] GAO-07-154.

[75] See GAO, *Homeland Security: Critical Design and Implementation Issues,* GAO-02-957T. (Washington, D.C.: July 17, 2002).

[76] GAO, *Financial Regulation: Industry Changes Prompt Need to Reconsider U.S. Regulatory Structure*, GAO-05-61 (Washington, D.C.: Oct. 6, 2004); and *Financial Regulation: Industry Trends Continue to Challenge the Federal Regulatory Structure*, GAO-08-32 (Washington, D.C.: Oct. 12, 2007).

In: Modernizing Financial Regulation
Editor: Lawrence P. Cowell
ISBN: 978-1-60741-442-1

Chapter 4

STATEMENT OF GENE L. DODARO, ACTING COMPTROLLER GENERAL OF THE UNITED STATES, BEFORE THE CONGRESSIONAL OVERSIGHT PANEL ON FINANCIAL REGULATION

United States Government Accountability Office

Chair Warren and Members of the Panel:

I am pleased to be here today to discuss our January 8, 2009, report that provides a framework for modernizing the outdated U.S. financial regulatory system.[1] We prepared this work under the authority of the Comptroller General to help policymakers weigh various regulatory reform proposals and consider ways in which the current regulatory system could be made more effective and efficient. My statement today is based on our report, which (1) describes how regulation has evolved in banking, securities, thrifts, credit unions, futures, insurance, secondary mortgage markets and other important areas; (2) describes several key changes in financial markets and products in recent decades that have highlighted significant limitations and gaps in the existing regulatory system; and (3) presents an evaluation framework that can be used by Congress and others to shape potential regulatory reform efforts. To do this work, we synthesized existing GAO work and other studies and met with representatives of financial regulatory agencies, industry associations, consumer advocacy organizations, and others. The work upon which the report is based was conducted in accordance with generally accepted government auditing standards. Those standards require that we plan and perform the audit to obtain sufficient, appropriate evidence to provide a reasonable basis for our findings and conclusions based on our audit objectives. We believe that the evidence obtained provides a reasonable basis for our findings and conclusions based on our audit objectives. This work was conducted between April 2008 and December 2008.

The report was enhanced by input from representatives of 29 agencies and other organizations, including federal and state financial regulatory agencies, consumer advocacy groups, and financial service industry trade associations, who reviewed and commented on a draft of the report prior to its release. A list of organizations that reviewed the draft report is included at the end of my statement. In general, reviewers commented that the report represented an important and thorough review of the issues related to regulatory reform.

SUMMARY

The current U.S. financial regulatory system has relied on a fragmented and complex arrangement of federal and state regulators—put into place over the past 150 years—that has not kept pace with major developments in financial markets and products in recent decades. Today, almost a dozen federal regulatory agencies, numerous self-regulatory organizations, and hundreds of state financial regulatory agencies share responsibility for overseeing the financial services industry. As the nation finds itself in the midst of one of the worst financial crises ever, it has become apparent that the regulatory system is ill-suited to meet the nation's needs in the 21st century.

Several key changes in financial markets and products in recent decades have highlighted significant limitations and gaps in the existing regulatory system.

- First, regulators have struggled, and often failed, to mitigate the systemic risks posed by large and interconnected financial conglomerates and to ensure they adequately manage their risks.
- Second, regulators have had to address problems in financial markets resulting from the activities of large and sometimes less-regulated market participants—such as nonbank mortgage lenders, hedge funds, and credit rating agencies—some of which play significant roles in today's financial markets.
- Third, the increasing prevalence of new and more complex investment products has challenged regulators and investors, and consumers have faced difficulty understanding new and increasingly complex retail mortgage and credit products.
- Fourth, standard setters for accounting and financial regulators have faced growing challenges in ensuring that accounting and audit standards appropriately respond to financial market developments, and in addressing challenges arising from the global convergence of accounting and auditing standards.
- Finally, as financial markets have become increasingly global, the current fragmented U.S. regulatory structure has complicated some efforts to coordinate internationally with other regulators.

These significant developments have outpaced a fragmented and outdated regulatory structure, and, as a result, significant reforms to the U.S. regulatory system are critically and urgently needed. The current system has significant weaknesses that, if not addressed, will continue to expose the nation's financial system to serious risks. Our report offers a framework for crafting and evaluating regulatory reform proposals consisting of nine characteristics that should be reflected in any new regulatory system. By applying the elements of the framework, the relative strengths and weaknesses of any reform proposal should be better revealed, and policymakers should be able to focus on identifying tradeoffs and balancing competing goals. Similarly, the framework could be used to craft proposals, or to identify aspects to be added to existing proposals to make them more effective and appropriate for addressing the limitations of the current system.

As the administration and Congress continue to take actions to address the immediate financial crisis, determining how to create a regulatory system that reflects new market realities is a key step to reducing the likelihood that the United States will experience another financial crisis similar to the current one.

Table 1. Framework for Crafting and Evaluating Regulatory Reform Proposals

	Characteristic	Description
✓	Clearly defined regulatory goals	Goals should be clearly articulated and relevant, so that regulators can effectively carry out their missions and be held accountable. Key issues include considering the benefits of re-examining the goals of financial regulation to gain needed consensus and making explicit a set of updated comprehensive and cohesive goals that reflect today's environment.
✓	Appropriately comprehensive	Financial regulations should cover all activities that pose risks or are otherwise important to meeting regulatory goals and should ensure that appropriate determinations are made about how extensive such regulations should be, considering that some activities may require less regulation than others. Key issues include identifying risk-based criteria, such as a product's or institution's potential to create systemic problems, for determining the appropriate level of oversight for financial activities and institutions, including closing gaps that contributed to the current crisis.
✓	Systemwide focus	Mechanisms should be included for identifying, monitoring, and managing risks to the financial system regardless of the source of the risk. Given that no regulator is currently tasked with this, key issues include determining how to effectively monitor market developments to identify potential risks; the degree, if any, to which regulatory intervention might be required; and who should hold such responsibilities.
✓	Flexible and adaptable	A regulatory system that is flexible and forward looking allows regulators to readily adapt to market innovations and changes. Key issues include identifying and acting on emerging risks in a timely way without hindering innovation.
✓	Efficient and effective	Effective and efficient oversight should be developed, including eliminating overlapping federal regulatory missions where appropriate, and minimizing regulatory burden without sacrificing effective oversight. Any changes to the system should be continually focused on improving the effectiveness of the financial regulatory system. Key issues include determining opportunities for consolidation given the large number of overlapping participants now, identifying the appropriate role of states and self-regulation, and ensuring a smooth transition to any new system.
✓	Consistent consumer and investor protection	Consumer and investor protection should be included as part of the regulatory mission to ensure that market participants receive consistent, useful information, as well as legal protections for similar financial products and services, including disclosures, sales practice standards, and suitability requirements. Key issues include determining what amount, if any, of consolidation of responsibility may be necessary to streamline consumer protection activities across the financial services industry.
✓	Regulators provided with independence, prominence, authority, and accountability	Regulators should have independence from inappropriate influence, as well as prominence and authority to carry out and enforce statutory missions, and be clearly accountable for meeting regulatory goals. With regulators with varying levels of prominence and funding schemes now, key issues include how to appropriately structure and fund agencies to ensure that each one's structure sufficiently achieves these characteristics.
✓	Consistent financial oversight	Similar institutions, products, risks, and services should be subject to consistent regulation, oversight, and transparency, which should help minimize negative competitive outcomes while harmonizing oversight, both within the United States and internationally. Key issues include identifying activities that pose similar risks, and streamlining regulatory activities to achieve consistency.
✓	Minimal taxpayer exposure	A regulatory system should foster financial markets that are resilient enough to absorb failures and thereby limit the need for federal intervention and limit taxpayers' exposure to financial risk. Key issues include identifying safeguards to prevent systemic crises and minimizing moral hazard.

Source: GAO.

Today's Financial Regulatory System Was Built over the Course of More Than a Century, Largely in Response to Crises or Market Developments

As a result of 150 years of changes in financial regulation in the United States, the regulatory system has become complex and fragmented. Today, responsibilities for overseeing the financial services industry are shared among almost a dozen federal banking, securities, futures, and other regulatory agencies, numerous self-regulatory organizations, and hundreds of state financial regulatory agencies. In particular, five federal agencies—including the Federal Deposit Insurance Corporation, the Federal Reserve, the Office of the Comptroller of the Currency, the Office of Thrift Supervision, and the National Credit Union Administration—and multiple state agencies oversee depository institutions. Securities activities are overseen by the Securities and Exchange Commission and state government entities, as well as by private sector organizations performing self-regulatory functions. Futures trading is overseen by the Commodity Futures Trading Commission and also by industry self-regulatory organizations. Insurance activities are primarily regulated at the state level with little federal involvement. Other federal regulators also play important roles in the financial regulatory system, such as the Public Company Accounting Oversight Board, which oversees the activities of public accounting firms, and the Federal Trade Commission, which acts as the primary federal agency responsible for enforcing compliance with federal consumer protection laws for financial institutions, such as finance companies, which are not overseen by another financial regulator.

Much of this structure has developed as the result of statutory and regulatory changes that were often implemented in response to financial crises or significant developments in the financial services sector. For example, the Federal Reserve System was created in 1913 in response to financial panics and instability around the turn of the century, and much of the remaining structure for bank and securities regulation was created as the result of the Great Depression turmoil of the 1920s and 1930s. Changes in the types of financial activities permitted for depository institutions and their affiliates have also shaped the financial regulatory system over time. For example, under the Glass-Steagall provisions of the Banking Act of 1933, financial institutions were prohibited from simultaneously offering commercial and investment banking services, but with the passage of the Gramm-Leach-Bliley Act of 1999 (GLBA), Congress permitted financial institutions to fully engage in both types of activities.

Changes in Financial Institutions and Their Products Have Significantly Challenged the U.S. Financial Regulatory System

Several key developments in financial markets and products in the past few decades have significantly challenged the existing financial regulatory structure. (See figure 1.) First, the last 30 years have seen waves of mergers among financial institutions within and across sectors, such that the United States, while still having large numbers of financial institutions, also has several very large globally active financial conglomerates that engage in a wide range of activities that have become increasingly interconnected. Regulators have struggled, and often failed, to mitigate the systemic risks posed by these conglomerates, and to ensure they adequately manage their risks. The portion of firms that conduct activities across the financial sectors of banking, securities, and insurance increased significantly in recent years, but none of the regulators is tasked with assessing the risks posed across the entire financial system.

A second dramatic development in U.S. financial markets in recent decades has been the increasingly critical roles played by less-regulated entities. In the past, consumers of financial products generally dealt with entities such as banks, broker-dealers, and insurance companies that were regulated by a federal or state regulator. However, in the last few decades, various entities—nonbank lenders, hedge funds, credit rating agencies, and special-purpose investment entities—that are not always subject to full regulation by such authorities have become important participants in our financial services markets. These unregulated or less regulated entities can sometimes provide substantial benefits by supplying information or allowing financial institutions to better meet demands of consumers, investors or shareholders, but pose challenges to regulators that do not fully or cannot oversee their activities. For example, significant participation in the subprime mortgage market by generally less-regulated nonbank lenders contributed to a dramatic loosening in underwriting standards leading up to the current financial crisis.

A third development that has revealed limitations in the current regulatory structure has been the proliferation of more complex financial products. In particular, the increasing prevalence of new and more complex investment products has challenged regulators and investors, and consumers have faced difficulty understanding new and increasingly complex retail mortgage and credit products. Regulators failed to adequately oversee the sale of mortgage products that posed risks to consumers and the stability of the financial system.

Fourth, standard setters for accounting and financial regulators have faced growing challenges in ensuring that accounting and audit standards appropriately respond to financial market developments, and in addressing challenges arising from the global convergence of accounting and auditing standards.

Finally, with the increasingly global aspects of financial markets, the current fragmented U.S. regulatory structure has complicated some efforts to coordinate internationally with other regulators. For example, the current system has complicated the ability of financial regulators to convey a single U.S. position in international discussions, such the Basel Accords process for developing international capital standards, and international officials have also indicated that the lack of a single point of contact on, for example, insurance issues has complicated regulatory decision making.

A Framework for Crafting and Assessing Alternatives for Reforming the U.S. Financial Regulatory System

As a result of significant market developments in recent decades that have outpaced a fragmented and outdated regulatory structure, significant reforms to the U.S. regulatory system are critically and urgently needed. The current system has important weaknesses that, if not addressed, will continue to expose the nation's financial system to serious risks. As early as 1994, we identified the need to examine the federal financial regulatory structure, including the need to address the risks from new unregulated products.[2] Since then, we have described various options for Congress to consider, each of which provides potential improvements, as well as some risks and potential costs.[3] Our report offers a framework for crafting and evaluating regulatory reform proposals; it consists of the following nine characteristics that should be reflected in any new regulatory system. By applying the elements of this framework, the relative strengths and weaknesses of any reform proposal should be better revealed, and policymakers should be able to focus on identifying trade-offs and balancing competing goals. Similarly, the framework could be used to craft proposals, or to identify aspects to be added to existing proposals to make them more effective and appropriate for addressing the limitations of the current system.

1. ***Clearly defined regulatory goals.* A regulatory system should have goals that are clearly articulated and relevant, so that regulators can effectively conduct activities to implement their missions.**

A critical first step to modernizing the regulatory system and enhancing its ability to meet the challenges of a dynamic financial services industry is to clearly define regulatory goals and objectives. In the background of our report, we identified four broad goals of financial regulation that regulators have generally sought to achieve. These include ensuring adequate consumer protections, ensuring the integrity and fairness of markets, monitoring the safety and soundness of institutions, and acting to ensure the stability of the overall financial system. However, these goals are not always explicitly set in the federal statutes and regulations that govern these regulators. Having specific goals clearly articulated in legislation could serve to better focus regulators on achieving their missions with greater certainty and purpose, and provide continuity over time.

Given some of the key changes in financial markets discussed in our report—particularly the increased interconnectedness of institutions, the increased complexity of products, and the increasingly global nature of financial markets—Congress should consider the benefits that may result from re-examining the goals of financial regulation and making explicit a set of comprehensive and cohesive goals that reflect today's environment. For example, it may be beneficial to have a clearer focus on ensuring that products are not sold with unsuitable, unfair, deceptive, or abusive features; that systemic risks and the stability of the overall financial system are specifically addressed; or that U.S. firms are competitive in a global environment. This may be especially important given the history of financial regulation and the ad hoc approach through which the existing goals have been established.

We found varying views about the goals of regulation and how they should be prioritized. For example, representatives of some regulatory agencies and industry groups emphasized the importance of creating a competitive financial system, whereas members of one consumer advocacy group noted that reforms should focus on improving regulatory effectiveness rather than addressing concerns about market competitiveness. In addition, as the Federal Reserve notes, financial regulatory goals often will prove interdependent and at other times may conflict.

Developments in financial markets and products		Examples of how developments have challenged the regulatory system
	Emergence of large, complex, globally active, interconnected financial conglomerates	Regulators sometimes lack sufficient authority, tools, or capabilities to oversee and mitigate risks.
		Identifying, preventing, mitigating, and resolving systemic crises has become more difficult.
	Less-regulated entities have come to play increasingly critical roles in financial system	Nonbank lenders and a new private-label securitization market played significant roles in subprime mortgage crisis that led to broader market turmoil.
		Activities of hedge funds have posed systemic risks.
		Overreliance on credit ratings of mortgage-backed products contributed to the recent turmoil in financial markets.
		Financial institutions' use of off-balance sheet entities led to ineffective risk disclosure and exacerbated recent market instability.
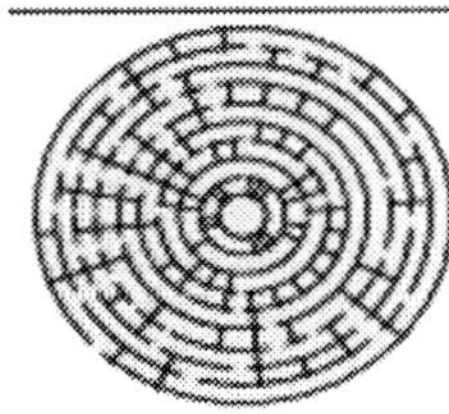	New and complex products that pose challenges to financial stability and investor and consumer understanding of risks.	Complex structured finance products have made it difficult for institutions and their regulators to manage associated risks.
		Growth in complex and less-regulated over-the-counter derivatives markets have created systemic risks and revealed market infrastructure weaknesses.
		Investors have faced difficulty understanding complex investment products, either because they failed to seek out necessary information or were misled by improper sales practices.
		Consumers have faced difficulty understanding mortgages and credit cards with new and increasingly complicated features, due in part to limitations in consumer disclosures and financial literacy efforts.
		Accounting and auditing entities have faced challenges in trying to ensure that accounting and financial reporting requirements appropriately meet the needs of investors and other financial market participants.
	Financial markets have become increasingly global in nature, and regulators have had to coordinate their efforts internationally.	Standard setters and regulators also face new challenges in dealing with global convergence of accounting and auditing standards.
		Fragmented U.S. regulatory structure has complicated some efforts to coordinate internationally with other regulators, such as negotiations on Basel II and certain insurance matters.

Sources: GAO (analysis); Art Explosion (images).

Figure 1. Key Developments and Resulting Challenges That Have Hindered the Effectiveness of the Financial Regulatory System

Revisiting the goals of financial regulation would also help ensure that all involved entities—legislators, regulators, institutions, and consumers—are able to work jointly to meet the intended goals of financial regulation. Such goals and objectives could help establish agency priorities and define responsibility and accountability for identifying risks, including those that cross markets and industries. Policymakers should also carefully define jurisdictional lines and weigh the advantages and disadvantages of having overlapping authorities. While ensuring that the primary goals of financial regulation—including system soundness, market integrity, and consumer protection—are better articulated for regulators, policymakers will also have to ensure that regulation is balanced with other national goals, including facilitating capital raising, innovation, and other benefits that foster long-term growth, stability, and welfare of the United States.

Once these goals are agreed upon, policymakers will need to determine the extent to which goals need to be clarified and specified through rules and requirements, or whether to avoid such specificity and provide regulators with greater flexibility in interpreting such goals. Some reform proposals suggest "principles-based regulation" in which regulators apply broad-based regulatory principles on a case-by-case basis. Such an approach offers the potential advantage of allowing regulators to better adapt to changing market developments. Proponents also note that such an approach would prevent institutions in a more rules-based system from complying with the exact letter of the law while still engaging in unsound or otherwise undesirable financial activities. However, such an approach has potential limitations. Opponents note that regulators may face challenges to implement such a subjective set of principles. A lack of clear rules about activities could lead to litigation if financial institutions and consumers alike disagree with how regulators interpreted goals. Opponents of principles-based regulation note that industry participants who support such an approach have also in many cases advocated for bright-line standards and increased clarity in regulation, which may be counter to a principles-based system. The most effective approach may involve both a set of broad underlying principles and some clear technical rules prohibiting specific activities that have been identified as problematic.

Key issues to be addressed

- Clarify and update the goals of financial regulation and provide sufficient information on how potentially conflicting goals might be prioritized.
- Determine the appropriate balance of broad principles and specific rules that will result in the most effective and flexible implementation of regulatory goals.

2. ***Appropriately comprehensive.* A regulatory system should ensure that financial institutions and activities are regulated in a way that ensures regulatory goals are fully met. As such, activities that pose risks to consumer protection, financial stability, or other goals should be comprehensively regulated, while recognizing that not all activities will require the same level of regulation.**

A financial regulatory system should effectively meet the goals of financial regulation, as articulated as part of this process, in a way that is appropriately comprehensive. In doing so, policymakers may want to consider how to ensure that both the breadth and depth of regulation are appropriate and adequate. That is, policymakers and regulators should consider how to make determinations about which activities and products, both new and existing, require some aspect of regulatory involvement to meet regulatory goals, and then make determinations about how extensive such regulation should be. As we noted in our report, gaps in the current level of federal oversight of mortgage lenders, credit rating agencies, and certain complex financial products such as CDOs and credit default swaps likely have contributed to the current crisis. Congress and regulators may also want to revisit the extent of regulation for entities such as banks that have traditionally fallen within full federal oversight but for which existing regulatory efforts, such as oversight related to risk management and lending standards, have been proven in some cases inadequate by recent events. However, overly restrictive regulation can stifle the financial sectors' ability to innovate and stimulate capital formation and economic growth. Regulators have struggled to balance these competing objectives, and the current crisis appears to reveal that the proper balance was not in place in the regulatory system to date.

Key issues to be addressed

- Identify risk-based criteria, such as a product's or institution's potential to harm consumers or create systemic problems, for determining the appropriate level of oversight for financial activities and institutions.
- Identify ways that regulation can provide protection but avoid hampering innovation, capital formation, and economic growth.

3. ***Systemwide focus.* A regulatory system should include a mechanism for identifying, monitoring, and managing risks to the financial system regardless of the source of the risk or the institutions in which it is created.**

A regulatory system should focus on risks to the financial system, not just institutions. As noted in our report, with multiple regulators primarily responsible for individual institutions or markets, none of the financial regulators is tasked with assessing the risks posed across the entire financial system by a few institutions or by the collective activities of the industry. The collective activities of a number of entities—including mortgage brokers, real estate professionals, lenders, borrowers, securities underwriters, investors, rating agencies and others—likely all contributed to the recent market crisis, but no one regulator had the necessary scope of oversight to identify the risks to the broader financial system. Similarly, once firms began to fail and the full extent of the financial crisis began to become clear, no formal mechanism existed to monitor market trends and potentially stop or help mitigate the fallout from these events.

Having a single entity responsible for assessing threats to the overall financial system could prevent some of the crises that we have seen in the past. For example, in its Blueprint for a Modernized Financial Regulatory Structure, Treasury proposed expanding the responsibilities of the Federal Reserve to create a "market stability regulator" that would have broad authority to gather and disclose appropriate information, collaborate with other regulators on rulemaking, and take corrective action as necessary in the interest of overall financial market stability. Such a regulator could assess the systemic risks that arise at financial institutions, within specific financial sectors, across the nation, and globally. However, policymakers should consider that a potential disadvantage of providing the agency with such broad responsibility for overseeing nonbank entities could be that it may imply an official government support or endorsement, such as a government guarantee, of such activities, and thus encourage greater risk taking by these financial institutions and investors.

Regardless of whether a new regulator is created, all regulators under a new system should consider how their activities could better identify and address systemic risks posed by their institutions. As the Federal Reserve Chairman has noted, regulation and supervision of financial institutions is a critical tool for limiting systemic risk. This will require broadening the focus from individual safety and soundness of institutions to a systemwide oversight approach that includes potential systemic risks and weaknesses.

A systemwide focus should also increase attention on how the incentives and constraints created by regulations affects risk taking throughout the business cycle, and what actions regulators can take to anticipate and mitigate such risks. However, as the Federal Reserve Chairman has noted, the more comprehensive the approach, the more technically demanding and costly it would be for regulators and affected institutions.

Key issues to be addressed

- Identify approaches to broaden the focus of individual regulators or establish new regulatory mechanisms for identifying and acting on systemic risks.
- Determine what additional authorities a regulator or regulators should have to monitor and act to reduce systemic risks.

4. ***Flexible and adaptable.* A regulatory system should be adaptable and forward-looking such that regulators can readily adapt to market innovations and changes and include a mechanism for evaluating potential new risks to the system.**

A regulatory system should be designed such that regulators can readily adapt to market innovations and changes and include a formal mechanism for evaluating the full potential range of risks of new products and services to the system, market participants, and customers. An effective system could include a mechanism for monitoring market developments— such as broad market changes that introduce systemic risk, or new products and services that may pose more confined risks to particular market segments—to determine the degree, if any, to which regulatory intervention might be required. The rise of a very large market for credit derivatives, while providing benefits to users, also created exposures that warranted actions by regulators to rescue large individual participants in this market. While efforts are under way to create risk-reducing clearing mechanisms for this market, a more adaptable and responsive regulatory system might have recognized this need earlier and addressed it sooner. Some industry representatives have suggested that principles-based regulation would provide such a mechanism. Designing a system to be flexible and proactive also involves determining whether Congress, regulators, or both should make such determinations, and how such an approach should be clarified in laws or regulations.

Important questions also exist about the extent to which financial regulators should actively monitor and, where necessary, approve new financial products and services as they are developed to ensure the least harm from inappropriate products. Some individuals commenting on this framework, including industry representatives, noted that limiting government intervention in new financial activities until it has become clear that a particular activity or market poses a significant risk and therefore warrants intervention may be more appropriate. As with other key policy questions, this may be answered with a combination of both approaches, recognizing that a product approval approach may be appropriate for some innovations with greater potential risk, while other activities may warrant a more reactive approach.

Key issues to be addressed

- Determine how to effectively monitor market developments to identify potential risks; the degree, if any, to which regulatory intervention might be required; and who should hold such a responsibility.
- Consider how to strike the right balance between overseeing new products as they come onto the market to take action as needed to protect consumers and investors, without unnecessarily hindering innovation.

5. ***Efficient and effective*. A regulatory system should provide efficient oversight of financial services by eliminating overlapping federal regulatory missions, where appropriate, and minimizing regulatory burden while effectively achieving the goals of regulation.**

A regulatory system should provide for the efficient and effective oversight of financial services. Accomplishing this in a regulatory system involves many considerations. First, an efficient regulatory system is designed to accomplish its regulatory goals using the least amount of public resources. In this sense, policymakers must consider the number, organization, and responsibilities of each agency, and eliminate undesirable overlap in agency activities and responsibilities. Determining what is undesirable overlap is a difficult decision in itself. Under the current U.S. system, financial institutions often have several options for how to operate their business and who will be their regulator. For example, a new or existing depository institution can choose among several charter options. Having multiple regulators performing similar functions does allow for these agencies to potentially develop alternative or innovative approaches to regulation separately, with the approach working best becoming known over time. Such proven approaches can then be adopted by the other agencies. On the other hand, this could lead to regulatory arbitrage, in which institutions take advantage of variations in how agencies implement regulatory responsibilities in order to be subject to less scrutiny. Both situations have occurred under our current structure.

With that said, recent events clearly have shown that the fragmented U.S. regulatory structure contributed to failures by the existing regulators to adequately protect consumers and ensure financial stability. As we note in our report, efforts by regulators to respond to the increased risks associated with new mortgage products were sometimes slowed in part because of the need for five federal regulators to coordinate their response. The Chairman of the Federal Reserve has similarly noted that the different regulatory and supervisory regimes for lending institutions and mortgage brokers made monitoring such institutions difficult for both regulators and investors. Similarly, we noted in our report that the current fragmented U.S. regulatory structure has complicated some efforts to coordinate internationally with other regulators.

One first step to addressing such problems is to seriously consider the need to consolidate depository institution oversight among fewer agencies. Since 1996, we have been recommending that the number of federal agencies with primary responsibilities for bank oversight be reduced.[4] Such a move would result in a system that was more efficient and improve consistency in regulation, another important characteristic of an effective regulatory system. In addition, Congress could consider the advantages and disadvantages of providing a federal charter option for insurance and creating a federal insurance regulatory entity. We have not studied the issue of an optional federal charter for insurers, but have through the years noted difficulties with efforts to harmonize insurance regulation across states through the NAIC-based structure. The establishment of a federal insurance charter and regulator could help alleviate some of these challenges, but such an approach could also have unintended consequences for state regulatory bodies and for insurance firms as well.

Also, given the challenges associated with increasingly complex investment and retail products as discussed earlier, policymakers will need to consider how best to align agency responsibilities to better ensure that consumers and investors are provided with clear, concise, and effective disclosures for all products.

Organizing agencies around regulatory goals as opposed to the existing sector-based regulation may be one way to improve the effectiveness of the system, especially given some of the market developments discussed earlier. Whatever the approach, policymakers should seek to minimize conflict in regulatory goals across regulators, or provide for efficient mechanisms to coordinate in cases where goals inevitably overlap. For example, in some cases, the safety and soundness of an individual institution may have implications for systemic risk, or addressing an unfair or deceptive act or practice at a financial institution may have implications on the institution's safety and soundness by increasing reputational risk. If a regulatory system assigns these goals to different regulators, it will be important to establish mechanisms for them to coordinate.

Proposals to consolidate regulatory agencies for the purpose of promoting efficiency should also take into account any potential trade-offs related to effectiveness. For example, to the extent that policymakers see value in the ability of financial institutions to choose their regulator, consolidating certain agencies may reduce such benefits. Similarly, some individuals have commented that the current system of multiple regulators has led to the development of expertise among agency staff in particular areas of financial market activities that might be threatened if the system were to be consolidated. Finally, policymakers may want to ensure that any transition from the current financial system to a new structure should minimize as best as possible any disruption to the operation of financial markets or risks to the government, especially given the current challenges faced in today's markets and broader economy.

A financial system should also be efficient by minimizing the burden on regulated entities to the extent possible while still achieving regulatory goals. Under our current system, many financial institutions, and especially large institutions that offer services that cross sectors, are subject to supervision by multiple regulators. While steps toward consolidated supervision and designating primary supervisors have helped alleviate some of the burden, industry representatives note that many institutions face significant costs as a result of the existing financial regulatory system that could be lessened. Such costs, imposed in an effort to meet certain regulatory goals such as safety and soundness and consumer protection, can run counter to other goals of a financial system by stifling innovation and competitiveness. In addressing this concern, it is also important to consider the potential benefits that might result in some cases from having multiple regulators overseeing an institution. For example, representatives of state banking and other institution regulators, and consumer advocacy organizations, note that concurrent jurisdiction— between two federal regulators or a federal and state regulator—can provide needed checks and balances against individual financial regulators who have not always reacted appropriately and in a timely way to address problems at institutions. They also note that states may move more quickly and more flexibly to respond to activities causing harm to consumers. Some types of concurrent jurisdiction, such as enforcement authority, may be less burdensome to institutions than others, such as ongoing supervision and examination.

Key issues to be addressed

- Consider the appropriate role of the states in a financial regulatory system and how federal and state roles can be better harmonized.
- Determine and evaluate the advantages and disadvantages of having multiple regulators, including nongovernmental entities such as SROs, share responsibilities for regulatory oversight.
- Identify ways that the U.S. regulatory system can be made more efficient, either through consolidating agencies with similar roles or through minimizing unnecessary regulatory burden.
- Consider carefully how any changes to the financial regulatory system may negatively impact financial market operations and the broader economy, and take steps to minimize such consequences.

6. ***Consistent consumer and investor protection.* A regulatory system should include consumer and investor protection as part of the regulatory mission to ensure that market participants receive consistent, useful information, as well as legal protections for similar financial products and services, including disclosures, sales practice standards, and suitability requirements.**

A regulatory system should be designed to provide high-quality, effective, and consistent protection for consumers and investors in similar situations. In doing so, it is important to recognize important distinctions between retail consumers and more sophisticated consumers such as institutional investors, where appropriate considering the context of the situation. Different disclosures and regulatory protections may be necessary for these different groups. Consumer protection should be viewed from the perspective of the consumer rather than through the various and sometimes divergent perspectives of the multitude of federal regulators that currently have responsibilities in this area.

As discussed in our report, many consumers that received loans in the last few years did not understand the risks associated with taking out their loans, especially in the event that housing prices would not continue to increase at the rate they had in recent years. In addition, increasing evidence exists that many Americans are lacking in financial literacy, and the expansion of new and more complex products will continue to create challenges in this area. Furthermore, regulators with existing authority to better protect consumers did not always exercise that authority effectively. In considering a new regulatory system, policymakers should consider the significant lapses in our regulatory system's focus on consumer protection and ensure that such a focus is prioritized in any reform efforts. For example, policymakers should identify ways to improve upon the existing, largely fragmented, system of regulators that must coordinate to act in these areas. This should include serious consideration of whether to consolidate regulatory responsibilities to streamline and improve the effectiveness of consumer protection efforts. Another way that some market observers have argued that consumer protections could be enhanced and harmonized across products is to extend suitability requirements—which require securities brokers making recommendations to customers to have reasonable grounds for believing that the recommendation is suitable for the customer—to mortgage and other products. Additional consideration could also be given to determining whether certain products are simply too complex to be well understood and make judgments about limiting or curtailing their use.

Key issues to be addressed

- Consider how prominent the regulatory goal of consumer protection should be in the U.S. financial regulatory system.
- Determine what amount, if any, of consolidation of responsibility may be necessary to enhance and harmonize consumer protections, including suitability requirements and disclosures across the financial services industry.
- Consider what distinctions are necessary between retail and wholesale products, and how such distinctions should affect how they are regulated.
- Identify opportunities to protect and empower consumers through improving their financial literacy.

7. ***Regulators provided with independence, prominence, authority, and accountability.* A regulatory system should ensure that regulators have independence from inappropriate influence; have sufficient resources, clout, and authority to carry out and enforce statutory missions; and are clearly accountable for meeting regulatory goals.**

A regulatory system should ensure that any entity responsible for financial regulation is independent from inappropriate influence; has adequate prominence, authority, and resources to carry out and enforce its statutory mission; and is clearly accountable for meeting regulatory goals. With respect to independence, policymakers may want to consider advantages and disadvantages of different approaches to funding agencies, especially to the extent that agencies might face difficulty remaining independent if they are funded by the institutions they regulate. Under the current structure, for example, the Federal Reserve primarily is funded by income earned from U.S. government securities that it has acquired through open market operations and does not assess charges to the institutions it oversees. In contrast, OCC and OTS are funded primarily by assessments on the firms they supervise. Decision makers should consider whether some of these various funding mechanisms are more likely to ensure that a regulator will take action against its regulated institutions without regard to the potential impact on its own funding.

With respect to prominence, each regulator must receive appropriate attention and support from top government officials. Inadequate prominence in government may make it difficult for a regulator to raise safety and soundness or other concerns to Congress and the administration in a timely manner. Mere knowledge of a deteriorating situation would be insufficient if a regulator were unable to persuade Congress and the administration to take timely corrective action. This problem would be exacerbated if a regulated institution had more political clout and prominence than its regulator because the institution could potentially block action from being taken.

In considering authority, agencies must have the necessary enforcement and other tools to effectively implement their missions to achieve regulatory goals. For example, in a 2007 report we expressed concerns over the appropriateness of having OTS oversee diverse global financial firms given the size of the agency relative to the institutions for which it was responsible.[5] It is important for a regulatory system to ensure that agencies are provided with adequate resources and expertise to conduct their work effectively. A regulatory system should also include adequate checks and balances to ensure the appropriate use of agency authorities. With respect to accountability, policymakers may also want to consider different governance structures at agencies—the current system includes a combination of agency heads and independent boards or commissions— and how to ensure that agencies are recognized for successes and held accountable for failures to act in accordance with regulatory goals.

Key issues to be addressed

- Determine how to structure and fund agencies to ensure each has adequate independence, prominence, tools, authority and accountability.
- Consider how to provide an appropriate level of authority to an agency while ensuring that it appropriately implements its mission without abusing its authority.
- Ensure that the regulatory system includes effective mechanisms for holding regulators accountable.

8. ***Consistent financial oversight.* A regulatory system should ensure that similar institutions, products, risks, and services are subject to consistent regulation, oversight, and transparency, which should help minimize negative competitive outcomes while harmonizing oversight, both within the United States and internationally.**

A regulatory system should ensure that similar institutions, products, and services posing similar risks are subject to consistent regulation, oversight, and transparency. Identifying which institutions and which of their products and services pose similar risks is not easy and involves a number of important considerations. Two institutions that look very similar may in fact pose very different risks to the financial system, and therefore may call for significantly different regulatory treatment. However, activities that are done by different types of financial institutions that pose similar risks to their institutions or the financial system should be regulated similarly to prevent competitive disadvantages between institutions.

Streamlining the regulation of similar products across sectors could also help prepare the United States for challenges that may result from increased globalization and potential harmonization in regulatory standards. Such efforts are under way in other jurisdictions. For example, at a November 2008 summit in the United States, the Group of 20 countries pledged to strengthen their regulatory regimes and ensure that all financial markets, products, and participants are consistently regulated or subject to oversight, as appropriate to their circumstances. Similarly, a working group in the European Union is slated by the spring of 2009 to propose ways to strengthen European supervisory arrangements, including addressing how their supervisors should cooperate with other major jurisdictions to help safeguard financial stability globally. Promoting consistency in regulation of similar products should be done in a way that does not sacrifice the quality of regulatory oversight.

As we noted in a 2004 report, different regulatory treatment of bank and financial holding companies, consolidated supervised entities, and other holding companies may not provide a basis for consistent oversight of their consolidated risk management strategies, guarantee competitive neutrality, or contribute to better oversight of systemic risk.[6] Recent events further underscore the limitations brought about when there is a lack of consistency in oversight of large financial institutions. As such, Congress and regulators will need to seriously consider how best to consolidate responsibilities for oversight of large financial conglomerates as part of any reform effort.

Key issues to be addressed

- Identify institutions and products and services that pose similar risks.
- Determine the level of consolidation necessary to streamline financial regulation activities across the financial services industry.
- Consider the extent to which activities need to be coordinated internationally.

9. ***Minimal taxpayer exposure.* A regulatory system should have adequate safeguards that allow financial institution failures to occur while limiting taxpayers' exposure to financial risk.**

A regulatory system should have adequate safeguards that allow financial institution failures to occur while limiting taxpayers' exposure to financial risk. Policymakers should consider identifying the best safeguards and assignment of responsibilities for responding to situations where taxpayers face significant exposures, and should consider providing clear guidelines when regulatory intervention is appropriate. While an ideal system would allow firms to fail without negatively affecting other firms— and therefore avoid any moral hazard that may result—policymakers and regulators must consider the realities of today's financial system. In some cases, the immediate use of public funds to prevent the failure of a critically important financial institution may be a worthwhile use of such funds if it ultimately serves to prevent a systemic crisis that would result in much greater use of public funds in the long run. However, an effective regulatory system that incorporates the characteristics noted above, especially by ensuring a systemwide focus, should be better equipped to identify and mitigate problems before it become necessary to make decisions about whether to let a financial institution fail.

An effective financial regulatory system should also strive to minimize systemic risks resulting from interrelationships between firms and limitations in market infrastructures that prevent the orderly unwinding of firms that fail. Another important consideration in minimizing taxpayer exposure is to ensure that financial institutions provided with a government guarantee that could result in taxpayer exposure are also subject to an appropriate level of regulatory oversight to fulfill their responsibilities.

Key issues to be addressed

- Identify safeguards that are most appropriate to prevent systemic crises while minimizing moral hazard.
- Consider how a financial system can most effectively minimize taxpayer exposure to losses related to financial instability.

Finally, although significant changes may be required to modernize the U.S. financial regulatory system, policymakers should consider carefully how best to implement the changes in such a way that the transition to a new structure does not hamper the functioning of the financial markets, individual financial institutions' ability to conduct their activities, and consumers' ability to access needed services. For example, if the changes require regulators or institutions to make systems changes, file registrations, or other activities that could require extensive time to complete, the changes could be implemented in phases with specific target dates around which the affected entities could formulate plans. In addition, our past work has identified certain critical factors that should be addressed to ensure that any large-scale transitions among government agencies are implemented successfully.[7] Although all of these factors are likely important for a successful transformation for the financial regulatory system, Congress and existing agencies should pay particular attention to ensuring there are effective communication strategies so that all affected parties, including investors and consumers, clearly understand any changes being implemented. In addition, attention should be paid to developing a sound human capital strategy to ensure that any new or consolidated agencies are able to retain and attract additional quality staff during the transition period. Finally, policymakers should consider how best to retain and utilize the existing skills and knowledge base within agencies subject to changes as part of a transition.

Chair Warren and Members of the Panel, I appreciate the opportunity to discuss these critically important issues and would be happy to answer any questions that you may have. Thank you.

Appendix I: Agencies and Other Organizations That Reviewed the Draft Report

American Bankers Association
American Council of Life Insurers
Center for Responsible Lending
Commodity Futures Trading Commission
Conference of State Bank Supervisors
Consumer Federation of America
Consumers Union
Credit Union National Association
Department of the Treasury

Federal Deposit Insurance Corporation
Federal Housing Finance Agency
Federal Reserve
Financial Industry Regulatory Authority
Financial Services Roundtable
Futures Industry Association
Independent Community Bankers of America
International Swaps and Derivates Association
Mortgage Bankers Association
National Association of Federal Credit Unions
National Association of Insurance Commissioners
National Consumer Law Center
National Credit Union Administration
National Futures Association
Office of the Comptroller of the Currency
Office of Thrift Supervision
Public Company Accounting Oversight Board
Securities and Exchange Commission
Securities Industry and Financial Markets Association
U.S. PIRG

Related GAO Products

Financial Regulation: A Framework for Crafting and Assessing Proposals to Modernize the Outdated U.S. Financial Regulatory System. GAO-09-216. Washington, D.C.: January 8, 2009.

Troubled Asset Relief Program: Additional Actions Needed to Better Ensure Integrity, Accountability, and Transparency. GAO-09-161. Washington, D.C.: December 2, 2008.

Hedge Funds: Regulators and Market Participants Are Taking Steps to Strengthen Market Discipline, but Continued Attention Is Needed. GAO-08-200. Washington, D.C.: January 24, 2008.

Information on Recent Default and Foreclosure Trends for Home Mortgages and Associated Economic and Market Developments. GAO-08-78R. Washington, D.C.: October 16, 2007.

Financial Regulation: Industry Trends Continue to Challenge the Federal Regulatory Structure. GAO-08-32. Washington, D.C.: October 12, 2007.

Financial Market Regulation: Agencies Engaged in Consolidated Supervision Can Strengthen Performance Measurement and Collaboration. GAO-07-154. Washington, D.C.: March 15, 2007.

Alternative Mortgage Products: Impact on Defaults Remains Unclear, but Disclosure of Risks to Borrowers Could Be Improved. GAO-06-1021. Washington, D.C.: September 19, 2006.

Credit Cards: Increased Complexity in Rates and Fees Heightens Need for More Effective Disclosures to Consumers. GAO-06-929. Washington, D.C.: September 12, 2006.

Financial Regulation: Industry Changes Prompt Need to Reconsider U.S. Regulatory Structure. GAO-05-61. Washington, D.C.: October 6, 2004.

Consumer Protection: Federal and State Agencies Face Challenges in Combating Predatory Lending. GAO-04-280. Washington, D.C.: January 30, 2004.

Long-Term Capital Management: Regulators Need to Focus Greater Attention on Systemic Risk. GAO/GGD-00-3. Washington, D.C.: October 29, 1999.

Bank Oversight: Fundamental Principles for Modernizing the U.S. Structure. GAO/T-GGD-96-117. Washington, D.C.: May 2, 1996.

Financial Derivatives: Actions Needed to Protect the Financial System. GAO/GGD-94-133. Washington, D.C.: May 18, 1994

End Notes

[1] GAO, *Financial Regulation: A Framework for Crafting and Assessing Proposals to Modernize the Outdated U.S. Financial Regulatory System,* GAO-09-216 (Washington, D.C.: Jan. 8, 2009).

[2] GAO, *Financial Derivatives: Actions Needed to Protect the Financial System,* GAO/GGD-94-133 (Washington, D.C.: May 18, 1994).

[3] GAO, *Financial Regulation: Industry Changes Prompt Need to Reconsider U.S. Regulatory Structure,* GAO-05-61 (Washington, D.C.: Oct. 6, 2004); and *Financial Regulation: Industry Trends Continue to Challenge the Federal Regulatory Structure,* GAO-08-32 (Washington, D.C.: Oct. 12, 2007).

[4] See GAO, *Bank Oversight: Fundamental Principles for Modernizing the U.S. Structure,* GAO/T-GGD-96-117 (Washington, D.C.: May 2, 1996).

[5] GAO, *Financial Market Regulation: Agencies Engaged in Consolidated Supervision Can Strengthen Performance Measurement and Collaboration,* GAO-07-154 (Washington, D.C.: Mar. 15, 2007).

[6] GAO-05-61.

[7] See GAO, *Homeland Security: Critical Design and Implementation Issues,* GAO-02-957T (Washington, D.C.: July 17, 2002).

In: Modernizing Financial Regulation
Editor: Lawrence P. Cowell

ISBN: 978-1-60741-442-1

Chapter 5

SPEECH BY TIMOTHY F. GEITHNER, PRESIDENT AND CEO, FEDERAL RESERVE BANK OF NEW YORK, AT THE ECONOMIC CLUB OF NEW YORK, JUNE 9, 2008

Timothy F. Geithner

REDUCING SYSTEMIC RISK IN A DYNAMIC FINANCIAL SYSTEM

Since the summer of 2007, the major financial centers have experienced a very severe and complex financial crisis. The fabric of confidence that is essential to the viability of individual institutions and to market functioning in the United States and in Europe proved exceptionally fragile. Money and funding markets became severely impaired, impeding the effective transmission of U.S. monetary policy to the economy. Central banks and governments, here and in other countries, have taken dramatic action to contain the risks to the broader economy.

Why Was the System so Fragile?

Part of the explanation was the size of the global financial boom that preceded the crisis. The larger the boom, the greater the potential risk of damage when it deflates.

The underpinnings of this particular boom include a large increase in savings relative to real investment opportunities, a long period of low real interest rates around the world, the greater ease with which capital was able to flow across countries, and the perception of lower real and inflation risk produced by the greater apparent moderation in output growth and inflation over the preceding two decades.

This combination of factors put upward pressure on asset prices and narrowed credit spreads and risk premia, and this in turn encouraged an increase in leverage across the financial system.

This dynamic both fed and was fed by a wave of financial innovation. As the magnitude of financial resources seeking higher returns increased around the world, products were created to meet this demand. Financial innovation made it easier for this money to flow around the constraints of regulation and to take advantage of more favorable tax and accounting treatment.

The U.S. financial system created a lot of lower quality mortgage securities, many of which were packaged together with other securities into complex structured products and sold to institutions around the world. Many of these securities and products were held in leveraged money or capital market vehicles, and financed with substantial liquidity risk. And yet, by historical standards, the overall level of risk premia in financial markets remained extraordinarily low over this period.

The structure of the financial system changed fundamentally during the boom, with dramatic growth in the share of assets outside the traditional banking system. This non-bank financial system grew to be very large, particularly in money and funding markets. In early 2007, asset-backed commercial paper conduits, in structured investment vehicles, in auction-rate preferred securities, tender option bonds and variable rate demand notes, had a combined asset size of roughly $2.2 trillion. Assets financed overnight in triparty repo grew to $2.5 trillion. Assets held in hedge funds grew to roughly $1.8 trillion. The combined balance sheets of the then five major investment banks totaled $4 trillion.

In comparison, the total assets of the top five bank holding companies in the United States at that point were just over $6 trillion, and total assets of the entire banking system were about $10 trillion.

This parallel system financed some of these very assets on a very short-term basis in the bilateral or triparty repo markets. As the volume of activity in repo markets grew, the variety of assets financed in this manner expanded beyond the most highly liquid securities to include less liquid securities, as well. Nonetheless, these assets were assumed to be readily sellable at fair values, in part because assets with similar credit ratings had generally been tradable during past periods of financial stress. And the liquidity supporting them was assumed to be continuous and essentially frictionless, because it had been so for a long time.

The scale of long-term risky and relatively illiquid assets financed by very short-term liabilities made many of the vehicles and institutions in this parallel financial system vulnerable to a classic type of run, but without the protections such as deposit insurance that the banking system has in place to reduce such risks. Once the investors in these financing arrangements—many conservatively managed money funds—withdrew or threatened to withdraw their funds from these markets, the system became vulnerable to a self-reinforcing cycle of forced liquidation of assets, which further increased volatility and lowered prices across a variety of asset classes. In response, margin requirements were increased, or financing was withdrawn altogether from some customers, forcing more de-leveraging. Capital cushions eroded as assets were sold into distressed markets. The force of this dynamic was exacerbated by the poor quality of assets—particularly mortgage-related assets—that had been spread across the system. This helps explain how a relatively small quantity of risky assets was able to undermine the confidence of investors and other market participants across a much broader range of assets and markets.

Banks could not fully absorb and offset the effects of the pullback in investor participation—or the "run"—on this non-bank system, in part because they themselves had sponsored many of these off-balance-sheet vehicles. They had written very large contingent commitments to provide liquidity support to many of the funding vehicles that were under pressure. They had retained substantial economic exposure to the risk of a deterioration in house prices and to a broader economic downturn, and as a result, many suffered a sharp increase in their cost of borrowing.

The funding and balance sheet pressures on banks were intensified by the rapid breakdown of securitization and structured finance markets. Banks lost the capacity to move riskier assets off their balance sheets, at the same time they had to fund, or to prepare to fund, a range of contingent commitments over an uncertain time horizon.

The combined effect of these factors was a financial system vulnerable to self-reinforcing asset price and credit cycles. The system appeared to be more stable across a broader range of circumstances and better able to withstand the effects of moderate stress, but it had become more vulnerable to more extreme events. And the change in the structure of the system made the crisis more difficult to manage with the traditional mix of instruments available to central banks and governments.

First Repair, Then Reform

What Should Be Done to Reduce These Vulnerabilities?

Our first and most immediate priority remains to help the economy and the financial system get through this crisis.

A range of different measures of liquidity premia and credit risk premia have eased somewhat relative to the adverse peaks of mid-March.

Part of this improvement—this modest and tentative improvement—is the result of the range of policy actions by the Federal Reserve System, the U.S. Treasury and other central banks. Part is the consequence of the substantial adjustments already undertaken by financial institutions to reduce risk, raise capital and build liquidity.

These actions by institutions and by the official sector have helped to reduce the risk of a deeper downturn in economic activity and of a systemic financial crisis.

But the U.S. economy and economies worldwide are still in the process of adjusting to the aftermath of rapid asset price growth and unsustainably low risk premiums. This process will take time.

As we continue to work with other central banks to ease the adjustment now under way in the U.S. economy and globally, we are working to make the financial system more resilient and to improve its capacity to deal with future crises.

We are working closely with the Securities and Exchange Commission (SEC), with banking supervisors in the United States and the other major economies, and with the U.S. Treasury to strengthen the financial foundation of the major investment and commercial banks. We have encouraged a significant increase in the quality of public disclosure. We have supported efforts that have brought a very substantial amount of new equity capital into many financial institutions. These efforts will help mitigate the risk of a deeper credit crunch. And even as the Federal Reserve has worked to mitigate the liquidity pressures in markets by implementing a new set of lending facilities, we have worked with the SEC and others to ensure that the major institutions are strengthening their liquidity positions and funding strategies.

We are also initiating important steps to strengthen the financial infrastructure. We are in the process of encouraging a substantial increase in the resources held against the risk of default by a major market participant across the set of private sector and cooperative arrangements for funding, trading, clearing and settlement of financial transactions that form the "centralized infrastructure" of the financial system. We have begun to review how to reduce the vulnerability of secured lending markets, including triparty repo by reducing, in part, the scale of potentially illiquid assets financed at very short maturities.

This afternoon, 17 firms that represent more than 90 percent of credit derivatives trading, meet at the Federal Reserve Bank of New York with their primary U.S. and international supervisors to outline a comprehensive set of changes to the derivatives infrastructure. This agenda includes:

- the establishment of a central clearing house for credit default swaps,
- a program to reduce the level of outstanding contracts through bilateral and multilateral netting,
- the incorporation of a protocol for managing defaults into existing and future credit derivatives contracts, and
- concrete targets for achieving substantially greater automation of trading and settlement.

These changes to the infrastructure will help improve the system's ability to manage the consequences of failure by a major institution. Making these changes will take time, but we expect to make meaningful progress over the next six months.

The set of ongoing and near-term initiatives I just outlined are only the beginning and should be considered a bridge to a broader set of necessary changes to the regulatory framework in the United States and globally.

I believe the severity and complexity of this crisis makes a compelling case for a comprehensive reassessment of how to use regulation to strike an appropriate balance between efficiency and stability. This is exceptionally complicated, both in terms of the trade-offs involved and in building the necessary consensus in the United States and the world. It is going to require significant changes to the way we regulate and supervise financial institutions, changes that go well beyond adjustments to some of the specific capital charges in the existing capital requirement regime for banks.

We have to recognize, however, that poorly designed regulation has the potential to make things worse. We have to distinguish carefully between problems the markets will solve on their own and those markets cannot solve. We have to acknowledge not just that regulation comes with costs, but that if not carefully crafted it can distort incentives in ways that may make the system less safe. And we have to focus on ways regulation can mitigate the moral hazard risk created by the actions central banks and governments have taken and may take in the future to avert systemic financial crises.

I am going outline some broad proposals for reform, focusing on the aspects of our system that are most important to reducing systemic risk. These proposals do not address a myriad of other important aspects of regulatory policy, including consumer protection issues in the mortgage origination business, the future role of government and government-sponsored enterprises in our housing markets, and many others.

Any agenda for reform has to deal with three important dimensions of the regulatory system.

- *Regulatory policy.* These are the incentives and constraints designed to affect the level and concentration of risk-taking across the financial system. You can think of these as a financial analog to imposing speed limits and requiring air bags and antilock brakes in cars, or establishing building codes in earthquake zones.

- *Regulatory structure.* This is about who is responsible for setting and enforcing those rules.

- *Crisis management.* This is about when and how we intervene and about the expectations we create for official intervention in crises.

Here are a few broad points on each of these.

Regulatory Policy

The objectives of regulatory policy should be to improve the capacity of the financial system to withstand the effects of failure and to reduce the overall vulnerability of the system to the type of funding runs and margin spirals we have seen in this crisis.

First, this means looking beyond prudential supervision of the critical institutions to broader oversight of market practices and the market infrastructure that are important to market functioning. Two obvious examples: we need to make it much more difficult for institutions with little capital and little supervision to underwrite mortgages, and we need to look more comprehensively how to improve the incentives for institutions that structure and sell asset-backed securities and CDOs of ABS. And supervision will have to focus more attention on the extent of maturity transformation taking place outside the banking system.

Second, risk-management practices and supervisory oversight has to focus much more attention on strengthening shock absorbers within institutions and across the infrastructure against very bad macroeconomic and financial outcomes, however implausible they may seem in good times. After we get through this crisis and the process of stabilization and financial repair is complete, we will put in place more exacting expectations on capital, liquidity and risk management for the largest institutions that play a central role in intermediation and market functioning.

This is important for reasons that go beyond the implications of excess leverage for the fate of any particular financial institution. As we have seen, the process of de-leveraging by large but relatively strong institutions can cause significant collateral damage for market functioning and for other financial institutions.

Inducing institutions to hold stronger cushions of capital and liquidity in periods of calm may be the best way to reduce the amplitude of financial shocks on the way up, and to contain the damage on the way down. Stronger initial cushions against stress reduces the need to hedge risk dynamically in a crisis, reducing the broader risk of a self-reinforcing, pro-cyclical margin spiral, such as we have seen in this crisis.

How should we decide where to set these constraints on risk-taking? This is hard, but the objective should be to offset the benefits and the moral hazard risk that come from access to central bank liquidity in crises, without setting the constraint at a level that will only result in pushing more capital to the unregulated part of the financial system.

Risk management and oversight now focuses too much on the idiosyncratic risk that affects an individual firm and too little on the systematic issues that could affect market liquidity as a whole. To put it somewhat differently, the conventional risk-management framework today focuses too much on the threat to a firm from its own mistakes and too little on the potential for mistakes to be correlated across firms. It is too confident that a firm can adjust to protect itself from its own mistakes without adding to downward pressure on markets and takes too little account of the risk of a flight to safety—a broad-based, marketwide rush for the exits as the financial system as a whole de-leverages and tries collectively to move into more liquid and lower risk assets of government obligations.

Third, although supervision has to focus first on the stability of the core of financial institutions, it cannot be indifferent to the scale of leverage and risk outside the regulated institutions.

I do not believe it would be desirable or feasible to extend capital requirements to institutions such as hedge funds or private equity firms. But supervision has to ensure that counterparty-credit risk management in the regulated institutions contains the level of overall exposure of the regulated to the unregulated. Prudent counterparty risk management, in turn, will work to limit the risk of a rise in overall leverage outside the regulated institutions that could threaten the stability of the financial system.

Supervision has to explicitly focus on inducing higher levels of margin and collateral in normal times against derivatives and secured borrowing to better cover the risk of market illiquidity. Greater product standardization and improved disclosure can also help, as will changes to the accounting rules that govern what risks reside on and off balance sheets.

Finally, central banks, governments and supervisors have to look much more carefully at the interaction between accounting, tax, disclosure and capital requirements, and their effects on overall leverage and risk across the financial system. Capital requirements alone are rarely the most important constraint.

The President's Working Group on Financial Markets and the Financial Stability Forum has laid out a very detailed list of reforms to begin this process. And we are fortunate to have Jerry Corrigan engaged in working to shape a set of recommendations to help us get the balance right.

Regulatory Structure

Apart from the mix of incentives and constraints set by regulatory policy, the structure of the regulatory system in the United States needs substantial reform. Our current system has evolved into a confusing mix of diffused accountability, regulatory competition, an enormously complex web of rules that create perverse incentives and leave huge opportunities for arbitrage and evasion, and creates the risk of large gaps in our knowledge and authority.

This crisis gives us the opportunity to bring about fundamental change in the direction of a more streamlined and consolidated system with more clarity around responsibility for the prudential safeguards in the system. In this regard, Secretary Paulson's blueprint outlines a sweeping consolidation and realignment of responsibilities, with a clear set of objectives for achieving a better balance between efficiency and stability, between market discipline and regulation. This proposal has stimulated a very constructive set of discussions, and will help lay the foundation for action when the dust settles.

The most fundamental reform that is necessary is for all institutions that play a central role in money and funding markets—including the major globally active banks and investment banks—to operate under a unified framework that provides a stronger form of consolidated supervision, with appropriate requirements for capital and liquidity.

To complement this, we need to put in place a stronger framework of oversight authority over the critical parts of the payments system, not just the centralized payments, clearing and settlements systems but the infrastructure that underpins the decentralized over-the-counter markets.

The Federal Reserve should play a central role in this framework, working closely with supervisors here and in other countries. At present the Federal Reserve has broad responsibility for financial stability not matched by direct authority, and the consequences of the actions we have taken in this crisis make it more important that we close that gap.

CRISIS MANAGEMENT

No financial system will be free from crises, whatever the design of the regulatory framework or the rules of the game. The framework of lender-of-last-resort policies and the regime for facilitating an orderly resolution of a major non-bank financial institution are critical to our ability to contain financial crises.

In response to this crisis, the Federal Reserve has designed and implemented a number of innovative new facilities for injecting liquidity into the markets. These facilities have played a significant role in easing liquidity strains in markets and we plan to leave them in place until conditions in money and credit markets have improved substantially.

We are also examining what suite of liquidity facilities will be appropriate in the future, with what conditions for access and what oversight requirements to mitigate moral hazard risk. Some of the mechanisms we have employed during this crisis may become permanent parts of our toolkit. Some might be best reserved for the type of acute market illiquidity experienced in this crisis.

It would be helpful for the Federal Reserve System to have greater flexibility to respond to acute liquidity pressure in markets without undermining its capacity to manage the federal funds rates at the FOMC's (Federal Open Market Committee) target. The authority Congress has granted the Fed to pay interest on reserves beginning in 2011 will be very helpful in this regard. We welcome the fact that Congress is now considering accelerating that authority.

The major central banks should put in place a standing network of currency swaps, collateral policies and account arrangements that would make it easier to mobilize liquidity across borders quickly in crisis. We have some of the elements of this framework in place today, and these arrangements have worked relatively well in the present crises. We should leave them in place, refine them further and test them frequently.

The Federal Reserve Act gives us very broad authority to lend in crises. We used that authority in new and consequential ways, but in the classic tradition of central banks and lenders of last resort. As we broadened the range of collateral we were willing to finance, extended the terms of our lending and provided liquidity insurance to primary dealers, our actions were carefully calibrated to improve overall market functioning by providing an effective liquidity backstop and to avoid supplanting either the interbank market or the secured funding market.

In addition to these new facilities, the Fed made the judgment, after very careful consideration, that it was necessary to use its emergency powers to protect the financial system and the economy from a systemic crisis by committing to facilitate the merger between JPMorgan Chase and Bear Stearns. We did this with great reluctance, and only because it was the only feasible option available to avert default, and because we did not believe we had the ability to contain the damage that would have been caused by default.

Our actions were guided by the same general principles that have governed Fed action in crises over the years. There was an acute risk to the stability of the system; we were not confident that the damage could be contained through other means; we acted only to help facilitate an orderly resolution, not to preserve the institution itself; and the management of the firm and the equity holders of the institution involved suffered very substantial consequences.

Although we assumed some risk in this transaction, that risk is modest in comparison to the risk of very substantial damage to the financial system and the economy as a whole that would have accompanied default.

Conclusion

One of the central objectives in reforming our regulatory framework should be to mitigate the fragility of the system and to reduce the need for official intervention in the future. I know that many hope and believe that we could design our system so that supervisors would have the ability to act preemptively to diffuse pockets of risk and leverage. I do not believe that is a desirable or realistic ambition for policy. It would fail, and the attempt would entail a level of regulation and uncertainty about the rules of the game that would offset any possible benefit. I do believe, however, that we can make the system better able to handle failure by making the shock absorbers stronger.

This crisis exposed very significant problems in the financial systems of the United States and some other major economies. Innovation got too far out in front of the knowledge of risk.

It is very important that we move quickly to adapt the regulatory system to address the vulnerabilities exposed by this financial crisis. With the leadership of the Secretary of the Treasury, Hank Paulson, we are beginning the process of building the necessary consensus here and with the other major financial centers.

Let me just finish by saying that confidence in any financial system depends in part on confidence in the individuals running the largest private institutions. Regulation cannot produce integrity, foresight or judgment in those responsible for managing these institutions. That's up to the boards and shareholders of those institutions.

One of the great strengths of our system is the speed with which we adapt to challenge. We can do better, and I am reasonably confident we will.

Thank you.

CHAPTER SOURCES

The following chapters have been previously published:

Chapter 1 – This is an edited, reformatted and augmented edition of a Congressional Research Service publication, CRS Report RL33036, dated July 10, 2008.

Chapter 2 – This is an edited, excerpted and augmented edition of a United States Government Accountability Office report, Report GAO-08-32, dated October 2007.

Chapter 3 – This is an edited, excerpted and augmented edition of a United States Government Accountability Office report, Report GAO-09-216, dated January 2009.

Chapter 4 – This is an edited, excerpted and augmented edition of a United States Government Accountability Office report, Report GAO-09-310T, dated January 14, 2009.

Chapter 5 –This is an edited, reformatted and augmented edition of a speech made by Timothy F. Geithner (President and CEO of the Federal Reserve Bank of New York) at the Economic Club of New York on June 9, 2008.

INDEX

A

B

C

D

E

F

G

N

O

P

Q

R